Promoting Children's Well-Being in the Primary Years

Promoting Children's Well-Being in the Primary Years

Edited by Andrew Burrell and Jeni Riley

*A Network Educational Press publication
in collaboration with Right from the Start*

Published by Network Educational Press Ltd
PO Box 635, Stafford ST16 1BF

First published 2005
© Right from the Start 2005

ISBN 185539 119 8

Editor: Ann Baggaley
Design: Proof Books
Proofreader: Lynn Bresler

Printed in Great Britain by MPG Books Ltd, Bodmin, Cornwall

DEDICATION

Promoting Children's Well-Being in the Primary Years is dedicated to the memory of two of the contributors, Joan Webster and Virginia Gordon, both of whom sadly died before this book went to the publisher, and to their shared conviction that sorting out people's feelings and emotions and how they live together and help each other stands way above everything else, in and out of school.

Photograph credits
Ashfield Nursery School: 44, 70, 71, 72; Bournemouth News and Picture Service: 122; Bristol United Press: 125; Cavell First and Nursery School: 102; Cherion Trust: 133; Coombes School: 2, 12, 20, 38, 41, 110, 167; Daphne Clarke: 173, 174, 175; Didi Ananda Kaumudi: 128; Dropmore Infant School: 8, 29, 30, 210, 211, 212, 213 (top, bottom), 214, 215, 216, 217, 218; Sally and Richard Greenhill: 98; Shelagh Hennigan: 118; Institute of Education, London: front and back cover, 107; Roots of Empathy: 63, 64; Aliki Sapountzi: 74, 81, 90; Elspeth Thompson: 93, 94; Tuckswood Community First School: 36, 40, 154, 178, 186, 188, 190, 193, 196, 204, 234

Childhood (beginning of Section 1)
Alliance of Childhood for permission to use *Childhood*.

Parenting and Child Development Education in Schools
Roots of Empathy for permission to use the case study of Tom's Pink Feather.

Teaching the heart: the emotional value of play and Charter for Play
'Teaching the heart: the emotional value of play' and 'Charter for Play' by Sally Jenkinson reprinted by kind permission of Hawthorn Press, Stroud. Originally published by Hawthorn Press in *The Genius of Play* by Sally Jenkinson.

What's normal? Using drama to challenge the culture of violence in which children are reared
Roger McGough for permission to use his poem 'Beatings' from his Puffin collection.

Towards a non-violent society: Checkpoints
George Varnava and the National Children's Bureau for permission to use Checkpoint 2 (Values) from *Towards a Non-violent Society: Checkpoints for schools* (2000 page 4).

Brain Gym®: Integrating mind and body through movement
1) Lorna Ross for permission to use the Brain Gym® illustrations.
2) Permission from the Brain Gym® Foundation UK to describe Brain Gym® exercises.

Tuckswood: the school as a community of enquiry
Hawthorn Press for the figures on pages 182, 190, 191.

'The Young Man and the Starfish' (beginning of Appendices)
United Nations Association for permission to use this short story inspired by Loren Eiseley.

Summary of UN Convention on the Rights of the Child from UNICEF UK (Appendix 1)
UNICEF UK for permission to use their summary of UN Convention on the Rights of the child (What Rights?).

Children's books (Appendix 2) and Contacts (Appendix 4)
Resources and contacts from Global Citizenship: The Handbook for Primary Teaching (pages 174, 176, 178 and 186) reproduced with permission of Oxfam Publishing, 274 Banbury Road, Oxford OX2 7DZ www.oxfam.org.uk

Contents

Foreword

I touch the future; I teach.

Christa McAuliffe, teacher/NASA astronaut

Everyone is in favour of giving children the best possible start in life. Who would vote against such an aspiration, in a show of hands? Yet even in twenty-first-century Britain, when child exploitation, poverty, disease and maltreatment are supposed to be nothing more than faint memories of a tragic and distant past, many children still miss out, one way or another, despite everyone's stated best intentions.

That is why this book is so important. Children should have a whole series of entitlements, basic human rights. Providing these need not require a fortune. Many are fundamental and inexpensive, more about better ways of treating children within existing institutions and relationships, rather than purchasing costly equipment or premises. Imaginative play, for example, is a central means of learning pleasantly as you grow up. Other creatures engage in it, whether they are kittens learning to use their claws, or young bears enjoying a rough and tumble, so it is an entirely natural phenomenon. None the less, some children are denied these basic opportunities to flourish in a beneficial and appealing way, so I am glad that some of the authors have written about a topic as important as the thoughtful and intelligent use of play.

Life in the twenty-first century is not going to be easy. The qualifications required for employment have escalated, as thousands of unskilled and semi-skilled jobs evaporated during the last few years of the twentieth century. Furthermore, the personal demands on applicants have increased. Stick a pin in any employer's recruitment pamphlet nowadays and you will soon hit phrases like 'we are looking for people who are willing to learn...who can be members of a team...adaptable to the rapid changes in our field...get on well with their fellows...good communicators...reliable, punctual, trustworthy...able to use their initiative...'

These are all valuable personal qualities. As the numbers of jobs that merely involve standing next to a noisy machine in a factory declined, those working with their fellow human beings increased, so employers asked for more on both sides of the balance sheet: qualifications and personality. The entrance fee to adult society simply went up, very sharply. Those unable to pay it became outsiders, trampled in the headlong rush. In this kind of rapidly changing society, ill-equipped youngsters can soon become victims of the many unscrupulous predators who prey on the vulnerable – the loan sharks, the exploiters, the greedy.

That is why it is important to give every child a flying start during the years of primary schooling. Leave it until they are about to enter adult life and it is far too late, the damage has already been done. Only when people feel confident and positive about themselves can they begin to fulfil their potential. Many a promising talent has been smothered by contempt, ignorance, ridicule or neglect. Imagine a pair of identical twins separated at birth. One is given love and stimulus at home, goes to a good primary school, reaches secondary education full of enthusiasm. The other is neglected, humiliated, ridiculed, goes to a lousy primary school where nobody cares much. Would it be surprising, years later, if their genetic endowment counted for little?

This book offers a series of ideas and practices that have actually been tried out with children, for it is not a compendium of armchair speculation. It will be very handy for busy teachers and their support staff, who are often more persuaded by one enthusiastic description of something that appeared to work than a hundred dry policy documents conceived in a fusty office, a million miles from daily reality. The more teachers are given formulae and prescriptions by politicians, the more essential it is for them to reflect on their own practice, so that their craft skills do not fade away.

The good thing about books dealing with classroom and school practice is that the reader has at least three choices. First, you can like the idea and simply try it out for yourself. Second, the spirit of what is being suggested may appeal to you, but you believe it would not fit your own situation, personality or approach, so you modify it. Third, you might hate the idea, feeling that anyone could do better, and so be driven to improvise something of your own that is quite different. Most of us need help to come up with fresh ideas. I have lost count, over the years, of the many teachers I have watched, or spoken to, whose practices have given me ideas I could try out for myself.

My only reservation is about people taking over someone else's idea uncritically, or over-enthusiastically. Trying to be responsive to children's needs, understand their problems, offer them support, can spill over into self-indulgence, patronage, or even turn into cloying treacle, instead of rational behaviour. The ideas in this book are most engaging when used intelligently. Implement them mechanically, believe that your own input does not matter, or allow them to dominate when they should merely influence, and you demean their originators.

There are dozens of viable ideas and practices described in this book. It should make a valuable contribution to giving children what they all deserve as a fundamental human right: a flying start, so that they can be in with a chance of becoming the person that their potential promises them. The greatest crime anyone can perpetrate is to rob children of their childhood. The greatest gift anyone can bestow is to help them enjoy it to the full and then bounce off it into the future with confidence.

Children are born with a metaphorical learning switch firmly in the 'on' position. It is essential that they leave primary education with it still switched on. After all, they may live for eight or more decades in the twenty-first century after they have left childhood.

Professor Ted Wragg, Exeter University

Acknowledgements

The production of this book has involved collaboration on a grand scale. We applaud Sarah Woodhouse on, first, having the vision and then her tireless and diligent effort to see through this *Right from the Start* book for primary teachers (see the Introduction for the project details). There could hardly be a more important and admirable aim. As *Right from the Start*'s chief executive Sarah has successfully brought together a number of individuals in order to create this book. She has also been wonderfully supported by the Charity's trustees and would like to record her particular gratitude to Ailsa Moore, who has been involved in the project since 1988.

As editors we would like to express our gratitude, along with that of Sarah, to all the contributors who have responded with enthusiasm and concern to assure the success of this publication. Together these authors represent great commitment to the topic, also a wealth of professional knowledge and experience. The contributors include primary school teachers, university lecturers, consultants, life trainers and those individuals representing particular organizations concerned with personal and organizational well-being. Each has taken time from their busy lives to share both insight and expertise.

We would like to thank the following individuals who have provided the technical support during the production of the manuscript – Alison Newman, James O'Toole and Heather Wicks. Josie MacKenzie ensured that the entire manuscript was correctly formatted before it was submitted to the publisher. We are particularly grateful to Rachel Jenkins for her care and advice on the manuscript. As the book began to be a reality, we are grateful to Jim Houghton, the managing director at Network Educational Press Ltd for recognizing the real need for this publication. Our thanks go to Bridget Gibbs, the publishing manager for NEP who has been supportive and empathic, Ann Baggaley who meticulously edited the copy and Lynn Bresler for her thorough proofreading. We have enjoyed greatly working with Peter Bailey of Proof Books who undertook the design work; his patience and professionalism have made this final stage a pleasure.

Finally, it is our hope that this book will provide a thought-provoking and valuable resource to all those readers concerned about children's well-being in the primary years and without which no individual is able to achieve his or her potential.

Andrew Burrell and Jeni Riley
December 2004

Introduction

Children Learn What They Live
By Dorothy Law Nolte

If children live with criticism, they learn to condemn.

If children live with hostility, they learn to fight.

If children live with ridicule, they learn to feel shy.

If children live with shame, they learn to feel guilty.

If children live with encouragement, they learn confidence.

If children live with tolerance, they learn patience.

If children live with praise, they learn appreciation.

If children live with acceptance, they learn to love.

If children live with approval, they learn to like themselves.

If children live with honesty, they learn truthfulness.

If children live with security, they learn to have faith in
themselves and in those about them.

If children live with friendliness, they learn the world is a
nice place in which to live.

Right from the Start: purpose and vision

Sarah Woodhouse and Andrew Burrell

"The world will not change and there will be no peace if there is not a new education."

U Thant, former Secretary General to the United Nations

Where does this project come from?

Right from the Start is a charitable company (registration no. 327989) set up in order to 'promote the physical, intellectual, moral and spiritual education and development of children and adults' and to 'support innovative ventures at all levels of education'. To achieve these objectives, *Right from the Start* initiated a human rights education project for children from conception to 12 and all the adults in their lives. It responds to the changing mood and growing anxiety in the country about children's troubled or destructive behaviour, and parental and school helplessness in the face of it. It is an over-arching response to the present strains, confusion and peacelessness in so many children's lives.

The *Right from the Start* project was developed originally in response to a three-year research programme set up by the Schools' Council in the 1980s. That study looked at the emotional and mental health and the behaviour of children in inner-city and council estate primary schools throughout England and Wales. The main focus of the research was on five year olds as they first came into school, and again on the children during their last year or two before moving on to secondary school.

Two specific and clear-cut findings in the final report carried a powerful message. The first was that over 70 per cent of the five year olds coming into those primary schools already showed some signs of disturbed or violent behaviour. The second was that those children who had, from the very start of their lives, experienced love, acceptance and a creative family life, combined with security at school, showed an extraordinary 'peaking' of human qualities between the ages of 9 and 12. During this period these children showed a striking capacity for openness, helpfulness, kindness and generosity; also a high degree of sensitivity towards others, and freedom from cruelty, prejudice and dishonesty.

The prospects for these children's future is golden because, whatever their situation, they have absorbed the art of making strong, warm, trusting and lasting human relationships. This is the one most vital key to a peaceful and creative community anywhere in the world.

The original aim of the *Right from the Start* project was to ensure that this 'peaking' of human qualities is achieved for many more children before they come face-to-face with the upheavals of puberty and the pressures of a larger school.

Right from the Start spent six years investigating educational initiatives, parenting education and support programmes, and relevant research in Holland, Denmark, Sweden, Germany, Italy, the USA, India and Japan, as well as in the UK. It is these searchings and discoveries that have supported the development of the *Right from the Start* series of books for teachers and parents. Every one of these research undertakings and initiatives shows the extent to which early intervention and the help and encouragement given to parents will protect and bring out the best in children and so help teachers enormously when those children come to school.

What is the project's philosophy?

Right from the Start believes:

- that the newborn child has a wholeness and a unique spiritual, loving and creative potential;
- that a sense of identity, of trust, of justice

and of loving kindness is paramount in the life of every child and that this early learning is both powerful and permanent;

- that it is the responsibility of individuals, schools, communities, and local and national government, to enable children to fulfil this potential.

U Thant, former Secretary General to the United Nations, describes spirituality in these words:

Spirituality is a state of connectedness to life. It is an experience of being, belonging and caring. It is sensitivity and compassion, joy and hope. It is the harmony between the innermost life and the outer life, or the life of the world and the life universal. It is the supreme comprehension of life in time and place, the tuning of the inner person with the great mysteries and secrets that are around us. It is the belief in the goodness of life and possibility of each person to contribute goodness to it. It is the belief in life as part of the eternal stream of time, that each of us came from somewhere and is destined somewhere, that without such belief there could be no prayer, no meditation, no peace and no happiness.

The *Right from the Start* dolphin-and-child logo comes from the 5.5m (18ft) bronze sculpture by David Wynne on London's Albert Embankment, overlooking the River Thames. It has been chosen because a dolphin has a high level of emotional intelligence, a close affinity with human beings and a special instinct to heal and comfort. A dolphin also has a great sense of fun. The picture of child and dolphin playing together symbolizes trust, affection, adventure and the sense of unity in all creation.

What are the project's aims?

The project's aims are:

- To introduce tried and tested initiatives and strategies that are known to help children grow up more confident, capable and kind.

- To bring back more enchantment, joy and satisfaction into teaching and parenting.
- To help parents and teachers grow more understanding and skilful in their response to children's moods, and variations in their behaviour and energy.
- To help people to recognize the spirituality for children in their educational experience.
- To help prevent children's lives from becoming invaded by stress and violence.
- To affirm the crucial role of men as well as women in parenting and teaching in the early years.
- To draw parents and teachers into a fuller working partnership.

How is *Right from the Start* working to achieve these aims?

RESOURCE BOOKS

The project presents an integrated series of educational aids for parents and teachers. It consists of a number of wide-ranging, single-focus yet closely interrelated resource books for parents, child carers, nursery and primary teachers. The parenting resource books are also written for child and family care organizations, parenting groups and parenting education courses in secondary schools.

All the resource books surround and support this book. They are full of pictures and stories, and present a wealth of useful information, new knowledge, age-old wisdom, fresh ideas, enterprises, activities, strategies, stories, games, skills, tools and troubleshooting tactics.

PARTNERSHIP WITH PARENTS

The happiest and most successful schools are those that have a close working partnership with parents. For this reason, many of the *Right from the Start* books are written for parents and teachers together. It is equally important that *Right from the Start* should be an international project, sharing outstanding good practice, new knowledge and critical research findings across national boundaries.

The series will be regularly reappraised and updated through a feedback invitation in each book so that they will always be a continuing and valuable resource for parents and teachers over the years. Everything that has been written for the project is concerned, first and foremost, with respect for the children. We can only work from the standpoint of love. We can only begin and continue slowly and gently with all possible variety of ideas and experiences for the children so that each of them is caught up somewhere, somehow, some day, by something we have done for them.

"Peace is being without crime and violence and hating. It is love that is passed on from generation to generation."

Clifford, aged 8

THE UNITED NATIONS CONVENTION ON THE RIGHTS OF THE CHILD

The baseline for this project is provided by the United Nations Convention on the Rights of the Child (UN General Assembly 1989), agreed to and signed by the British government on 16 December 1991. All but two of the world's countries have ratified the UN Convention, making it a truly global aspect of citizenship that young children around the world share (UNICEF). The key provisions covered by the Convention can be summarized in four broad categories:

> survival rights
> developmental rights
> protection rights
> participation rights.

The Convention consists of 54 Articles that together offer an effective framework for understanding and respecting children's rights. Articles 3, 12, 29, 31 and 36 are particularly relevant to *Right from the Start* because they are concerned with the spiritual, emotional, mental and moral protection and development of a child, and the essential educational, leisure and cultural provisions to be made for them (see Appendix 1 for a summary).

However, the Convention can only work for children as central and local government and non-government organizations achieve changes in the law, and then at local level, that will truly reflect and put into practice the principles of the Convention and so bring them to life. The International Committee on the Rights of the Child undertakes a watchdog check-up at five-year intervals to see how genuinely and imaginatively each nation is responding to the Convention. But this committee can only use persuasion, offer strong advice and put on the pressure, up to a point.

Because of this, the Convention can only really work for children when individual people, above all, parents and teachers, begin to take each relevant Article a step further. This means recognizing and responding to the developing needs and rights of childhood in more exact and everyday detail than would be possible to present within the United Nations framework. Primary schools can, for example, raise awareness of rights and responsibilities by using them as shared values. This can then support a whole-school ethos of respect for everyone's rights and so help to bring about improvements in their pupils' attitude, behaviour and participation in school life.

PROMOTING WELL-BEING THROUGH THIS BOOK

The book's various authors share a commitment to the personal development and education of children and adults. Many of the authors have been at the forefront of innovative ventures concerned to promote well-being.

This book has been divided into seven main chapters. The first of these, 'Educating the whole person', examines the child's needs and rights. The complex process of personal development is also examined in relation to the child's understanding of himself or herself, others and society. Each of these aspects of personal development is illustrated by case studies. Reference is made to relevant policy and planning documents.

'Partnerships for learning and well-being' are the focus of the second chapter. The first four contributions in this chapter examine the well-being of staff and children. They are written from a variety of perspectives and explore emotional literacy, self-esteem and work–life balance, and offer practical and emotional support for staff in education. Underpinning these contributions is the belief that a healthy school environment is essential if teachers and children are to perform to the best of their ability. Jenny Mosley's contribution, for example, examines how teachers can help staff morale and self-esteem so that they have the energy to help others. Kevin Avison draws on his experience of Steiner education to discuss how mentoring facilitates teachers' professional development. Developing partnerships beyond the school is a feature of the final two contributions in this chapter. The first of these provides details about two successful parenting education programmes that require a commitment to community involvement. The final contribution describes a nursery school's developing partnership with parents and the local community, and the links forged with a school in Italy.

Chapter 3, 'Play and natural wonder', introduces a wide range of initiatives and contemporary issues that seek to promote children's well-being and enhance learning. The contributions examine fundamental aspects of childhood and the need to nurture these within educational settings so that children will continue to develop their sense of wonder and excitement of the world. The inclusion of a charter for children's play reflects the increasing pressure on children to grow up fast through more and hurried adult controlling which allows children less time and almost no freedom to play and explore – thus denying them a true experience of childhood.

Chapter 4, 'Peace and conflict resolution', contains contributions that seek to develop positive relationships. Joan Webster's 'talking out' strategy demonstrates how even very young children are capable of peaceful conflict-solving. The message that children can be trusted to help in the resolution of each other's problems is also a feature of the Circle of Friends approach, based on the notion of inclusion. Here, Gill Taylor describes through the use of case studies how this approach can support children with social and emotional difficulties. John Airs describes several drama exercises he has used with children to challenge attitudes towards violence. The promotion of non-violence in school is the focus of George Varnava's contribution. He describes a series of publications known as 'Checkpoints'. Used as an auditing tool, Checkpoints can raise awareness and enable schools to add a violence-prevention perspective to their work.

Several of the contributions in chapter 5, 'Reflection and contemplation', focus on the benefits of quietening the mind. Primary school teacher Anne D'Souza provides a brief description of how she introduced Tai chi to the small village school where she teaches. This ancient exercise is performed in a slow and controlled manner. The benefits of Tai chi are both physical and emotional. Laura Hyde describes how meditation is introduced on a voluntary basis to ten year olds at her school. Included are views from pupils on how this way of focusing, being quiet and still, has benefited them. The two contributions that follow this describe a larger-scale initiative known as 'A Quiet Place' that began in Liverpool. In this holistic approach, designed to improve children's emotional well-being, a room is set aside by the school. Decorated to offer a pleasant and nurturing environment, these quiet havens are designed as a multisensory experience for

children who are experiencing difficulties with their emotions or their behaviour. This very specific programme is characterized by the supervised practice of therapists trained to a professional level through nationally recognized training programmes. The practice of story-telling has always featured in primary schools. Two contributions offer different perspectives on story-telling. The first examines the important role oral story-telling has on children's development and how it helps children to construct their identities. The second describes the use of story by a therapist who worked in primary schools and other contexts.

The first two contributions in chapter 6, 'Enhancing learning', have a distinct focus on the ideas and methods practised by teachers in Steiner Waldorf schools. These schools bring both a gentleness and a thoughtful structure to early childhood education. They seek to protect the child's right to a healthy and appropriate childhood that acknowledges the significance of play and the need for a balance of artistic, practical and intellectual content in the curriculum. In recent years, there has been increasing concern over the emphasis given to the core national curriculum subjects and related testing in our primary schools. It is important that the arts are not sidelined or ignored as they have a significant role in promoting the education and development of children's well-being. Susan Digby's contribution provides such an example. She outlines a music education programme, which has helped those primary schools involved to transform the atmosphere, all relationships in the school community and the children's ability to learn. Sarah Woodhouse examines the effect of nutrition on children's brains and their behaviour. The final contribution in this chapter reminds us that using movement and physical activity can help many primary school children to absorb, process and understand information. Daphne Clarke provides an introduction to Brain Gym® exercises, which integrate the mind and body through movement. Her contribution includes several exercises she has found to be particularly helpful to children.

Chapter 7 describes work undertaken at Tuckswood Community First School, providing an example of a school that has successfully implemented a range of initiatives to support children's social, emotional and cognitive development. Furthermore, it underlines the importance of having vision and purpose…right from the start.

The resource lists that form part of the Appendices
are intended to be a valuable part of the book in
terms of other openings and extending support. In
addition to this, each contribution concludes with a
list of resources and suggested further reading to
enable readers to develop further their interest or
commitment to a particular initiative to promote
children's well-being.

Feedback invitation

Promoting Children's Well-Being in the Primary Years and the other associated *Right from the Start* resource books (see list on page 235) present a wide-ranging, integrated series of educational aids for teachers and parents.

Many teachers and educationists have shared their experiences so that these books will help in sensitive ways to bring out the best in our children, whatever the circumstances in which we live or teach. This sharing has been a gift to the *Right from the Start* project from many extraordinary people whose understanding of children and responses to them are exceptional.

If your own teaching experience or understanding seem especially relevant to any of the books in the series and you feel you have valuable insights or suggestions to offer, please write to:

Right from the Start Feedback
C/o Network Educational Press Ltd
P.O. Box 635, Stafford ST16 1BF
email: enquiries@networkpress.co.uk
website: http://www.networkpress.co.uk

The *Right from the Start* trustees are grateful to Network Educational Press Ltd for making possible the publication and distribution of this handbook and the other forthcoming titles in the series.

"Peace is being without crime and violence and hating. It is love that is passed on from generation to generation."
Clifford, aged 8

1 *Educating the whole person*

Childhood

Childhood is a time for learning about the essentials – about the heavenly world and the earthly, about goodness, beauty and truth.

Childhood is a time to be loved and to love – to express fear and to learn trust – to be allowed to be serious and calm and to celebrate with laughter and joy.

Children have a right to dream, and they need time to grow at their own pace. They have the right to make mistakes and the right to be forgiven.

Children need help to develop self-mastery, to transform themselves and bring forth their highest capacities.
Children have a right to be spared violence and hunger to have a home and protection.
They need help to grow up healthily, with good habits and sound nutrition.

Children need people to respect,
Adults whose example and loving authority they follow.
They need a range of experience – tenderness and kindness, boldness and courage, and even mischief and misbehaviour.

Children need time for receiving and giving, for belonging and participating.
They need to be part of a community, and they need to be individuals.
They need privacy and sociability.
They need time to rest and time to play, time to do nothing and time to work.

They need moments for devotion and room for curiosity. They need protective boundaries and freedom for creativity.
They need to be introduced to a life of principles and given the freedom to discover their own.
They need a relationship to the earth – to animals and to nature, and they need to unfold as human beings within the community.

The spirit of childhood is to be protected and nurtured. It is an essential part of every human being and needs to be kept alive.

 The Alliance for Childhood, partners working together to create a healthy childhood, International Joint Alliance Working Group – New York 1999

Educating the whole person:
children's needs and rights

Priscilla Alderson

This contribution considers meanings in the charity's title 'Right from the Start'. When does 'the Start' begin? How can we best understand and respect children's rights so that, as caring adults, we 'get it right' in our relationships with children? Priscilla Alderson discusses how we can 'educate the whole person' by attending to children's needs and rights and their own knowledge. She reviews the benefits of approaches based on rights and respect when working and researching with children. The examples are drawn from the literature and from Priscilla Alderson's experiences as a teacher, researcher, mother and helper in early years groups.

When does 'the Start' begin?

Howard Gardner (1993), a professor of education in New York, describes a study of physics graduates. When they were asked complex questions about trajectory, they gave the complex replies that physicists understand. When asked the same questions, but in simple terms, they forgot their specialist knowledge. They answered in the common-sense ways that a four or five year old would talk, such as about throwing things.

Gardner shows how we all rely most of the time on the basic knowledge we have acquired before five years of age, about ourselves and others, time and space, language and morality, art and science. Gardner argues that our minds are often 'unschooled'. Our formal schooling slips off our minds like water off a duck's back, unless teachers start from the deep knowledge we bring to our first day at school. Instead, they tend to ignore that, and behave as if real learning begins on day one at nursery or infant school. When school lessons seem to contradict our basic knowledge, we usually ignore or forget them, unless we can explore the contradictions.

For 25 years at their New York school, Gardner and his team have researched how to work with young children, beginning at the high levels they have already reached and taking these further. Adults and children are both respectful co-learners. Gardner admires the 'whole person', such as our creative, technical and social intelligences, besides our IQ. For many years, Gardner and other psychologists (Donaldson 1978) have deplored the way school lessons are so often abstract. Many lessons take tiny bits of remote ideas out of context and away from the personal relationships, feelings and experiences that give them real meaning and interest. Children struggle to understand taught ideas that they would quickly grasp, or already know about, through their own activities. In contrast, Gardner shows how school subjects can be linked in practical ways that children enjoy and understand when, for instance, a team of young children of mixed ages build a bicycle together.

The mention of personal relationships, feelings and experiences returns to the question: when does 'the Start' begin? We learn everything through our bodies and feelings, our five senses, and how we experience, perceive, remember and imagine what we have sensed. In our current research in intensive care units for premature and sick babies, the babies learn about pain (they learn to expect their heels to be pricked when their feet are held) and about pleasure (their body rhythms change when their parents cuddle them). They recognize and prefer their parents' voices. Some babies can get into comfortable positions (curled up, hands near their mouths) that help them to calm down and sleep and grow, whereas other babies need much more help to learn how to comfort themselves. The babies are beginning to work out how to use their hands, through countless little efforts (Murray and Andrews 2000). Educationists often write about children at school having to 'learn how to learn', how to attend, persevere, analyse, remember, refine skills and so on. Yet people close to babies know how brilliant babies and young children already are at these learning skills. Learning begins very early in life.

Why should we respect children's rights?

There are several reasons for respecting children's rights. As members of the human family, from birth all children have certain inalienable human rights, for example, the right to life and to protection from abuse. We are all sensitive, feeling, reacting people who can easily be hurt. We are not like objects or even pets. From the start, babies behave in uniquely human ways. For example, they share in the micro-dance that happens whenever two people talk to one another. They nod their heads in time to the speech, and take turns to listen and to make sounds (Murray and Andrews 2000). Adults therefore have duties and responsibilities towards children to ensure that their human rights are respected. The United Nations 1989 Convention on the Rights of the Child (United Nations 1989) enshrines these agreed rights in 54 Articles.

Another reason for respecting the children's rights in the UN Convention is that the Convention gives an ideal plan for educating everyone to respect and care for one another. The Convention states that respecting the inherent worth and dignity and the inalienable rights of all members of the human family promotes social progress and better standards of life in larger freedoms, and lays foundations for justice and peace in the world.

A third reason for respecting human rights goes back to the first thinking about human rights some 400 years ago. At first, it was argued that independent men should have the right to lead their own lives in the way they choose, because they are rational persons and no one else can make better decisions for them. Gradually, other groups have claimed their equal rights: working men, ethnic minorities, women and disabled people. They argued that they, too, could make the best decisions about their own lives. However, children have always been seen as not able to reason – as used to happen to women. This chapter argues that children are very often reasonable and should be involved in matters that affect them.

RETHINKING CHILDHOOD

Much if not most of the literature about children implies or openly states that they are inadequate. Very often double standards are assumed (see box below).

The double adult–child standards

ADULTS	CHILDREN
Strong	Weak
Informed	Ignorant
Reasonable	Unreasonable
Reliable	Unreliable
Supportive	Dependent
Competent	Incompetent

The idea of child development assumes that children will gradually move from the second column towards the first. A widely used book on observing young children (Sharman, Cross and Vennis 1995) advises students to see how children meet their milestones at each age. The only 'key features' given for 9 to 18 months are:

'Growing independence can lead to rage when thwarted. Shows anxiety when left alone. Emotionally more stable but can be jealous of adults' attention to other children. Can be defiant – learns NO.'

All the key features are negative. They ignore the very many positive exciting things that children aged 9 to 18 months are doing. The features imply that young children are tiresome and troublesome, and therefore that adults are kind to look after them and put up with them. The text slips over the ways that the adults might be thwarting or leaving the children or in other ways annoying them or upsetting them. So the text masks the two-way relationship between adults and children.

The text also ignores any reasons that children may have for their behaviour. And when children's reactions are noticed, without an understanding of what they are reacting to, their behaviour can easily look silly, naughty and unreasonable. Worse still, the double standards lead adults to assume that, if adults and children disagree, the adults are always right, and children always wrong simply because they are children.

However, when adults try to understand and respect the child's point of view, being 'thwarted' might look quite sensible. People of any age who are deeply absorbed in painting or making something or talking with friends, and are suddenly dragged away, are likely to feel 'thwarted'. That is part of being enthusiastic, creative and deeply absorbed, which children are good at being.

Another problem with the milestones is that they imply that children are incomplete and are gradually working their way up to being complete adults, real people. Yet adults, too, can feel rage and jealousy, whereas many children can sympathize with and help people who feel angry or upset. The double standards listed above are misleading. People at every age tend to have a mixture of qualities across both columns. Even very young children are concerned when others are upset and try to comfort them (Dunn 1993).

If we are to take children's rights seriously, we have to rethink the many false prejudices about childhood – that often used to be held against women, too. And taking rights seriously can help us to think about children more fairly and realistically.

How can we best understand and respect children's rights?

The earlier examples of babies show how the UN Convention rights apply from birth. These rights are about providing for children's needs, not for luxuries. Children's right to life involves ensuring that they have an adequate standard of living and the best available health care if they need it. Another basic provision right is education, that in so many ways begins from birth. So do the protection rights, which safeguard children from neglect, cruel and degrading treatment, abuse and discrimination. Protection includes treating every child fairly, not discriminating against children or withholding services because their parents are, say, asylum seekers or drug addicts.

All the protection and provision rights can equally well be discussed as children's needs, welfare or best interests, which adults decide for children. As one psychologist wrote, defining children's needs can be a way of saying 'as an expert I know what is best for you' whether the child agrees or not (Woodhead 1997). But rights bring in new dimensions.

Firstly, rights are basic entitlements. They are not about kind adults giving out favours, or about children being good or clever enough to earn their rights. Instead, rights express the justice that equally respects every child. Far from setting children against

each other to compete for resources, many of the basic rights, such as to clean water or to play-space, can benefit the whole community.

Secondly, rights are legal ideas. They therefore involve actions that can be enforced by law. For example, no child has the right to have loving parents, because no one can enforce love. A very fraught, depressed mother cannot be taken to court for not loving her children enough. Instead, rights are realistic. Parents can be judged, for example, if they behave in obviously cruel or neglectful ways, and therefore children have rights to protection from this treatment. The UN Convention recognizes that love is a need, though not a right, and all the Convention's rights are intended to support and promote loving families.

Thirdly, rights centre on respecting and listening to the rights-holders (women, disabled people, children), instead of to the usually more powerful people who may respect or ignore less powerful people's rights. The Convention includes participation rights: to a name, an identity and a family; to be informed in many ways; to have freedom of peaceful association and assembly, of thought, conscience and religion. In other words, no one should be able to stop children and their parents attending, for example, their local mosque, or having family gatherings or partying with friends and neighbours, or working together to improve local amenities. Disabled children should be able 'to enjoy a full and decent life, in conditions which ensure dignity, promote self-reliance and facilitate the child's active part in the community' (Article 23). The Convention repeats its concern to respect the worth and dignity of every child.

The key right is about assuring

'...to the child who is capable of forming his or her own views the right to express those views freely in all matters affecting the child, the views of the child being given due weight in accordance with the age and maturity of the child (Article 12).'

Article 12 is very often misquoted. Children's 'opinions' are often mentioned instead of their 'views'. An opinion is lighter, less reliable, less real than a view. I have a view of the Millennium Wheel from my window. I do not simply have an opinion that it is there. 'Decisions' affecting the child are sometimes mentioned instead of the actual phrase 'all matters', which cover everything. 'Decisions' tend to be narrowed down to the rare times when a choice seems to arise that a child might be able to have a view about. However, children's lives are organized by countless decisions that have already been made and are no longer seen as decisions at all – where they live, the school they attend, their parents' careers, the family income and whole lifestyle.

Surely children can hold and express views about these 'matters' that affect them so much, even though no overt 'decision' is being considered at the time. By talking about things that seem fixed and unchangeable, such as rules and routines in a school, people may come to realize that things can be changed and improved, and that they can share in this creative process.

It took ten years to write the Convention, which has been ratified by every government except in the USA and in Somalia, which has no government. This extremely carefully written document provides the best principled but also flexible framework for understanding and respecting children's rights.

EDUCATING THE WHOLE PERSON BY ATTENDING TO CHILDREN'S NEEDS AND RIGHTS

One of the strengths of many early years services is the attention given to the 'whole child', mind, body and spirit, and thereby to the wide range of children's needs and rights. However, it is not always easy for staff in under-resourced services to achieve this. Helen Penn (1997) gave examples of their difficulties in her study comparing British and continental nursery care (see Case study, above).

The differences between the nurseries that Penn observed show how young children, their bodily, emotional, social and cultural needs and rights, as well as the adults caring for them, are valued, or not valued, in their communities. The differences also illustrate the point made earlier about how hidden decisions in early years national and local policies and economics can affect many detailed matters in young children's daily needs and rights.

Recently, in line with Article 12, the government's Children's and Young People's Unit has advocated that children should be consulted about all the public services they use. Ofsted asks children about the services they use, and so do local authorities. (It is important that careful, reliable methods are used, to prevent sham and misleading consultations. We have

---

Case study:
Public policies affect the quality of early years care

Helen Penn (1997) compared publicly funded nurseries in Italy, Spain and Britain. In Britain, disadvantaged and often disturbed children attended for a few slots a week. They tended to be lonely and anxious, unable to get to know the changing shifts of staff and groups of children well. Outdoor play areas were vandalized and strewn with rubbish. Staff dressed in plastic aprons and gloves kept the children inside, for fear that they might find needles infected with HIV.

In the Mediterranean nurseries, the children enjoyed continuity and warm friendships, lovely toys and gardens, fine music and art, delicious food, which they helped to cook. (British children were not allowed into the kitchens.) The staff were well educated and well respected in their communities. In Italy, the Mayor attended a banquet with all the families when a new member of staff was appointed.

---

a long way to go in devising good methods of consulting children – and adults.) These new moves offer valuable ways of learning about children's all-round needs and rights so that their education may become more holistic.

RIGHTS AND RESPONSIBILITIES

Rights are often linked to responsibilities; usually adults' responsibilities, to ensure that children's provision and protection rights are honoured. We tend to think of this being a one-way process, from adults to young children. Yet it can be two-way. The participation rights are showing that many children would like to have more share and responsibility in helping to plan and provide their local services. Early years policies can be far better informed by listening to and observing young children, seeing whether they are happy or sad, inspired or frustrated.

People's views tend to be limited to their own experiences. So when asking children about early years centres, it is important to inform them about a range of options, and perhaps show them videos or take them on visits to other centres. Children can use a mosaic of methods to collect information and express their views, such as taking photographs of the places and things they like most and least (Clark and Moss 2001).

Case study:

Young children and planning services

A council planned to upgrade a run-down housing estate and to build a playground. They chose a site on the edge of the estate and across a busy road. Luckily, ten children aged three to eight years became involved in the planning. They did a survey of the other children's views, and wrote a report with maps, drawings and photos. On their advice, the playground was built in the middle of the estate, away from traffic and passing strangers. Children could easily reach and enjoy the playground without having to rely on their parents to stay with them (Newson 1995).

When are children old enough to begin to form and express their own views? Save the Children asked me to do an international review about Article 12, and how children from babyhood to eight years of age can participate and be consulted (Alderson 2000). Gradually, I found younger and younger examples. At all ages, rights often relate to bodily comfort: protection from pain or fear; provision of basic physical needs; freedoms to move around and enjoy positive experiences and relationships. So rights are not simply ideas in our heads or complicated choices to think through; they have physical and emotional aspects, too.

Babies are very aware of their bodily needs and can express 'sensible' views. For example, breastfeeding works best when the mother lets the baby decide the timing and pace of feeds. Babies let us know vividly if they are hungry, too hot or cold, tired or bored, and when they are happy and excited. Young children express their needs and choices sensibly, when they are listened to respectfully.

Problems often begin when adults rush in to provide for children, ignore or override children's views, and do not trust or respect them as sensible people. The web page called 'Watch, wait and wonder' shows how greatly we can learn from being more patient and respectful (www.solgen.gov).

Listening to a child's views can benefit that child and often potentially others, too, when adults learn how to improve general policies and practices. For example, in the baby units, some of the hospital staff have learned from the babies how they need quiet, low-lit nurseries, and how babies cope better with painful procedures when someone talks to them gently. A few units adopt these 'baby-led' policies and constantly train the staff to follow them (Als 1999). Many reports vividly show the rewards of working with children instead of against them (see Suggested further reading, page 31).

Sharing views and decisions with children

The following is a review of what is involved when sharing more formal decision making with children. The examples are taken mainly from health care, because most research about decision making has been undertaken in this area.

There are four levels in decision making (Alderson and Montgomery 1996):

1. to be informed
2. to express an informed view
3. to have that view taken into account when decisions are made
4. to be the main decider.

The fourth level includes making and signifying the decision, acting on it and taking responsibility for it whatever the outcome. It is often argued that children cannot and should not make major decisions, for reasons linked to the levels listed above:

1. they cannot understand the relevant information;
2. they cannot evaluate information in the light of lasting personal values;
3. they cannot know their own best interests, so adults must act for them;
4. if things go wrong, children do not yet have the courage and resolve to stand by a decision, and they need to blame other people instead of risking guilt and blame themselves.

Doctors used all these arguments, in the past, to protect adult patients. The UN Convention recognizes the first three levels as rights without any age barrier (Articles 12 and 13). Children have the right to all kinds of useful information. We should take account of children's views as soon as they are old enough to form and express them. As already mentioned, babies form and express views about feeding. Toddlers share in choosing what to wear, and learn when to wear warm or cool clothes. Some two year olds are able to make complex decisions about their health care, such as actively co-operating with taking unpleasant cancer treatments (Kendrick et al. 1986), or physiotherapy and diet to treat their cystic fibrosis. Children aged four with diabetes can share in administering daily blood tests and insulin injections, and in managing their diet to control blood sugar levels. This requires children to be informed and committed if, for example, they are to be able to refuse the sweet foods that their friends are enjoying.

The fourth level of decision making is to be the main decider. This level is not covered in the UN Convention, but it is part of English law following the 1985 Gillick case. The Gillick ruling was that children can make valid decisions if they are able and willing to do so, and can make an informed decision in their own best interests. Children and their parents and doctors usually all agree about health care decisions. Occasionally they disagree.

One example is vaccinations, when children might be afraid of the needle and are also unable to understand about the illnesses that the vaccination will prevent. The adults can explain and reassure, support and comfort the child, and perhaps use a cream to stop the sting. They can justify insisting that the child has the vaccination by saying they are protecting the best interests and health rights of the child, and also of all the other children who might become infected if a non-vaccinated child develops measles or rubella and passes it on.

While an overriding of the child's views might work on a rare occasion, such as vaccinations, it will not work well if needles are to be used daily, such as when a child has diabetes. Then, it is vital to avoid daily fights. So it is very important to help children to feel informed, respected and involved, and willing to take an active part in their daily health care. The courage and good sense that so many young children show illustrates that this is possible and worthwhile. Sometimes young children's very serious decisions are trusted, as in the case of Samantha, who chose to forgo prolonged medical treatment (see Case study, below).

Samantha's story is not told because she was an unusual child, quite the opposite. It is told to suggest that she became unusual because of her unusual experiences. Most young children probably have these great reserves of wisdom and courage. However, many children live safe, fortunate lives. They may never need to know about, or show, the courage and hard thinking that Samantha showed. From hundreds of examples of children's decision making, the case of Susan (see Case study, page 28) illustrates one about education.

In some ways, at four and at ten years, Susan was the only person who could make a fully informed decision that took account of her experiences, values and plans. Many other girls and boys with average abilities, and some with learning difficulties, have talked to me with great insight into their own and their families' and friends' interests. They showed how their understanding was gained through their experiences, rather than from age or assessed intelligence.

Adults often assume that the high-flying, healthy, intelligent, 'successful' children are the most informed, brave and wise. Perhaps the reverse is true. Children who are asylum seekers (Candappa 2002), or who experience racism, poverty or disability, gain deep hard-earned knowledge. They develop capable ways of coping with adversity. If we really want to know how competent children can be, if they have to, maybe we should listen more closely to these disadvantaged groups. There is much we could learn from them, on how to tackle their problems with them, instead of simply seeing them as passive victims that adults must rescue.

Case study:

A young child's serious decisions

Samantha aged six years agreed to have a liver transplant (Irwin 1996). She wanted to look pink instead of yellow, to be able to run about and feel well, and to wear nice clothes. She explained clearly to her class at school what was going to happen to her. The transplant was unsuccessful. Samantha agreed to go through a second transplantation, and bravely did so. Sadly, the second one also failed, and Samantha became very anxious and depressed. She refused to eat, or to look at her scar. The doctors wanted to try a third transplant with, they said, a 2 per cent chance of success. Her parents longed to try any chance of hope, but gradually her mother felt that they must respect Samantha's wish to stop treatment. Being so ill and close to death, Samantha probably knew profoundly what not having the operation would mean, as other young children can know (Alderson 1993; Judd 1989; Sourkes 1995). Samantha's parents took her home and she died two days later, the most stressful but important time of their lives.

RESEARCH WITH INSTEAD OF ON CHILDREN

There is growing interest in collecting children's own views (Christensen and James 2000). There are important questions to ask when you do research, or read other people's research reports, or think about whether to use their findings in your own practice.

Researchers tend to find whatever they are looking for: incompetent young children or competent ones. Much depends on the assumptions and questions that researchers start out with, and they may not explain these. So when reading a research report, the first question to ask is: What are the researchers' views about childhood?

The three Ps in the UN Convention are often helpful here. At heart, people's views about children tend to be a desire to *protect* them or to *provide* for them. Other people prefer to respect children, and increase their *participation* in society and in having a say about their own lives.

The protectors and providers tend to worry about risk and need, and want to show how children depend on adults' services. The participators aim to show how actively young children can form and express views and share responsibilities, including as young researchers. For example, we asked young asylum seekers aged 5 to 12 years to take photos and make a video about aspects of their school that made them feel welcome and that respected their rights. They matched their photos to articles in the UN Convention and made scrapbooks about their rights (Alderson, Clarke-Jones and Schaumberg 2002). The value of asking for children's own explanations is illustrated by an example from Miller (1998) (see Case study, below).

TRADITIONAL AND NEW RESEARCH METHODS AND VALUES

One reason that researchers tend to find what they are looking for is their choice of research methods. Traditional methods tend to undermine and underestimate children. Over much of the twentieth century, researchers have:

- observed children with methods based on an animal model of research;
- examined them in laboratory conditions isolated from their everyday context;
- given them artificial tests and hypothetical questions;
- tested them against norms;
- designed questionnaires about the children for adults to answer;
- used adult-centred units of analysis such as the family;
- searched for causes for children's behaviour without asking for the children's views;
- proposed a scientific universal model of child development.

Newer methods of research with children tend to:

- observe and also, crucially, talk with children as people;
- meet them in their everyday contexts and relationships where they have expert knowledge;
- avoid tests and assessments and adult-assumed norms;
- try to see children's perspectives and how they organize and make sense of their lives;
- ask the children and not rely wholly on their parents' or teachers' views;
- see the child as the unit of analysis, and how resources are often unequally shared within the family or the school;
- search for motives and contextual reasons for children's behaviour;
- compare greatly varying childhoods around the world, and especially note the 'adult' competencies of so many children in the poorer majority world.

These newer approaches begin from and/or produce evidence to support certain values:

- Children's lives are worthwhile and matter now, in the present, not simply for their future effects.
- Children are not merely developing and practising, they are also accomplishing and contributing competently (Hutchby and Moran-Ellis 1998).
- Adulthood is not the perfect endpoint after childhood. We all change and learn and make mistakes throughout our lives.
- Therefore, childhood and adulthood are in many ways similar and equally important parts of our lives.
- The value of life cannot be measured by its length but by its quality.

Children enjoying a class picnic

All children have a right to relax and play

EDUCATIONAL BENEFITS OF APPROACHES BASED ON RIGHTS AND RESPECT

Some educators assume that children can and must behave 'properly' so that they can concentrate on learning. If they cannot or will not behave, these children should be excluded, for the sake or the rights of everyone else in the group. Others believe that the adults should make allowances. They should support disturbed or disturbing children as much as possible, using exclusion as a last resort. A third approach sees helping children to tackle their problems together as a central topic and method for learning (McNamara and Moreton 1995; Alderson 1999).

Right from the start, children are learning the real, crucial lessons in life:

- how to live together with peace and justice
- how to resolve conflicts
- how to understand and care for one another
- how to respect and celebrate difference and diversity.

Punishing and excluding the children with difficulties can make everyone else feel anxious about being rejected too. It sets negative hostile examples of human relationships, instead of 'laying the

Case study:
Working with disturbed children

In one nursery, Janet aged 22 months ran about frenetically. The staff decided not to wait months for a medical diagnosis – this would not necessarily provide any extra support or ideas on how to help Janet. They saw the issue as an educational one, not simply a medical one.

Janet's key worker Helen listed many things that Janet could do, which made the staff and Janet's mother feel more hopeful. Helen began running about with Janet around the garden holding her hand. She helped Janet to slow down, and to gain more skill and control over her movements. She held Janet in her arms until Janet relaxed and began to play, at first like a younger child, mouthing toys. After a few days of intensive help, Janet became more like an ordinarily energetic child, and the staff found ways to help her to be calm and attentive (Goldschmeid and Jackson 1994).

foundations for peace and justice in the world' that the Convention advocates. This can take imagination and energy (see Case study, page 30).

Countless young children struggle with serious 'adult' problems, and need friendly support to help them to cope and to help to reduce future problems. Here are just two, from many general examples. Young children in Northern Ireland learn very early that they are living in the midst of bitter political conflicts (Connolly et al. 2002). And, in Britain, the soaring numbers of prisoners means that many more children have a parent in prison. Sometimes they have to keep this secret, but sometimes their school can help. One prisoner said, 'The nursery has even got my daughter to do a tape to send me, telling me all about her day and what she has done, and what she is going to do. It's lovely to hear her voice whenever I want to' (Katz 2002, page 22).

Adults working with young children can assume that it is 'normal' for many of them to have obvious or hidden problems. Effective education involves accepting and respecting the children as whole people, with all their needs and difficulties, their rights, strengths and potential contributions, right from the start.

The key points

- Education and rights are vital concerns from birth.

- Formal education needs to build on the deep knowledge that children have already gained informally as expert learners.

- The UN 1989 Convention on the Rights of the Child offers the best framework for understanding and respecting children's rights.

- Children's crucial rights to express their views freely in all matters that affect them, and for due account to be taken of their views, are integral parts of effective education.

- The way adults ignore and punish, or else value and respect, children with problems set potent negative or positive educational examples.

- Listening to children can help adults to improve services for individuals and groups of children, and to work with them on reducing and resolving problems.

Resources

A summary of the UN Convention on the Rights of the Child can be found at the back of this book (see Appendix 1).

Suggested further reading

Edwards, C., Gandini, L. and Forman, G. (eds) (1998), *The Hundred Languages of Children: The Reggio Emilia approach to childhood education*, Ablex, Norwood, New Jersey
Reggio Emilia has evolved into a distinctive and innovative approach that supports children's well-being and has become recognized and acclaimed as one of the best systems of education in the world.

Finch, S. (1998), *An Eye for an Eye Leaves Everyone Blind: Teaching young children to settle conflicts without violence*, National Early Years Network in association with Save the Children, London
This handbook contains guidance on creating an environment that discourages violence, and suggestions for practical activities on non-violent conflict resolution.

Mayall, B. (2002), *Towards a Sociology for Childhood*, Routledge, London
This book examines some critical issues in the current development of childhood studies. It argues for an improved social status of childhood, including respecting children's rights.

Miller, J. (1997), *Never Too Young: How young children can take responsibility and make decisions*, National Early Years Network/Save the Children, London
A practical handbook showing how young children, under the age of eight, can participate, make decisions and take responsibility for their actions.

Nutbrown, C. (ed.) (1996), *Respectful Educators – Capable Learners: Children's rights and early education*, Paul Chapman, London
This book draws attention to early childhood issues in relation to the UN Convention on the Rights of the Child.

References

Alderson, P. (1993), *Children's Consent to Surgery*, Open University Press, Buckingham

Alderson, P. (1999), *Learning and Inclusion: The Cleves School experience*, David Fulton, London

Alderson, P. (2000), *Young Children's Rights*, Jessica Kingsley, London

Alderson, P. and Goodey, C. (1998), *Enabling Education: Experiences in special and ordinary schools*, Tufnell Press, London

Alderson, P. and Montgomery, J. (1996), *Health Care Choices: Making decisions with children*, IPPR, London

Alderson, P., Clarke-Jones, L. and Schaumberg, H. (2002), *Evaluation of the Office of Children's Rights Commissioner for London*, part 1. Social Science Research Unit, Institute of Education, London

Als, H. (1999), Reading the premature infant. In Goldson, E. (ed.) *Nurturing the Premature Infant*, Oxford University Press, New York

Candappa, M. (2002), Human rights and refugee children in the UK. In Franklin, B. (ed.) *The New Handbook of Children's Rights*, Routledge, London

Christensen, P. and James, A. (eds) (2000), *Research with Children*, Routledge Falmer, London

Clark, A. and Moss, P. (2001), *Listening to Young Children: The mosaic approach*, National Children's Bureau, London

Connolly, P., Smith, A. and Kelly, B. (2002), *Too Young to Notice? The cultural and political awareness of 3–6 year olds in Northern Ireland*, Northern Ireland Community Relations Council/Channel 4, Belfast

Donaldson, M. (1978), *Children's Minds*, Fontana, Glasgow

Dunn, J. (1993), *Young Children's Close Relationships: Beyond attachment*, Sage, London

Gardner, H. (1993), *The Unschooled Mind: How children think and how schools teach*, Fontana Press, London

Goldschmeid, E. and Jackson, S. (1994), *People Under Three: Young children in day care*, Routledge, London

Hutchby, I. and Moran-Ellis, J. (eds) (1998), *Children and Social Competence: Arenas of action*, Falmer, London

Irwin, C. (1996), 'Samantha's wish', *Nursing Times*, 4 92 (36), pages 30–31

Judd, D. (1989), *Give Sorrow Words: Working with a dying child*, Free Association Books, London

Katz, A. (ed.) (2002), *Parenting Under Pressure: Voices of prisoners and their families*, Young Voice, London

Kendrick, C. et al. (1986), 'Children's understanding of their illness and treatment within a paediatric oncology unit', *ACP Newsletter*, 8 (2), pages 16–20

McNamara, S. and Moreton, G. (1995), *Changing Behaviour: Teaching children with emotional and behavioural difficulties in primary and secondary classrooms*, David Fulton, London

Miller, J. (1998), 'But we didn't mean to do that!' *Co-ordinate*, 67, pages 5–6

Murray, L. and Andrews, L. (2000), *The Social Baby: Understanding babies' communication from birth*, Children's Project Publishing, Richmond

Newson, C. (1995), 'The patio project.' *Co-ordinate*, 45, pages 10–11

Penn, H. (1997), *Comparing Nurseries: Staff and children in Italy, Spain and the UK*, Paul Chapman, London

Sharman, C., Cross, W. and Vennis, D. (1995), *Observing Children: A practical guide to case studies*, Cassell, London

Sourkes, B. (1995), *Armfuls of Time: The psychological experience of the child with a life-threatening illness*, University of Pittsburgh Press, Pittsburgh

United Nations (1989), *Convention on the Rights of the Child* (available at http://www.cirp.org/library/ethics/UN-convention)

Woodhead, M. (1990/1997), Psychology and the cultural construction of children's needs. In James, A. and Prout, A. (eds) *Constructing and Reconstructing Childhood*, Falmer Press, Basingstoke

Getting it right:
supporting children's personal, social and emotional development in the primary years

Liz Brooker

Liz Brooker sets the scene for the many and varied contributions that constitute the heart of this book. She suggests a framework for thinking about the way we work with children on their identity and relationships, from the time when we first meet them in nursery until the end of their primary years. The framework builds on both the guidance offered by recent government documents, and on the principles set out in the United Nations Convention.

Introduction

If such 'guidance' already exists, why does it need discussion? Perhaps there are two reasons. Firstly, few of us, looking at the difficulties our young people currently experience, would claim that we are actually 'getting it right' as a society, in the sense of preparing them adequately for the roles, responsibilities and relationships they encounter in adolescence and beyond. Schools and teachers have always tried to support children's personal, social and emotional development (PSE), but the challenges of an increasingly complex global society require increasingly informed and sophisticated responses from educators. We can no longer be guided simply by our own personal convictions and life-experiences in planning appropriate support for children's development in these areas.

Secondly, though the advice we have may be excellent, it is not statutory. From the United Nations Convention to the scheme of work for citizenship, the principles and guidance are non-compulsory. Many teachers, while agreeing with the recommendations, will feel that the pressures to comply with statutory requirements – pressures which increase as children progress through the school system – prevent them from giving priority to the social and affective areas of learning. This contribution is a reminder to prioritize children's needs throughout their school careers.

The complex process of children's personal development is presented here as three aspects, all of them interlinked and concurrent: 'understanding myself', 'understanding others' and 'understanding society'. Each aspect is illustrated by case study stories, some about the planned curriculum and some about the unplanned incidents through which children and their teachers learn from each other.

Foundations

Four documents provide the rationale and content for our planning for children's personal, social and emotional development in schools: the United Nations Convention on the Rights of the Child (UN General Assembly 1989); *Curriculum Guidance for the Foundation Stage* (QCA 2000); the revised *National Curriculum* (DfES/QCA 1999); and the scheme of work for citizenship (QCA 2002). All four offer common threads on which our approach to PSE can be based.

THE UNITED NATIONS CONVENTION ON THE RIGHTS OF THE CHILD

Though concerned with far more than education, the Convention offers important principles for all services for children. Its Preamble notes that it aims for 'the protection and harmonious development of the child', while Article 29 describes the universal goals of education as 'the development of the child's personality'; 'respect for human rights'; 'respect for the child's parents, his or her own cultural identity, language and values'; and 'respect for the natural environment'. All these may be seen as part of what Article 29 calls 'the preparation of the child for responsible life in a free society', and all are included in our own curricula for children aged 3 to 11.

CURRICULUM GUIDANCE FOR THE FOUNDATION STAGE

The introduction of a new framework for the education of children aged three to five has helped to prioritize PSE for this age group, and to lay foundations for the subsequent Key Stages. Personal, social and emotional development is the first of the six curriculum areas outlined, and is viewed as the context for all successful learning. The document (QCA 2000, page 28) explains that this area of learning is about:

...emotional well-being, knowing who you are and where you fit in and feeling good about yourself. It is also about developing respect for others, social competence and a positive disposition to learn.

The guidance contains six strands, with related 'goals':

- Dispositions and attitudes
- Self-confidence and self-esteem
- Making relationships
- Behaviour and self-control
- Self-care
- Sense of community

Together they create an image of the child described by the educators of Reggio Emilia – a child who is 'rich in potential, strong, powerful, competent and, most of all, connected to adults and other children' (Malaguzzi 1993, page 10).

NATIONAL CURRICULUM 2000

The non-statutory guidance for the revised national curriculum makes clear statements of aims and values for work on PHSE and citizenship, which should:

- contribute to the development of pupils' sense of identity;
- promote pupils' self-esteem and emotional well-being; and
- help them to form worthwhile and satisfying relationships, based on
- respect for themselves and others.

These four emphases – identity, self-esteem, relationships and respect – are the foundations for the citizenship scheme of work and the themes for this contribution.

CITIZENSHIP

The scheme of work for citizenship extends the national curriculum guidelines into units of study for children in Key Stages 1 and 2. Their 'aims' are those of the earlier document – that children should:

- develop confidence and responsibility, and make the most of their abilities;
- prepare to play an active role as citizens;
- develop a healthy, safer lifestyle; and
- develop good relationships and respect the differences between people.

The 12 units include topics such as 'Taking part' (communication and participation), 'Choices' (making decisions, learning right from wrong), 'Living in a diverse world' (on similarities and differences) and 'Children's rights – human rights', which distinguishes needs, wants and rights. Topics like these clearly build on the values of the United Nations Convention, and on the Foundation Stage guidance, and help us to envisage a programme of learning for children from 3 to 11, based on identity, self-esteem, relationships and respect.

Understanding myself: working towards self-identity and self-esteem

DEVELOPING A SENSE OF IDENTITY

Research has told us a great deal about how babies and young children acquire their identity, or rather – because we all have such multifaceted experiences – the various components of their identity (Trevarthen 1977; Dunn 1988; Schaffer 1992). Babies develop their sense of self through seeing themselves mirrored in the looks and behaviour of others, especially their closest caregivers. Their spontaneous sounds and gestures are mimicked by the people around them, and become incorporated in the shared repertoire of infant and carer. Before long, they learn to distinguish their own self from the selfhood of those they interact with and to identify their own impact on the environment. From 15 months they demonstrate awareness of their own appearance, and by 24 months they can identify themselves by name and gender – they hear themselves labelled by adults ('big boy', 'good girl') long before they know what the labels mean.

Education should develop each child's personality and talents to the full

The home environment, for most children, is a safe and protective one in which the child is known, loved and accepted for what she or he is. Starting school or pre-school is another matter. At this point the child has, for the first time, to present herself to strangers: to let them know, by her behaviour, her appearance, her speech, what kind of person she is. For the first time, a child may have to articulate for herself, as well as for others, who she is – name, sex, ethnicity, age, status, relationships and sense of belonging.

Some of these labels can be problematic. Children's names (especially non-English ones) may be mispronounced, or their full names used instead of the nicknames they know. The age-label confuses many. Children who are addressed by a teacher as 'You four' may protest indignantly, 'I'm not four, I'm three!' (three what?). Children who have never given much thought to their colour discover with surprise that they are 'black', and that this is not seen by everyone as a desirable label. Those with developmental delays, and those who are different in any way, may have their inadequacies of speech or skills, their oddities of dress or behaviour, pointed out to them by peers in ways that are distressing and confusing. Since the child's sense of self is inextricably linked with that of her family and community, any reconsideration of her own identity means re-thinking her whole familiar world, just at the point when she may be missing it and longing for it.

But research shows us, too, that the transition to a new environment, if it is well managed, is a positive step in a child's development (Bronfenbrenner 1979). Separation from the familiar environment offers an opportunity to expand one's sense of self. The child can now see herself as someone who drinks from the family's mugs at home, but from a beaker with her name on at nursery; who throws her cardigan over a chair at home, but hangs it on her peg at pre-school; who tips her toys into a toybox at home, but tidies things into separate crates in daycare; someone who exists in more than one place. This awareness of one's different roles enables the child to reflect more consciously on her own identity: on occasion she may have to introduce herself to new adults in the setting – 'I'm Katie but I'm in Patti's group' – and supply information on her life outside the setting – 'I get picked up later because my mum goes to work'. Through these experiences the child's own self-

Case study:
Preethi's trousers

Preethi settled into nursery without difficulty and formed good friendships. Her family were well-educated and articulate, so her nursery workers had no reason to suspect that she would be vulnerable on account of her bilingualism or her family culture. In her early months in the nursery she seemed to have a very positive sense of self.

Around Easter, Preethi's demeanour began to change. She became reserved and diffident, and often declined an adult's invitation to join a group activity. At outside time, she drifted against the fence and watched from a distance while other girls played. A key worker investigated, and gradually discovered what had gone wrong. Preethi's playmates had been showing off their summer skirts and dresses, and had challenged her statement that 'you got to always have trousers on your legs' by saying that only boys had to wear trousers. Preethi was desolate and very confused. A practitioner with some picture books of children from different cultures was able to help all the children understand that in fact, 'everyone was right, no one had got it wrong'.

concept is broadened, helped by adults who are attentive to her growing understanding, and ready to support her when her identity is threatened.

SELF-ESTEEM

Self-esteem has been described as the value a child assigns herself or himself. Attempts to 'measure' it have focused on the disparity between what a child would like to be like and that child's view of how he or she actually is. But in early childhood, self-esteem principally reflects the value the child perceives she has in the eyes of others, particularly those 'significant others' whose opinions really count. And although children in the later pre-school years can separate and evaluate different aspects of themselves (being good at football, or drawing, or making up stories), young children have a simpler, 'global' self-concept. For this reason, early childhood practitioners work hard to promote self-esteem through the ethos of the setting and the social interactions it provides. As Roberts (1998, page 161) argues, 'Children's self-esteem is a key factor not only for their well-being but also for learning outcomes', and low self-esteem has long-term consequences.

Young children's self-esteem can be affirmed (see the Case study on Preethi, left) by affirming the 'rightness' of their own and their family's identity. But all children also need to know that their significant adults – first family, then friends and teachers – are interested in them and value them for their unique combination of attributes. Teachers often send out unintentional signals to children that some kinds of child are appreciated more than others; that girls' behaviour is generally preferable to boys'; that quiet activities are more worthy of adult attention than noisy ones; that tidiness and conformity are more welcome than exploration and mess. Boys, and children who have difficulty settling to quiet activities, may notice that they receive less attention, and fewer tokens of approval, than girls and settled children; and having noticed, rather than becoming quieter, are likely to become more challenging.

One unfortunate consequence of many practitioners' concern for self-esteem, however, has been a tendency to offer children indiscriminate praise, seeking to encourage and reassure them by a constant stream of approval – 'Well done!' 'Good girl!' 'Super!' 'You're a star!' Such expressions of enthusiasm, if habitual, soon cease to hold meaning for the child, and may even do harm. First, they make the child dependent on adult approval, showing her that the way adults judge her efforts is what counts. Second, they give the child no information on which to base her own independent assessments of her efforts. As Roberts (2002, page 106) argues, 'strategies such as habitual empty praise, gold stars, smiley stickers and meaningless statements are more likely to feed children's self-preoccupation and narcissism than to help them form a genuine sense of their own worth'.

In the end, real self-esteem comes from a realistic assessment of one's efforts and outcomes. In the end, too, when children are praised for efforts of which they are not particularly proud, they may come to question the trustworthiness of the adults (Gura 1996). The better alternative is to make time to give every child your full attention and some informative feedback. Spending time sitting with a child, asking questions about what she has done and how she did it, and commenting in detail on the outcome, will reward her far more than an enthusiastic cry of 'Lovely!'.

Another important source of self-esteem, while children are growing up, is the gradual acquisition of responsibility. Teachers often attempt to inculcate this sense by involving children in 'helping' with

Case study:

Kuldeep at the gurdwara

Kuldeep seemed a difficult and unco-operative pupil. He rarely made eye contact or appeared to take any notice of adults, and spent much of his time in giggly, clowning behaviour with his group of particular friends. Comments in his school reports indicated that he was generally regarded as 'immature' and hinted that he was probably not helped by an over-indulgent family.

A class outing to the local Sikh gurdwara (temple) overturned these assumptions. As the children entered the foyer, Kuldeep sprang into action, fetching scarves for his classmates to cover their heads and showing them where to leave their shoes. He took himself into the worship hall and paid his respects to the guru granth sahib before selecting a place and sitting attentively. When the children subsequently filed into the langar (dining room) and sat down for lunch, his teacher discovered that Kuldeep had disappeared. Moments later, he emerged from the kitchen with some elderly men, all of them carrying containers of food that they proceeded to dish into trays and serve to the children at their tables. Kuldeep was kept busy for the next 20 minutes. He circulated among the long tables, explaining to children what was in each dish, inviting them to taste, fetching more chapattis and jugs of water from the kitchen. When he finally sat down to eat himself, he maintained a watchful eye on his classmates and jumped up twice more to see to their needs. It was clear that he took his responsibilities both naturally and seriously.

classroom tasks (fetching the register, counting the pencils). Often, however, these tasks are quite limited and undemanding. When children volunteer to help with a real task, such as lifting equipment, switching on a plug at a socket, or fetching a sharp knife, they may be shooed away and told not to touch. Yet these same children may be used to taking responsibility at home: caring for a younger sibling or handling tools, alongside responsible adults. Teachers need to be alert to the roles children may be accustomed to outside school and give them credit for their sense of responsibility.

Understanding others: working towards relationships

Personal and social learning, as we have seen, begins in interactions, so that in learning about herself, the child is simultaneously learning to understand the role of others in her life. Adult–child interactions in the early weeks of life are a sophisticated demonstration of turn-taking, in which the child, apparently instinctively, alternately utters and attends. From the early games of peek-a-boo onwards, as Dunn (1988) has shown, relations with parents and siblings lay the foundations for children's subsequent ability to share the perspectives of others, and prepare them for the world outside the home. As a result, Trevarthen (1998, page 97) claims: 'A three-year-old is a socially aware person who is capable of making and keeping friends and of negotiating interesting co-operations and tests of understandings with a wide range of acquaintances.'

PLAY AND FRIENDSHIP

In the school and pre-school years, as children's play behaviour demonstrates, relationships with peers become increasingly important. Studies of children's self-directed play (Sylva et al. 1980) confirm that, from around the age of three, children who have previously been observed in 'solitary' or 'parallel' play gradually spend more time playing sociably with others. From the age of five, peer friendships can play an important role in children's lives, eventually supplanting the influence of family members for some. As Dowling (2000, page 24) points out, friendships are crucial in facilitating children's curriculum learning as well as their social development: 'A child's ability to form good relationships not only enhances her personal development but helps her progress intellectually.'

Children exploring ideas and materials

In the pre-school phase, socio-dramatic or 'pretend' play has been viewed as the pre-eminent vehicle for social learning. The theories of Piaget, who saw symbolic play as the characteristic activity for three to six year olds, and Vygotsky, who taught us to look at the value of peer interactions for learning language and culture, support this view, and research has consistently shown associations between children's engagement in pretend play and their social and cognitive progress (Smilansky 1990). However, Faulkner (1995) argues that all forms of play and games can contribute to children's development of social competence. Vygotsky, she points out, 'saw play between children as creating a zone in which their performance is in advance of their actual developmental level'. This 'zone of proximal development' (the ZPD) can be seen as 'a sort of inter-psychological, social space in which children can explore new knowledge and ideas through conversation and other forms of interaction' (Faulkner 1995, page 241). Not only pretend play, but social play of all kinds, lends itself to such explorations.

As children move into middle childhood, both teachers and parents will notice their growing enthusiasm for 'games with rules', described by Piaget as the characteristic form of play for these years. Children's genuine involvement in game-playing provides opportunities for learning across the curriculum: board and card games, quizzes and puzzles, and computer games, can supply much of the curriculum content in Key Stages 1 and 2. Although many other play opportunities have disappeared from the classroom, involvement in game-playing can allow children to continue to construct their own learning through social interactions, in an environment where direct teaching may otherwise predominate. We need to remind ourselves that play can still serve as a zone of proximal development when the game is snakes and ladders or computer chess, rather than 'dressing-up'.

CIRCLE TIME

In order to sustain social relationships, children need to use a range of related 'skills': skills of turn-taking, sharing, negotiating, co-operating and empathizing. These skills develop gradually, aided both by the modelling behaviour of adults and the perspective-taking abilities practised in infancy. By discussing them explicitly, teachers can enable all children to develop as individuals whose social strategies are based, at least in part, on an understanding of the needs of others. Starting the year in a new school or classroom is a good time to initiate such discussions, and circle time is a good context for them.

The rules for circle time must first be negotiated – everyone sits on the floor, all are equal; one person talks, everyone listens; everyone may speak, no one has to speak; and so on. After this, the children's own 'golden rules' for their classroom may be constructed: a task that everyone can see is 'real' and essential, rather than simply another topic from the teacher's repertoire. In a large class, with whole-class as well as group activities, sharing resources and taking turns, and respecting the space and needs of others, are priorities for everyone and require everyone's assent and understanding. Children generally find it easy to generate a long list of 'don'ts' – don't fight, don't poke, don't shout, don't throw rubbers – but they can be encouraged to re-think their prohibitions as positive statements. Positive

Case study:
Rickie's maths

Rickie was not enjoying his progress through the primary school. A cheerful, independent boy in Nursery and Reception, he had begun to flounder in Year 1, when literacy and numeracy sessions dominated the school day, and went into Year 2 with low expectations, low self-esteem and a generally weary look. His mornings, particularly the numeracy hour, continued to be a trial, but his teacher noticed that he really came to life when playing games in the short session before the lunch register. Not only did the chance to pit his wits at draughts, dominoes and Connect Four transform his facial expression and body language completely, but he was thinking aloud, calculating, adding and subtracting, estimating and predicting in a non-stop stream of mathematical talk.

Rickie's teacher took advice from a maths adviser, who suggested that, rather than using games as a follow-up to direct instruction in maths, she could introduce the games first, as a form of exploratory learning, and then build on the knowledge the children had constructed through playing, in her follow-up teaching. She also appointed Rickie the 'class calculator', inviting him to estimate the dinner numbers and snack money, keep a tally of equipment issued and suggest what quantities of materials would need to be set out for various maths tasks. Rickie's written maths was slow to improve, but his enthusiasm for mathematical challenges kept him involved until his pencil skills began to mature, and his new standing in the class supported his learning across the curriculum.

Close friends

Children's understanding of 'difference' begins in the early years, based on discussions of the ways that individuals – adults and children in the group – differ in appearance and in attributes. In Key Stages 1 and 2, their understanding should move beyond the personal and individual, towards the political and structural. They need to know and discuss the fact that 'being different' can bring disadvantages for whole groups of people in society, regardless of their individual needs and talents. Gradually, the important 'early years' rhetoric of universal friendship and equality must give way to the reality of inequality and prejudice – realities that most children will certainly be aware of by middle childhood.

The curriculum, and the daily life of schools, is full of opportunities for teaching about social justice in ways that children can understand. One class regularly worked on topics from black history

rules generally require us to think about the effect on others of our own (selfish, or simply thoughtless) behaviour. If children are regularly invited to take another person's perspective, to understand what it is like to be them, they will learn to manage their own feelings and behaviour far better than if they are simply responding to prohibitions.

Circle times, or class meetings, allow children to see for themselves that participating in a democratic process is effective, despite all the difficulties and frustrations associated with it.

Understanding society: working towards citizenship

We can view the curriculum for citizenship as a natural extension of earlier learning in the personal and social sphere. Its first aim (developing confidence and responsibility) affirms the continuing importance of self-esteem as children grow and acquire new aspects of their identity; the second (playing an active role) builds on the participatory experiences of circle times and class meetings – perhaps through a school council; the third emphasizes a safe and healthy lifestyle, echoing the 'self-care' of the Foundation Stage; while the fourth (developing relationships, respecting differences) expands the theme of 'understanding others' to include a developed understanding of diversity.

Case study:
Circle time

One Year 3 class developed such good participatory skills in class meetings that in time their teacher was able to hand over the entire running of the group to the children, while she stood aside and listened. Each child took the chair on a rota basis and implemented the class's rules for contributors. After any contribution, the chair would ask for 'comments or questions', and other children would respond 'I have a comment on that', 'I have a question for Marcie'. The child in the chair would decide when a topic was exhausted, and invite further topics for discussion.

The main difficulty with this process, in the teacher's eyes, was the children's rather harsh approach to discipline. It came to the point where children who squirmed or wriggled too much were being peremptorily dismissed from the circle by the chair, in ways that the teacher herself could not condone. One day she had to take back the chair and lead a discussion of why some children were not 'sitting properly' in the circle. All the children knew, as she soon realized: the discussion was not always interesting, children 'took too long', some people 'told us things we already know'. Further discussion helped to clarify these issues and gave children a new understanding of each others' behaviour, and a new basis for assessing their own and each others' contribution to the process.

Case study:
Rosa Parks and the bus boycott

A Year 2 class had spent several days working on the story of Rosa Parks, told to them by their teacher, who had a collection of photographs of the incident and its aftermath. They particularly enjoyed their drama sessions on the story, and devised their own version of the 'bus game', in which they lined up at the 'bus stop' and each took a paper-plate mask from a pile as they were about to board the makeshift 'bus'. Only when they turned the mask over and discovered whether they were 'black' or 'white' did they discover what their roles in the drama would be.

The effectiveness of the learning was demonstrated when they suggested showing the drama to the whole school in assembly. The class lined up; the teacher introduced Rosa Parks, the bus driver and the 'bus' to the school, and the children took on their roles – selecting a mask, holding it up, entering the appropriate 'door' and sitting in the appropriate seats. The drama was appreciated by the audience, but came to life when one child (who was himself black) picked up a black mask and absent-mindedly entered the 'whites only' door of the bus. The children shrieked, 'No Richard, you're black! Get off the bus!' Many, including Richard, saw the irony of the situation, and several teachers asked to have the drama presented again for their class's benefit. Discussions of 'rules' to prevent unfair treatment of different groups continued for many more weeks.

(incidentally, women's history, too). The stories of Harriet Tubman and the Underground Railroad, Phyllis Wheatley and the slave ships, Rosa Parks and the Montgomery bus boycott (see Case study, above), provided starting-points for looking at racism in their own class, school and neighbourhood, which carried over into school council meetings and the involvement of pupils in writing the school's anti-racist policy.

BELONGING AND PARTICIPATING
We can think of the whole of the PSE/citizenship curriculum as a matter of 'being' and 'belonging': finding out who we are, and what roles we have, in our family, class, school and community. In the years from birth to 11, children's sense of their own identity develops, becoming increasingly complex, and their sense of their place in the world comes to include many different roles. They need to recognize that 'belonging' is not a passive condition, but involves making a contribution to whatever social units they inhabit – helping in the home, collaborating in the classroom, expressing a view in school meetings. By Key Stage 2, most children are conscious of their place in the wider world. The mainstream curriculum teaches them their responsibility to protect the environment, conserve energy and recycle, and consider the rights of animals and humans. Many children develop passionate beliefs on these matters and will wish to save the whale single-handed; learning the limits to one's own power, and the potential for collective action, is another important lesson.

Children are commonly involved in planning and fund-raising for the benefit of their own school – creating a wildlife area or renovating a library – but whole-school projects for the benefit of communities outside the school should also have a place in their primary experience. One school always used their annual harvest celebrations as a focus for supporting development projects through Action Aid. One year

Playing in leaf fall

> **Case study:**
>
> ## Knitting for Red Nose Day
>
> Year 5 were into knitting. A school journey to a field centre, which had given them the opportunity to collect natural colours in the environment, was also the occasion of their discovering their teacher's love of knitting. On their return they had collected wools from parents, worked with colours in weaving and embroidery, and gradually started to take up knitting themselves. Their teacher decided the whole class should learn to knit, and set aside time each afternoon for practice. After six months the habit had spread and a school knitting club was launched.
>
> As Red Nose Day approached, someone had the idea of producing blankets for a development charity. A contact at Save the Children produced simple instructions and the children got started on their squares. On Red Nose Day itself the school was opened to everyone willing to knit – parents and grandparents, neighbours and helpers, and children. Most of the squares were unfinished on the day (and some were decidedly un-square), but two months later the school was able to invite an SCF speaker in to receive the two beautiful blankets they had created, and tell the children where they might be sent.

they raised money for vaccinations, another year for tree nurseries, another year for well-digging. A school council, with representatives from every class, should have a remit that includes outreach as well as in-school topics, so that children acquire a sense of scale and proportion. Encountering the living conditions of elderly people in the local care home, or of refugees using a neighbourhood centre, helps to contextualize the passions that are raised by school issues such as boys kicking balls into the quiet area of the playground, or the closure of a school tuck shop.

Conclusion

School is not 'life', and our institutions quite rightly aim to both protect children from the harsher aspects of life in society and prepare them for participation. This contribution has argued that by equipping children to understand and articulate their own identity, take the perspectives of others, and recognize their rights and responsibilities in the social worlds they inhabit, we are preparing them to cope confidently with their own future lives and to contribute to the future of their communities.

Resources

A summary of the UN Convention on the Rights of the Child can be found at the back of this book (see Appendix 1).

Suggested further reading

Claire, H. (2001), *Not Aliens: Primary school children and the citizenship/PSHE curriculum*, Trentham, Stoke-on-Trent
Based on research with 7 to 11 year olds, the author demonstrates how the Citizenship curriculum has been written with little regard for children's views and experiences and underestimates the level of debate that is possible with young children.

Dowling, M. (2000), *Young Children's Personal, Social and Emotional Development*, Paul Chapman Publishing, London
Drawing on everyday examples from early years settings, the author examines the need for personal and social development to be supported by sensitive interventions from adults who understand children's needs.

References

Bronfenbrenner, U. (1979), *The Ecology of Human Development*, Harvard University Press, Cambridge, MA

DfEE/QCA (1999), *The National Curriculum: Handbook for primary teachers in England*, DfEE, London

Dowling, M. (2000), *Young Children's Personal, Social and Emotional Development*, Paul Chapman Publishing, London

Dunn, J. (1988), *The Beginning of Social Understanding*, Blackwell, Oxford

Faulkner, D. (1995), Play, self and the social world. In Barnes, P. (ed.), *Personal, Social and Emotional Development of Children*, Blackwell/Open University, Oxford

Gura, P. (1996), What I want for Cinderella: self-esteem and self-assessment, *Early Education*, 19

Malaguzzi, L. (1993), For an education based on relationships, *Young Children*, Nov 1993, pages 9–13

QCA (2000), *Curriculum Guidance for the Foundation Stage*, QCA, London

QCA (2002), *Citizenship: A scheme of work for Key Stages 1 and 2*, DfES/QCA, London

Roberts, R. (1998), Thinking about me and them. In Siraj-Blatchford, I. (ed.) *A Curriculum Development Handbook for Early Childhood Educators*, Trentham Books, Stoke-on-Trent

Roberts, R. (2002), *Self-esteem and Early Learning*, Paul Chapman Publishing, London

Schaffer, H.R. (1992), Joint involvement episodes as contexts for cognitive development. In McGurk, H. (ed.) *Childhood Social Development: Contemporary perspectives*, Lawrence Erlbaum, Hove

Schaffer, H.R. (1996), *Social Development*, Blackwell, Oxford

Smilansky, S. (1990), Socio-dramatic play: its relevance to behaviour and achievement in school. In Klugman, E. and Smilansky, S. *Children's Play and Learning: Perspectives and policy implications*, Teachers College Press, New York

Sylva, K., Roy, C. and Painter, M. (1980), *Childwatching at Playgroup and Nursery School*, Grant McIntyre, London

Trevarthen, C. (1977), Descriptive analyses of infant communicative behaviour. In Schaffer, H.R. (ed.) *Studies in Mother–infant Interaction*, Academic Press, London

Trevarthen, C. (1998), A child's need to learn a culture. In Woodhead, M., Faulkner, D. and Littleton, K. (eds) *Cultural Worlds of Early Childhood*, Routledge, London

UN General Assembly (1989), *Convention on the Rights of the Child* (available at http://www.cirp.org/library/ethics/UN-convention/)

2 *Partnerships for learning and well-being*

Never doubt that a small group of people can change the world...indeed it is the only thing that ever has.

Margaret Mead

Why don't you just ask them?
Emotional literacy can transform schools

James Park

James Park is Director of Antidote, an organization that campaigns for emotional literacy in schools. Antidote describes emotional literacy as 'the capacity to manage our emotions and to draw on our feelings in ways to enrich our learning and interaction with others'. The promotion of emotional literacy can reduce stress among staff and pupils. It also has the potential to raise achievement and to improve well-being.

James Park's contribution conveys some of the real-life struggles and triumphs experienced in trying to encourage a more emotionally literate education system. Drawing on Antidote's experience of working closely with schools, he illustrates how staff and children can be expected to feel a sense of commitment to their schools only if they feel their voices are heard.

Introduction

Some teachers feel a sense of weariness when they hear the term 'emotional literacy'. Fearing that they are about to have dumped upon them yet another set of responsibilities, they reply that they are 'teachers, not therapists'. For them, the term triggers a surge of frustration at the extent to which targets, tests and the national curriculum can prevent them from responding as they would like to the emotional messages they receive from children. Barely concealing their anger, they declare that 'there is just not the time or the opportunity any more'.

More and more teachers, though, are coming to recognize that a focus on emotional literacy does not necessarily require them to develop a new set of skills. It does, however, provide a counter to the negative consequences of some government policies. Emotional literacy is, at heart, a strategy for creating school environments where teachers can deploy their existing skills in ways that promote children's natural curiosity and motivation to learn. An emotionally literate school works to ensure that every exchange between teachers and children has the potential to enhance mutual understanding of emotional experience. This understanding provides the basis for the sort of collaborative relationships that stimulate creativity.

How are such environments created? Some consider that it is by engaging in particular sorts of activities. Emotion lessons, they argue, can give pupils the opportunity to develop a language for talking about their feelings. Weekly circle time sessions apply this language to exploring current emotional issues within class groups. A peer mediation scheme enables peer conflicts to be explored and hopefully resolved, while a schools council empowers pupils to have a voice in the management of their school. This is what most people mean when they talk about having a whole-school emotional literacy strategy. But it is, in reality, only half the story.

Exploring emotional literacy at Fairbairn Primary

Janet used to talk proudly of the work she had done to establish just such a strategy at Fairbairn Primary[1], where she was head. The school is typical of many in our inner cities. Its newly constructed yellow brick walls and pine beams contrast strikingly with the drab concrete of the council estates that surround it. The pupils come from a wide range of different cultures, and some have been through traumatic experiences on their journeys to the UK. The level of economic deprivation in the area is reflected in the fact that over 80 per cent of the pupils are on free school meals.

Janet came to Fairbairn Primary with a commitment to giving its children real opportunities to build fulfilling lives. She felt that, by maximizing their capacity to understand their own feelings and those of others, the school could help them develop an enthusiasm for acquiring new knowledge and developing personal resources. But while the strategy had been welcomed by parents, staff and pupils, it did not seem to be generating the sort of qualitative shift in learning that Janet had hoped for. What more could she do? She happened to ask this question of a neighbour one Saturday morning in her local park. 'Why don't you just ask the teachers and pupils?' he said, before turning back to the football game with his son in which he was engaged. Janet was left to reflect on the obviousness of what had been suggested. If she wanted staff and children to be curious about each other, she needed to show that she herself was genuinely curious about what they were experiencing at an emotional level, and the ideas they had for improving things.

How could she ask her staff and pupils this question in a way that would lead to interesting answers? When you lead an organization, people tend to tell you what you already know or what they sense that you will find easy to hear. But Janet wanted answers that would surprise her, challenge her assumptions and provoke new thoughts about how to proceed. The only way to achieve this, she thought, was to engage outside consultants and to make this part of their brief. The team she employed was surprised by her apparent willingness to deal with whatever came up. Why was she so confident that there were things going on she could not see?

As it happened, it did not take the consultants long to identify Janet's blind spots. Much of their data pointed to the failure of the school's emotional literacy strategy to enable really open communication at any level. Teachers and other staff did not feel able to share with senior management, or with each other, their own ideas on how they could work more effectively together to improve the quality of their teaching. Nor did the children experience their weekly circle times and other classroom activities as opportunities to explore the things that really mattered to them.

There were understandable reasons for this lack of communication. Janet had a passionate belief in the new strategies that she and her young staff had developed. This made it hard for them to report what

was not working. She also promoted a very structured approach to lesson planning as an essential counter to the chaotic home environments from which many pupils came. But this prevented teachers from addressing the emotional issues that came up outside the times allocated to 'emotional literacy'.

Despite Janet's declared openness to whatever came up, the consultants felt nervous about presenting these findings to her. They had unearthed quite a lot of confusion and frustration among members of the school community, but they wanted to present this in ways that suggested positive ways of moving forward. They eventually decided to try and do this by describing their interview with a nine-year-old girl called Rana. It seemed to represent many of the issues that others – both staff and pupils – had described.

From the moment that Rana had arrived for her one-hour interview, she bubbled over with things she wanted to get off her chest – about how the boys in her class messed about, how they excluded girls from their various conspiracies, how girls tried to sort out some of their conflicts, how this sometimes led to the girls being blamed by teachers for causing disruption and how everyone got punished for the misbehaviour of the few. She also had strong views on how teachers often seemed overwhelmed by the challenges the young people presented to them, about the ideas she had about how they could manage their classes better.

'Do you ever get an opportunity to discuss these things in class?' the consultant interviewing her asked.
'No,' said Rana, as if she thought it strange that anyone could think this might happen.
'But you do have circle time, don't you?' the researcher went on.
'Yes. That's when we play games.'

Janet's initial response was a defensive one. We can arrange, she said, for the teacher to receive some additional training in listening skills. The consultants replied that many others – teachers and pupils – had articulated a sense that it was difficult to explore pressing emotional and social issues collectively. It seemed that, while teachers were being asked to listen to pupils in particular contexts, that did not make it a listening school. Janet was again struck by the obviousness of the insight she was being offered. If teachers feel they are not being listened to, how can they be expected to listen openly to what their pupils are thinking and feeling? She invited the consultants to facilitate a series of meetings to see how staff could find ways of becoming more open with each other.

The space that was created for staff to explore their thoughts on this question initially brought forth a jumble of different issues. Some talked about how little information they had about what other people in the school were doing; others riposted nervously that they did not feel the need to know everything that happened. Some spoke of feeling that they had taken on responsibilities they did not feel capable of handling, while others talked about feeling undervalued. The consultants observed that there was a common thread – people wanting to work out together how responsibilities should be allocated and where information needed to flow. All of this suggested that the group should meet more often to reflect on these issues.

While this first meeting felt quite sticky, the feedback to Janet was that people were glad of the opportunity to share such difficult issues. There was a much more positive 'can do' attitude at the subsequent sessions. To a degree that astonished Janet, the focus gradually switched away from internal blockages to the strategies that teachers could adopt to open up children's capacities to articulate and explore what was happening for them. Staff began to share ideas from their own experience and practice about how they could enable children to:

- be reflective about themselves;
- ask their own questions;
- engage in dialogue with each other;
- create meaningful narratives out of what emerged from reflection and dialogue.

It is all very well having this discussion, a small group of teachers complained at one meeting, but what's the point? We surely don't have the time. Janet was shocked by their negativity and the intensity of her riposte. Surely, we have to make the time. If this works, it will enable these young people to develop the capacities we are trying to help them develop. Janet was relieved when one of the older teachers, who had been at the school for 20 years, came in here. He commented that it was possible to think about these things now because, for the first time in his experience, they were starting to really talk with each other.

It was in this spirit that the teachers evolved their answers to the four issues: reflection; asking questions; engaging in dialogue; and making meaning.

REFLECTION

Teachers had discussed how they and the pupils experienced cycles of joy and disappointment, anger and affection in every school day. How could these emotions be addressed in a way that enabled learning to take place? In one group session, a Year 6 teacher described how she would sometimes tell her children coming in from playtime to close their eyes, sit very still and think about a time at playtime when it felt good. Several others wanted to try out the approach. They reported to others how much more relaxed and focused their pupils were afterwards. Soon 'reflection time' was a regular part of the day across many classes in the school.

ASKING QUESTIONS

The teachers discussed whether children were naturally curious about the world and each other or whether that curiosity had to be stimulated. Most believed that, when given the space in which to ask questions, children's curiosity enables them to work towards answers that are meaningful to them. One Fairbairn teacher had always been interested in the idea of philosophy for children as an approach to enabling pupils to ask their own questions about the world and use this as a jumping-off point to group exploration. This involves building a discussion around a story or a picture. What is happening? Why do different people see different things? With Janet's support, she invited a trainer to come and demonstrate the approach. Many teachers found that observing their classes respond to the approach gave them a new understanding of what they were capable of. One, in particular, commented on how her anxieties about behaviour prevented her from really listening to what was being said. 'What they say is amazing,' she remarked.

ENGAGING IN DIALOGUE

Encouraged by Janet, Fairbairn's teachers started using the enquiry approach in parts of all their lessons. What is power?, children asked in history. What is air?, they pondered in science. How did the world begin?, they considered in RE. This approach allowed children not only to describe their subjective experience of these issues, but also to talk about themselves in ways that sometimes touched emotional depths. Talking, for example, about the logical difficulties involved in believing that everything was created by God, one noted maker of mischief talked of his own desire to start life over again and behave this time around.

MAKING MEANING

Teachers at Fairbairn found that giving pupils the opportunity to share their own stories in relation to the people or issues they were studying gave them a window into the ways in which others experienced the world. What appeared at first to be a detour into personal narrative could be brought back to illuminate what subject was on the curriculum for that day. Pupils became increasingly excited by their learning because they could see its relevance to their own lives.

Schools are large and complex organizations operating within a whirlwind of pressures from government, parents and society at large. When staff and pupils are given regular opportunities to explore these feelings in conditions of safety, they learn to manage those forms of anxiety that cause people to close up, stop innovating and stop exploring new possibilities together. Janet's discovery was that, just as fear and anxiety can spread through an organization like a virus, so can processes of dialogue and reflection that sustain people's capacity to be interested in each other. The challenge of emotional literacy is to embed those processes into an organization's life in a way that is sustainable over the long term.

1. Fairbairn Primary is a composite of various schools whose explorations of emotional literacy are familiar to members of the Antidote team.

The ten key principles of emotional literacy

- Emotional literacy is a process rather than a goal.
- Emotional literacy involves releasing our capacity to learn with and from each other.
- Emotional literacy is generated through dialogue.
- Dialogue cannot happen without reflection.
- Dialogue enables us to develop new stories about ourselves as learners.
- Emotional literacy is sustained through our continuing curiosity about what is really going on.
- Small changes across a whole organization will have a bigger impact than a large change in one part of an organization.
- Adults need the same opportunities as young people to practise emotional literacy.
- Every interaction is an opportunity to facilitate or inhibit emotional literacy.
- Every organization has untapped resources for promoting emotional literacy.

Resources

Antidote, 3rd Floor, Cityside House, 40 Adler Street, London E1 1EE (Tel 020 7247 3355)
www.antidote.org.uk
Antidote campaigns for emotional literacy and is about realizing the potential of children through emotional education. It promotes the development of emotional literacy through consultancy, conferences, publications and training. Antidote produces a newsletter, *EL Update*, ten times a year, which captures the exciting emotional literacy work that is going on in schools and generates informed thinking about how schools can use emotional literacy to improve well-being, community and achievement.

Suggested further reading

Goleman, D. (1996), *Emotional Intelligence: Why it can matter more than IQ*, Bloomsbury, London
Goleman argues that our view of human intelligence is far too narrow, and that our emotions play a far greater role in thought, decision making and individual success than is commonly believed.

Park, J., Haddon, A. and Goodman, H. (2003), *The Emotional Literacy Handbook: Promoting Whole-School Strategies*, David Fulton Publishers, London
Drawing on Antidote's cutting-edge work, this book provides practical ideas for making schools more emotionally literate. It also provides a rich array of case studies to enable readers to benefit from the experience of other schools and to develop good practice.

Look after yourself

Jenny Mosley

Jenny Mosley is well known for her pioneering work on the use of circle time to enhance self-esteem, self-discipline and positive relationships. In this contribution she suggests how teachers can help staff morale and self-esteem so that they have the energy to help others. Drawing on her knowledge and experience of working with schools as a consultant, she offers practical suggestions to raise individual self-esteem and also to support staff well-being through her quality circle time approach.

Introduction

The success of an individual or of an organization is dependent on the energy and positivity of the people within it. As caring adults, we spend a great deal of time giving generous praise to the children whom we meet. We know that it gives them confidence and a positive attitude to their activities. Sometimes we are so busy encouraging others to feel good about themselves that we forget that we, however old we are, have exactly the same need for positive feedback. Luckily, as grown-ups, we are able to do two things that children are not usually empowered to do. Firstly, we have learned to recognize our own needs (even if we do not meet them) and, secondly, we are able to meet our needs if we assign enough importance to them. This is not selfish behaviour. The world needs us to feel good. Just as we nurture our children and colleagues, so we must learn to prepare a proper self-care plan for ourselves and ensure that we look after all our physical, spiritual, emotional, creative and intellectual needs. Self-care is not something we can take for granted. It is our right but it is also our responsibility.

Young or old, we hold an inner picture of ourselves, of our strengths and limitations. This self-picture has been, and is, contributed to by both the positive and negative responses we receive from people who are important to us. Our self-image influences the way in which we respond to all of life's challenges and choices.

If we have been encouraged and praised, and have been given some opportunities to experience personal and social success, we are more likely to see ourselves as capable, likeable and worthwhile people. Research suggests that success is dependent upon a positive mental attitude because people who have high self-esteem are more likely to work hard and have confidence in their skills and competence. They willingly work in teams because they firmly believe that they have plenty to contribute. They are not victims because they feel that they have a large measure of control over their lives. They believe that they can cope. They know that they deserve all the happiness, love and achievement that life has to offer them.

If we lose our self-esteem, we become doubtful and hesitant. Our state of uncertainty immobilizes us and we are unable to make the changes that we need to make. Individuals with low self-esteem are likely to view themselves as useless, unlikeable and incompetent. This lack of inner confidence can result in their constantly putting themselves down, an inability to relate in a warm, respectful and empathic way to others, and a fear of facing new learning experiences. Their personal view of themselves leads them to believe that is how others view them. They act defensively in order to protect themselves from further hurt – for example, by being the first to put other people down, by behaving aggressively or by withdrawing into a 'shell'. Secretly, people with poor self-esteem regard themselves as failures, or as misunderstood, and it seems to them that everyone else is more capable than they are. This negative thinking results in a pattern of negative behaviour that becomes a self-fulfilling prophecy, ensuring that they continue to fail.

Fortunately, self-esteem is not a 'fixed' thing: it can continually be influenced and improved. All you need is the conviction that your own self-esteem is well worth nourishing and the motivation to put yourself first for the very good reasons listed above.

Lift your spirits and raise your self-esteem

You need to look at all aspects of your life in detail to see whether they are working towards good health or negative health. Here are just a few of the questions you need to ask:

- **Diet** – Am I eating and drinking in a healthy way? Sharing food lifts the spirits, so some schools now have an 'exotic fruit day' as opposed to the doughnut day, or they start extra early in the morning with a bacon roll and end Friday with a special feast to which everybody contributes.

- **Exercise** – Am I getting enough (or any)? Again, there is plenty of advice available in bookshops. Most advice is in favour of something easy, like going for a walk – so no excuses. Each member of staff could contribute a few pounds and then they could buy in a weekly yoga teacher, a belly dancer, or a massage therapist to teach you all hand massage. The complementary therapies have a lot to offer tired staff.

- **Laughter** – Laughter and lightheartedness have been shown to be healing and make us feel good about ourselves; can I promote more of this in my life? Classic 'oldie' videos, humorous books or radio programmes might be worth investigating to put more laughter into our lives. We are too serious nowadays and there is not enough laughter at work. Put on a daft sketch or pantomime for the children at the end of term, organize a karaoke, get in a line dance – but laugh, and invite everyone to join in. Never leave out administrative staff or mid-day supervisors. Their resulting moods can knock down everyone. If you feel positive and happy you can keep everyone 'up' with you. Get a staff social committee going.

- **Social support** – Are the friends and others I mix with, including partners and relatives,

good for me? Do they support me when I take 'time out'? Do I feel better after being in their company? Do they give me positive messages about myself or do they reinforce negative feelings that I already have? Overall, am I getting enough good support from friends from whom I can share feelings and problems as well as bad times? Some clever schools have organized 'The Mystery Pal' – you all put your names in a hat, then each person is randomly assigned a mystery pal by taking a name out of the hat. Your task is to cheer up your 'special pal', but they do not know who you are. Mystery notes appear in pigeonholes and treats turn up on your desk. Because you are not sure who it is, you go around being smiley and positive to everyone – just in case.

- **Treats and pampering** – Could I be kinder to myself by giving myself regular treats? Things like luxuriating in a candle-lit bath, outings and good company are among the endless possibilities.

- **Golden moments** – Do I give myself quiet time, to be calm and to help me reflect and relax? Do I ensure that I have at least one 'golden moment' to myself every single day?

Create your own golden rules

Select one of these 16 golden rules to work on for yourself. You may wish to expand it to suit your own personal needs.

1. I should give myself the same care and attention that I give to others.

2. I have the right to express my feelings and opinions. I do not have to justify them but I have the right to stand up for my opinions if I choose.

3. I have the right to say 'yes' and 'no' for myself.

4. I have the right to change my mind.

5. I have the right to say 'I don't understand' and to ask for more information.

6. I have the right to ask for what I want.

7. I have the right to deal with others without being dependent on them for approval.

8. I am not an endless resource for others. I must stock up on reserves and not get too drained.

9. I have needs too, which may be different from the needs of my family, my friends or my colleagues.

10. I do not have to say 'yes' to all requests or feel guilty if I say 'no'.

11. The perfect person does not exist, making mistakes is permissible: I can learn from them, as can others.

12. I cannot solve all the problems I am confronted with. I can only do my best.

13. I have the right to be treated with respect as a worthwhile, intelligent and competent person.

14. I have the right to express my own needs and set my own priorities as a person, independent of the judgement of others.

15. I do not have to have everyone's approval all of the time to know that I am trying my hardest.

16. Time for unwinding is time well spent.

Quality circle time for teachers

The quality circle time approach offers staff a forum for constructing and maintaining a 'staff care plan' that will enable them to raise their own and group esteem. Quality circle time is a respectful group process. A circle is the best shape for encouraging a sense of equal right to full participation because it enables people to see, listen and empathize as they face each other and address the issues that are important to them. Quality circle time offers a structured problem-solving framework that becomes familiar and is, therefore, imbued with a sense of safety that fosters mutual support among the staff. Circle meetings are, metaphorically speaking, a 'holding situation', which means that they provide a form of emotional support, or 'containment', which is essential to our sense of well-being. They offer an opportunity for staff to share what they feel confident or pleased about in their work, and also offer an opportunity for them to receive the confirmation and praise that are so necessary if morale is to remain high.

Some schools hold brief circle meetings at the beginning of every working day. These need take only a few minutes but they provide a refreshing still-point between the hustle of preparing for the day and the tensions of the day itself. Mutual encouragement and 'team talk' can be offered and meetings can serve as a briefing session so that all staff are appraised of information that they may need during the day. Circle meetings can also be timetabled as a regular form of after-school meeting or as a shorter session preceding staff training or in-service meetings. It is important, however, that these circle meetings are clearly demarcated from sessions that are arranged to serve didactic purposes. Circle meetings work best if there are no handouts, no videos, no piles of government documents or graphs and flip charts. All the circle meeting needs is a group of people sitting together, facing one another, willing and ready to pay attention, listen and share their thoughts and feelings with the rest of the group.

The meeting must have a leader or facilitator. Initially, the leader may well be the headteacher or team leader but, as confidence and familiarity with the protocols grow, any member of the group can be enabled to take this role. The role of the leader is to facilitate a supportive climate and the status of leader does not include the right to control or dominate. In this context, the leader needs to be sensitive and perceptive in order to identify and elicit everyone's needs and points of view. He or she must aim to encourage a feeling of positive co-operation and trust within the circle to enable the group to develop. It is essential that leaders take their turn and are honest in their contributions. In order for this trust to develop, ground rules must be agreed during the first sessions. These are the golden rules that cannot be broken. For example: 'Do respect other people's rights to speak – don't use put-downs.' The focus or themes of the circle time should take into account the current concerns and anxieties of the participants. Every session must include a positive focus, for example, the formulation of an action plan or the celebration of an individual or collective success.

I am not saying that you can run this type of meeting every week; but certainly once a month or, even at the worst, once a half term. In the mid-1980s, I was running courses for Wiltshire LEA on staff self-esteem and circle time. Maybe now at last the time is right to bring them into your school.

Resources

Positive Press/Jenny Mosley Consultancies, 28A Gloucester Road, Trowbridge, Wiltshire BA14 0AA
(Tel 01225 719204); www.circle-time.co.uk
Quality circle time has been developed by Jenny Mosley as a whole-school approach to enhancing self-esteem and positive behaviour and relationships within the school community. For information about training by Jenny Mosley Consultancies telephone 01225 767157. Positive Press produces a range of books and resources.

Suggested further reading

Mosley, J. (1993), *Turn Your School Round: A circle-time approach to the development of self-esteem and positive behaviour in the primary staffroom, classroom and playground*, Learning Development Aids, Cambridge
This book draws on Jenny Mosley's 20 years' experience of using regular circle time sessions to involve all adults and children in the school community to develop, implement and review a self-esteem and positive behaviour policy.

Mosley, J. (1996), *Quality Circle Time in the Primary Classroom: Your essential guide to enhancing self-esteem, self-discipline and positive relationships*, Learning Development Aids, Cambridge
This book describes some effective ideas for enhancing the self-esteem of staff in addition to material for using circle time in the primary classroom.

Mosley, J. (2001), *Working Towards Whole-school Policy on Self-esteem and Positive Behaviour*, Positive Press, Trowbridge
This book presents ideas about self-esteem and respectful behaviour in relation to Mosley's whole-school quality circle time.

Work–life:
finding your balance and rhythm

James Butler

James Butler is a personal and business coach who works with individuals and companies to create and achieve their vision. This regularly involves tools and techniques to build a sustainable balance between all factors in people's lives – families, relationships, hobbies and, of course, work. His wife was a secondary maths teacher for 11 years, so he has 'enjoyed' many dinner parties discussing teacher workloads with her former colleagues. In this contribution, he blends his experience in business and coaching with that gained from nursing an exhausted spouse towards the end of term on a regular basis.

Introduction

Are you happy with the hours and intensity of your work at the moment? Do you have space in your life for things that matter to you – friends, family, children, spouses, the fortunes of Accrington Stanley Football Club? So-called work–life balance is an increasingly hot topic as the hours worked in all professions, and especially teaching, seem to creep ever upwards. Is there another way – is balance obtainable? The answer is 'yes' and what is even more exciting is that we have the power to strike that balance.

In doing that there are four fundamental steps to follow, which are looked at in detail in the following pages:

- Understand what balance means to you personally.
- Create a solid foundation upon which to build this new balanced life.
- Consider possible changes specific to your profession.
- Take action – make it happen.

Crushing myths

Why is work–life balance an issue in modern society? It seems so obvious that we should retain perspective on the various elements of our lives – especially work. Surely any society, employer or school would advocate ensuring your well-being? Sadly, our culture has developed over the last few decades to the point where this is not the case. Many myths exist around work–life balance, and it may be good to clear a couple up straight away.

Longer hours equals more success vs Productivity drops as working hours rise
The so-called 'work ethic' suggests that to be good teachers we should put the hours in, not complain and just get on with it. But as early as 1916 a government report identified that productivity rapidly declines in a long hours culture. The report, on fatigue in industrial premises, stated that output 'is lowered by the working of overtime. The diminution is often so great that the total daily output is less…thus overtime defeats its own object.' Presenteeism – the need to be in work early and stay late just to be seen to be making the effort – is increasingly seen as a dinosaur management style: let us hope it becomes extinct.

Work–life balance is for slackers vs Work smarter, not harder
Another myth surrounding this issue is that those who do take action to maintain a balance in their lives are just looking for excuses to work less hard than colleagues. On the contrary, work–life balance is all about maintaining or improving productivity by reducing conflict, stress, illness and inefficiencies.

What is work–life balance?

Before we can create a balanced life we need to answer this question on two levels: what is work–life balance in general; and what does it mean specifically for you? To paraphrase the government (who promote 'Work–life Balance Week every September – and then spend the other 51 weeks of the year introducing directives for teachers that keep you in the classroom until 10pm), finding work–life balance can be seen as creating working patterns to find a rhythm to help you combine work with your other responsibilities and aspirations. This wording suggests that it is right and proper to have a range of interests – or aspirations – and these can be combined through appropriate patterns of working to find the right rhythm. Rhythm is an interesting word to use, as it seems to suggest regularity, order and structure, as well as flow, naturalness and artistry.

How will that relate specifically to one individual, such as yourself? It would seem that if we are to determine the correct working pattern (I suggest that is our goal here), we need the other pieces of the jigsaw. What are your responsibilities and aspirations, what rhythm suits you? Every individual will have differing needs, but examples of responsibilities and aspirations could be:

- Children
- Elderly parent
- School governorship
- Spouse
- Chair/member of community group
- Being the breadwinner
- Continuing study
- Hobbies
- Relationships
- Leisure time
- Finally painting the spare room!
- Exercise/playing sports

What would be in your shopping basket for an ideal life? How do these things relate to each other? One way to determine what matters most to you – what you should prioritize when finding the right rhythm – is to consider yourself at your 80th birthday party. Imagine that there will be four speeches: one from a long-standing friend, one from your family (possibly your spouse), one from a work colleague (although hopefully you will not still be teaching at 80) and one from your community (church, local group). What would you want them to say about you as a person, your contribution? Experience with coaching clients suggests that this is often very different from what you might first think you aspire to – deeper and less material.

It is important not to let your current situation limit your expectations of the future. Some things will be immovable (most of us have to work for a living, and most of us have to teach to a timetable), but other things can be more flexible than you realize. Consider these words of wisdom:

If you only look at what is, you might never attain what could be.

Anonymous

Having created this shopping basket of responsibilities and aspirations, you can now consider how they interact and limit each other – you can set priorities for the various items in your basket. Remember that separate items need not be mutually exclusive or in conflict. By thinking laterally you can achieve more than one of your goals with one activity. For example, taking up a new evening class may allow you to continue your education as well as socialize or meet new people.

Strengthening your own foundation

Once we have the vision of what life we want to create, how it will look, feel and smell, we can start building it. However, hastily built constructions without sound foundations often crumble, so looking after yourself first is an important step. Elsewhere in this book (see pages 50–53) Jenny Mosley has excellent suggestions for how to prioritize looking after your well-being, and you may wish to consider what you are doing to sustain yourself physically, emotionally and spiritually. Look to build a healthy level in the following areas:

- Diet
- Exercise/fitness
- Sleep
- Time out

One way of integrating this into your routine is to have 'ten delicious daily habits'. Make a list of ten things you will aim to do each day that will be just for you – perhaps a short walk at lunchtime, a relaxing bath when you get home, time to spend with your spouse, reading the latest Harry Potter before you go to sleep – whatever will reward and invigorate you. Such daily action helps to make your new, balanced rhythm more sustainable, rather than a sticky plaster to help you through the last weeks of term.

Implementing your balanced rhythm

Perhaps you have a list of questions running through your head now:

- Has this guy ever been to a school?

- What chance have I got when the dragon I have as a headmistress asks for the Year 6 reports by tomorrow?

- Who is he to think his ideas could work in education?

- Why am I even reading this when I have to prepare my schemes of work for the staff meeting in an hour?

These are possibly reasonable questions, but are they about maintaining the status quo or moving forward? We could replace them with questions like:

- Am I just a victim here, or can I take responsibility for my own life?

- What is my current work–life imbalance costing me and those around me?

- How could it be different, if I applied myself?

- Just what would that mean to me, if I could create better balance and rhythm?

With these benefits in mind, we can turn to specific actions that could help to find better balance within the teaching environment.

WORK SMARTER, NOT HARDER

I like to believe we can achieve success through diligent laziness. We can all reduce our workloads by seeking out better ways of working. Can you share creation of schemes of work or lesson plans with colleagues – in your school or elsewhere? Can you automate or computerize some of the administrative tasks that eat up your time? Can you stop some tasks that have always been done but add limited value? Can you delegate other tasks to learning assistants or administrative staff (if you have them)?

MANAGE PEAKS AND TROUGHS

A recognized factor in stress for teachers is the intensity of work at certain points in the year. Teachers appear to work broadly similar hours annually compared to other professions, but they concentrate it into 40 weeks of the year, not 48 like most workers. This may change with revisions to the structure of the school year, but can you do anything to manage your workload and other responsibilities in recognition of the intensity in term time?

Can you manage some of your work to reflect busy times in the school calendar? If you have a particularly busy time (report writing, school production, Open Days), can you set homework that will reduce your marking load? Perhaps the homework can be assessed in class through presentations or discussion, or you can set right/wrong homework rather than essay or written project-based work, which will be easier to mark.

MAXIMIZING USE OF NON-CONTACT TIME

A perpetual frustration when my wife led a department was that so much of her time was timetabled and out of her control, leaving her to squeeze management tasks around lessons. She achieved a major breakthrough once she came to accept that this was outside her control, and she sought to maximize her non-contact time. Try to find distraction-free areas so that you can focus on your work. Schedule meetings with colleagues rather than catching them in the staffroom – this will improve focus for all of you. The flip side of this coin is, of course, to maximize use of contact time. While maintaining adequate supervision and teacher involvement, can you use time in class to perform some management tasks?

IN-TRAY AMNESTY

Something that causes a great deal of stress and prolongs working hours in any profession is the perennial backlog of projects or tasks. This can be especially true in teaching, where there always seems to be a new syllabus, different materials or more preparation you could be doing. Have you ever moved office and found all those pending projects that got lost behind filing cabinets or buried on the desk and never done? In reality, we can often cull a number of 'would like to' or 'the boss would like me to' projects from our job list without diminishing our effectiveness. If you need to reduce your workload to achieve your balance and rhythm, what can you cull?

GET A MENTOR

You must learn from the mistakes of others. You can't possibly live long enough to make them all yourself.

Sam Levenson

At any stage of our careers, but particularly in the first five to ten years, having a seasoned pro who can guide our development, remind us of what is important and give us perspective can provide immeasurable benefit. Does your school have an established mentor scheme? Can you find a mentor yourself – in your school or another?

Taking action

As educationists you will know that one of the most powerful ways to reinforce learning is for pupils to get on and do it (how many people learn to ride a bicycle from a book?). So now it is your turn:

- Create your vision of the balanced rhythm you want in life. Consider the shopping basket of responsibilities and aspirations you have, and how they relate to each other.
- Identify three actions that will take you towards that vision that you can take in the next seven days.
- Do them!
- Give yourself a small reward for getting started (in any march the first step is the biggest).

Summary

Work–life balance is an increasingly important topic, especially for teachers, and it is increasingly acceptable to have the right priorities in life. Having balance does not make you unprofessional, uncommitted or lazy, it is part of making you healthy, effective and best able to serve your pupils and your school.

That balance is achievable, but it will not happen by accident. If a lack of balance is costing you now, you can take the action to rectify that. The most important step is creating the space for you to understand what you truly want – to create that in your mind and, ideally, write it down. From there you can start to make that vision a reality, with simple practical steps, in themselves not necessarily astounding, but collectively they can change your life forever. Consider the words of Edmund Burke:

Nobody makes a greater mistake than he who does nothing because he could only do a little.

Resources

James Butler provides personal coaching on work–life balance, career management, confidence and relationships, helping successful people to achieve even more. (Tel 01491 659073) http://www.painlessbusiness.com

Suggested further reading

Covey, S. R. (1989), *The 7 Habits of Highly Effective People*, Simon and Schuster, London
This is a seminal work in personal effectiveness and one of the most influential books in helping people at all levels determine purpose in their lives and create the environment that allows them to fulfil that purpose. Full of practical steps to integrate the 7 Habits into your daily life, as well as powerful personal stories, this book has the power to transform lives and organizations.

Richardson, C. (2000), *Take Time for Your Life*, Bantam, London
A book for its time – an excellent, accessible guide to taking small actions to create balance in your life. A multitude of checklists and action plans guide the reader through overcoming limiting beliefs, smashing through their obstacles and building the right foundation for success.

The National Well-being Programme for staff in education

Ray Rumsby

Ray Rumsby has worked in education throughout his professional life as a teacher, as an Adviser in Suffolk Education Authority, later as a Senior Adviser in Norfolk, before moving into personnel work to initiate and co-ordinate Norfolk's Staff Well-being Project for two years. Currently, he is Manager of Worklife Support's Well-being Programme nationally. In the programme, all employees come together to develop strategies that will improve the well-being of their place of work as a community. He outlines the aims, principles and operation of this particular service.

Introduction

The Teacher Support Network is a charity (formerly the Teachers' Benevolent Fund) that wants all teachers to have access to practical help when they most need it. Worklife Support Ltd (WLS) has been established through the charity to provide a range of services aimed at improving the well-being and effectiveness of teachers, support staff and other employees in schools and the education service generally. The WLS Well-being Programme is based upon a highly successful two-year pilot project in Norfolk.

Aims and principles

The programme is indeed about well-being, having a positive approach rather than focusing on stress. The programme operates alongside counselling and other employee assistance services. Nationally its aims are:

- to make sustainable improvements in the well-being of all staff working in education;
- to promote supportive and well-informed managerial practice that actively develops healthy workplaces, focusing upon organizational progress;
- to enable staff as individuals and in groups to manage successfully the pressures they face;
- to use a range of evaluation methods in order to
  - identify strengths and weaknesses;
  - measure progress systematically;
  - inform action taken as a consequence;

  - establish effective means of achieving success in different contexts;
- to provide a means of networking information and research about best practice.

These aims are guided by the following principles:

- a no-blame culture, getting rid of 'us and them';
- a proactive rather than a reactive approach;
- use of collaborative problem solving;
- inclusive of all staff (not just teachers);
- focus on everyone helping to shoulder responsibilities;
- absolute protection of confidentiality;
- development of staff personally and professionally;
- networking and sharing expertise;
- an action-research approach;
- following national guidelines for health and safety in the workplace.

Local well-being co-ordinators

A well-being programme runs at a local level, such as a local education authority, with a central well-being co-ordinator appointed by the employer to manage its development for schools and LEA services. Every co-ordinator attends a three-day residential induction course provided by WLS, and then provides training, information and guidance based on confidential surveys of staff opinion. Several education authorities now have specially trained well-being co-ordinators, who have their own fast-growing network to share ideas and discuss common issues. Local LEA objectives are established by a Well-being Steering Group to reflect the programme's national aims.

Well-being facilitators

Each participating organization, such as a school, nominates at least one person to act as a well-being facilitator. This person is a volunteer – not necessarily a teacher – who has the respect and confidence of all the staff, including senior management, and who receives induction training and some resources. It is a role, not a job, and basically involves championing the cause of staff well-being across the organization. Some establishments develop four, five or even six facilitators in the course of time, reflecting the nature and structure of the organization. The Norfolk project found that the role of the facilitator and the support of senior managers are critical to the success of the programme in any organization.

How the programme operates

Every member of staff completes a confidential online questionnaire based on the Health and Safety Executive's detailed criteria for a healthy workplace. The local co-ordinator of the programme produces a supportive, written commentary including suggestions, based on the data, and feeds back the findings at a meeting with the headteacher (or head of service) and the facilitator. From there, the organization decides what its next steps should be. Arrangements are also made for feeding back the contents of the report to staff.

A programme of organizational development then takes place, focusing on one or two priority areas.

This programme usually includes an element of staff training and meetings for discussion but also, as time goes on, typically leads to the inclusion of well-being as an agenda item within meetings. The sorts of action taken vary widely, but can be categorized as:

- social and promotional events;
- organizational changes in routines and systems, or in ways of working;
- strategic change and development.

Often, all three types of action can be happening in parallel. A year later, the staff questionnaire is run again and comparative progress is measured.

Worklife Support's website (see below) provides information about national developments, but also allows special access to further information for those taking part directly. A programme that runs in several parts of the country has several advantages. It provides individuals with encouragement, ideas and confidence through the network. It can secure a wide range of case study information from people taking part and make it widely available. Finally, the programme is establishing a unique set of comparative data on staff well-being, in order to analyse what can be learned about progress and to develop a clearer understanding of best practice in this area – for example, ideas and activities that can be sustained and transferred successfully to other contexts.

It would seem common sense that staff with high morale, working in schools and departments where their own well-being is taken seriously and is nurtured, are likely to have a positive influence on the success of children's education. However, the main reason for Worklife Support's commitment to this programme is that all education employees, who give so much on behalf of others and whose work is so demanding, themselves deserve and need our care.

Resources

Teacher Support Network, Hamilton House, Mabledon Place, London WC1H 9BE (Tel 020 7554 5200, email services@teachersupport.info); www.teachersupport.info
The Teacher Support Network offers support to teachers, lecturers and their families, regardless of age, length of service or union affiliation. It provides information and newsletters about the range of services it offers in the UK.

Worklife Support: the well-being programme and other services, www.worklifesupport.com
Information about employee assistance programmes, the well-being programme, and training and development, as well as a password-access area for well-being programme participants and users of other contracted services.

The heart of the mentor

Kevin Avison

Reflection plays an important part in improving professional practice, especially when teachers draw on feedback from their colleagues. In Steiner Waldorf schools, as Kevin Avison's contribution indicates, teachers meet on a regular basis to discuss aspects of their work. This form of mentoring has benefits for both teachers and children. According to Fullan and Hargreaves (1992, page 111) 'Schools that actively monitor and strengthen the relationship between teacher and pupil well-being and development will find that both benefit in mutually escalating ways.'

Introduction

Picture a corner of a school library, music practice room or empty classroom, any available space. Three teachers sit together. One has a small pile of large, plain paper 'main lesson' books decorated with illustrations, handwritten poetry, coloured maps and charts, descriptive and narrative essays made by each child in a class of 12 year olds. The others are examining these while the older teacher talks about her work and its aims:

What I'm most concerned about is the rhythm of the lesson. As the children get older I'm finding it more difficult to balance the activities so there is a real breathing process. The last year it was much easier to introduce music or a movement exercise to keep the lesson flowing and stop us getting too 'heady'. Alan and Paul worry me especially.

The speaker is an experienced teacher in her fifties, her co-mentors a younger class teacher and a subject teacher (German and handwork in this case). They both give some lessons in the older colleague's class. In Steiner Waldorf schools, class teachers lead their classes (for the first, main lesson of the day) from ages 6 (Class 1) to 14. The speaker is in her sixth year with the same group of children.

The conversation that follows ranges from sharing observations of the children, a suggestion to visit some of them at home, discussion of lesson-planning objectives and exchange of useful teaching material, and includes some ideas for transitions between activities in the two-hour long 'main lesson'. These weekly meetings follow a similar pattern, but every one is different. After sharing reflections from the previous week's work, one of the three colleagues presents an aspect of her work, or details of a particular lesson, to the others and voices her professional concerns. The conversations are intended to allow each teacher to hear and be heard by a group of supportive and supportively critical friends on a regular basis. It is part of the ongoing learning the teacher must engage in if she is to continue to learn herself, with and from her class, and so manage to meet the challenge of eight years' class teaching (one hopes, as in the case of the teacher described, followed by a sabbatical before starting a new cycle). The meetings can be difficult, but are rarely without laughter. A genuine enthusiasm for learning and teaching pervades them, otherwise they would be worthless.

The art of teaching, if it is to become what Steiner Waldorf teachers aspire to, calls for constant refreshment. A scientific dedication to observation of the class and of oneself must inform it, and a 'religious mood', awe and wonder at the development of the child, sustains it. Mentor, in Homer's *Odyssey*, is the teacher of Odysseus' son, Telemachus, but also a vehicle for the goddess Athene, the true educator. In this context, we might call Athene the ideal of education. Mentoring, or co-mentoring, in the sense indicated here, is essential in a Steiner Waldorf school where there is no overt hierarchy (a College of Teachers takes the place of headteacher) or accompanying salary scale or such conventional outer differentiations. The colleagues described give some time to planning visits to one another's lessons occasionally to observe lessons – 'What aspect of your work, or that of the children, do you want me to make particular note of?' These colleagues will probably also attend class evenings with the parents. So far as possible, teaching styles and abilities of this collegial triad will be contrasting, for here the principle of complementary qualities is important and educative.

Just as Athene represents an ideal, the above characterizes an active ideal that Steiner Waldorf schools work towards, although there may be different ways of implementing it. Fundamental to the art of education in the classroom and in the school, if it is to have the qualities of a social 'organism' as distinct from that of a construct, an institution, is the art of conversation: listening-speaking and speaking-listening. Adult professionals assist one another to become more sensitive and responsive to the needs of the children and to their own pedagogical intuitions towards these. I prepare, I meet the class and what I have prepared is transformed in the teaching. I observe the transformation, evaluate what has happened and invite colleagues to help me appraise the process; their questions, disagreements, confirmations and reflections shape my future preparation. As I teach I learn. But I learn little or nothing until my learning is tested through my contact with others; then I find out what I did not know I knew and what I did not know at all. The children offer one type of reflection, my co-teachers help to articulate and recognize what is largely unconscious in the reactions of the class.

A school is woven out of relationships and, as in all relationships, challenges and failures present themselves along with success or affirmation. Among co-responsible colleagues a small sanctuary can be created in which we contemplate our trials and come to understand what makes us teachers (or sometimes why we might be better doing something else). Not supervision but intervision. Classroom advisers, parents with skills, educationists and researchers all have their place, but those who choose to travel the same road as one another and share their difficulties, insights and enthusiasms, create more than the sum total of their experience or knowledge. That is the heart of collegiality.

Suggested further reading

Rhodes, C., Stokes, M. and Hampton, G. (2004), *A Practical Guide to Mentoring, Coaching and Peer-networking: Teacher professional development in schools and colleges*, RoutledgeFalmer, London
This text emphasizes the importance of coaching, mentoring and peer-networking in assisting teachers, managers and leaders to provide and experience effective professional development.

Smith, P. and West-Burnham, J. (eds) (1993), *Mentoring in the Effective School*, Longman, London
This book raises issues concerning both the individual and the organization in relation to the effective management of mentoring in schools.

Reference

Fullan, M. and Hargreaves, A. (1992), *What's Worth Fighting For in Your School? Working together for improvement*, Open University Press, Buckingham
This book examines how to make schools more interesting and fulfilling places for pupils, teachers and heads.

Parenting and child development education in schools

Sarah Woodhouse

Sarah Woodhouse provides details about two parenting skills programmes developed and researched over the last eight to ten years. Both programmes require a commitment to community involvement through the establishment of partnerships for learning and well-being. The first of these centres around a neighbourhood parent and infant who make regular visits to the classroom. In the second, children make regular visits to a nursery or playgroup to help care for and play with younger children. These programmes aim to develop empathy in children by enabling them to watch a baby's development, celebrate milestones, interact with the baby and learn about baby and toddler care. These successful and long-running programmes recognize the importance of children developing and establishing respectful and caring relationships.

Introduction

The Gulbenkian report *Children and Violence* (1995) and the community study of physical violence to children in the home (Smith 1995) show that an increasing proportion of parents lack the knowledge, skills and confidence they need to give their children a secure foundation for their future development. The absence of good parenting is felt for generations to come. It now presents teachers in schools with a higher proportion of children than ever before who are distressed, distracted or violent.

Children at the primary stage can take pride in doing things gently and deftly. They catch on to the practicalities and skills of baby calming and care, and love the sense of responsibility involved. They learn that a baby is a very individual person, continually growing and changing. Still unselfconscious and open, they become unabashedly involved and show insights that are surprisingly penetrating. They are beginning to form for themselves images of strong and effective parenting.

The background to parenting education in the UK

Sir Keith Joseph, Secretary of State for Social Services in the early 1970s, devoted considerable energy to promoting the idea of Preparation for Parenthood and continuously emphasized the government's concern about the continuing increase in family breakdown and the quality of parenting.

In 1994 The Children's Society launched a resource pack called *Education for Parenthood* by Philip Hope for 14 to 18 year olds. This contained five topic books, a teachers' guide with 28 activities including questionnaires, project work, role plays and case studies all aimed towards stimulating class discussion. The pack, some of which can be drawn from and used with 10 to 12 year olds, has been revised (Hope with Sharland 1998). Following this introductory project for secondary schools, a report by Philip Hope and Penny Sharland was published in 1997 by the Gulbenkian Foundation: *Tomorrow's Parents, Developing Parenthood Education in Schools*.

A Home Office report in 1996 linked youth crime to the quality of parent–child relationships and the degree to which dysfunctional and disunited families result in child crime. In 1999, the UN Children's Rights Committee, with the task of monitoring the honouring of the United Nations Convention on the Rights of the Child, began pressing the British government strongly about its lack of any firm strategies for parenting education. The government's Guidelines for Schools on Parenting Education can be found on the Parenting Education and Support Forum website (see Resources, page 67).

Schools are still in the very early stages of developing parenthood teaching in the UK and there is a dearth of published materials for teachers, particularly for primary schools. The lead will need to be taken from successful and long-running programmes and training courses developed mainly in schools in the USA and Canada.

Current initiatives worldwide

ROOTS OF EMPATHY

This programme, used in Canada and now also in Japan, provides the first training course for parenthood education in primary schools to be made

Building empathy

available in the UK. It is highly recommended. To discover where and when Roots of Empathy training is available, check the Parenting Education and Support Forum website (see Resources, page 67).

The aim of Roots of Empathy in the long term is to build the parenting capacity of the next generation of parents. In the short term, the programme focuses on raising levels of empathy, which results in more respectful and caring relationships and reduced levels of disturbed and antisocial behaviour and violence.

Roots of Empathy offers an innovative classroom-based parenting programme for children aged 3 to 14 years; it aims to reduce aggression through the fostering of empathy and emotional literacy. The programme takes an inclusive approach, raising the level of empathy in the entire classroom and across age groups. When children understand how others feel, they are less likely to hurt each other through bullying, exclusion and violence. In the programme, children learn how to challenge cruelty and injustice. The experience of social inclusion and activities that are consensus-building contributes to a culture of caring that changes the tone of the classroom and improves children's learning in all areas.

The heart of the programme is a neighbourhood parent and infant who visit the classroom once a month for the full school year. Observations of a loving parent–child relationship give children a model of competent parenting. A qualified Roots of Empathy instructor helps the children to observe the baby's development, interact with the baby and learn about an infant's needs and unique temperament. The instructor also works with the class the week before and the week after each family visit to prepare and reinforce this teaching.

Roots of Empathy instructors plan lessons in the classroom and work closely with the teacher and the

Case study:

Tom's pink feather – making a difference, one child at a time

Tom, a seven-year-old boy who had been in and out of foster homes for many years, had exhibited consistently aggressive and antisocial behaviour throughout the year. He had not been able to make friends and was often very disruptive in class, displaying a hostile demeanour, always wearing a hat almost covering his eyes and never smiling.

When the Roots of Empathy instructor brought the parent and baby into the classroom, the class teacher was very concerned that Tom might harm the baby. He was placed with the instructor right next to the baby and, as a result, his reactions to the parent–baby exchanges revealed a completely different behaviour. During the first class visit, Tom smiled and interacted with the baby, during the second class visit he removed his hat, and at the third visit he brought in a dirty pink feather to tickle the bottom of the baby's feet. The contact with the baby and the observation of the exchanges between mother and child were the keys that unlocked his feelings and allowed him to display the gentle, sensitive person he was.

From that point on, both his fellow classmates and his teacher saw Tom from a new and kinder perspective. As his emotional literacy grew, so did his empathy. He gradually learned to mix with the children, made friends and learned how to talk about how he was feeling.

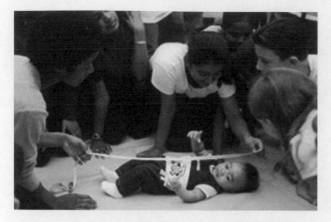

Gaining insights into the infant's growth and development

participating volunteer family. The instructors come from diverse professional backgrounds: teaching, health, early childhood education, social work, counselling, speech therapy and leisure activities. Having classroom experience is a major asset, as is having knowledge of infant development.

The advantages of having a visitor from outside the school as an instructor are considerable. It involves ongoing contact with the volunteer family between visits and the development of other community links that provide the children with wider opportunities for learning about child care. The visits also allow a teacher the chance to be an observer and learn new and often unexpected things about his or her pupils.

With the support of a trained instructor, schools may decide to approach the LEA to ask for half-day seminars on parenthood and child development education to be organized for all the staff, perhaps inviting teachers from other nearby schools.

Gonzaga Programme

The Gonzaga Programme was first developed by a Jesuit priest called Father Ed Durkin working with 7 to 12 year olds in elementary schools in Harlem in the 1980s and early 1990s. One unique ingredient of this parent education and child nurture programme is the secondment of individual children at the age of seven into a nursery or playgroup for a period each week for that year. Every child has an 'adopted' toddler to help care for and play with, and to make birthday gifts for. The children each keep and illustrate a diary about their experiences and report the toddler's activities and development back to the class. Home visits also take place, when advisable, so the pupil sees the toddler with the rest of the family.

The programme starts very simply and builds up steadily to a high standard of understanding and skills over four to five years. Certificates are awarded for parenting skills and knowledge of baby/child development.

The results of this programme over ten years were remarkable. The attitude and behaviour of the boys in particular were transformed; and in the harsh and violent circumstances in which most of the Harlem communities live, things changed radically. School-age pregnancies, street violence and drug-taking fell to a quarter of their former levels. This was partly due to better policing, but it was ascertained that the Gonzaga Programme had been the main contributor to this striking improvement.

This work with the children in Harlem is so intensive and continuous that further details of the way the programme is run were not yet available on a website at the time of going to print.

Other successful programmes have been developed over many years in the USA. The following two stand out – The Parenting Project, based in Florida and now serving six other states; and Educating Children for Parenting, based in Philadelphia (see Resources, page 67).

Setting up a parenting education programme in the primary school

School governors and staff will need to discuss the introduction of this new initiative into the school, the way it is handled and its aims and outcomes. Parents need to be informed and should be included in planning some aspects of the programme, such as the visits of a mother with her baby and the baby's father, too, if possible. Parents will also be able to provide useful contacts in the local area.

Schools can obtain valuable help from specialist organizations in the field of child care and parenting, both local and national. These organizations can sometimes provide trained advisers for the planning and delivery of parenthood education lessons, working with the class teacher. Parents in Partnership – Parent Infant Network (PIPPIN) may prove particularly helpful (see Resources, page 67).

Focusing on the family is an essential introduction to any programme of parenting education for children. Setting up displays about families in the main areas of school can encourage everyone who walks by or visits to think about families as an important topic.

Organizations and their resources

PARENTING EDUCATION AND SUPPORT FORUM

The Forum exists to raise awareness of the importance of parenting and its impact on the emotional, mental, social, intellectual and physical development of children. It is the prime source of information in the UK about organizations, training courses, conferences and publications; it also provides information about local Forum members and new initiatives and materials useful for supporting parenting education in schools. The Forum can help schools get in touch with local providers of courses in parenthood for adults that will assist those who are initiating a parenting education programme in their school. Membership of the Forum is therefore a practical first step.

The Forum believes that the main challenge for teachers is to be alert to the differences in each child's home and family circumstances and to prevent any child feeling stigmatized by the direction in which discussions may go. Awareness of cultural diversity and the different experiences of each child must be a priority, even though the fundamental needs of mothers, of fathers and of children remain the same throughout the world.

NATIONAL CHILDREN'S BUREAU

The Bureau provides support for teachers who want to undertake parenting education in their classes.

Young children show that they need to discuss on and on about what is a family; it matters so much to them, especially the problems of reconstituted families and adjustment to that. They often feel responsible for the loss of a parent through marriage breakdown. Their teacher may be the only person they can talk to.

Lin Poulton, National Children's Bureau

NATIONAL CHILDBIRTH TRUST

The Trust's members have a wealth of experience in preparing parents for the birth and care of their children. They have gathered ideas and practical experience on ways of teaching all aspects of birth education and baby care.

If it proves difficult to find a relaxed and experienced mother with a two- to three-month-old baby to act as a role model, the local branches of the National Childbirth Trust can ask members to help with the search. Local midwives and health visitors may also be able to advise.

THE OPEN UNIVERSITY WORLDWIDE

The Open University provides specific courses, modules and materials about child development and care that could be of value to teachers. Courses include Understanding Children (0–11), Child Development, Working with Children and Families, Childhood, and a Foundation Degree in Early Childhood (0–8). Every few years, courses are changed and new courses are added. A 30-day inspection of course material is allowed to educational establishments in the UK.

What are the benefits of parenting education in primary schools?

Among the benefits of parenting education in primary schools, the following are some of the most valuable:

- Such programmes confirm the human instincts for tenderness; for tending to someone or something smaller and more helpless than oneself; and for becoming competent and skilled in everyday family concerns.
- Understanding and sensitivity to others become part of a child's developing personality.
- Children become more committed to school, which immediately feels more approachable.
- Children enjoy the sessions and their mental health and motivation improve.
- Children are able to contribute on equal terms.
- Fewer children feel alienated. Bullying and dominant, aggressive and destructive behaviour fall away.
- Children are wide open to critically important learning experiences and become more competent in everyday family relationships.
- Reflective skills, communication skills and planning skills improve. These spread into the rest of the school day.
- Children become more willing to discuss family matters at home, are easier to communicate with and less jealous of a baby or younger sibling.
- There is direct stimulus to schools to involve parents more directly.
- The aims of the National Healthy Schools Standard Guidance are fulfilled. Successful parenthood education can become a school target.

BIRTH EDUCATION

Once the point has been reached when the children's curiosity and interest in the visiting baby turns into a real affection, the right time has come to consider introducing birth education (as opposed to sex education) into the programme. There are a number of excellent books, suitable for using with children, that explain how a baby grows in the womb and is born (see Suggested further reading, page 67).

What children and adults say about parenting education

I learned that babies have feelings just like us and we should respect them just like people give us respect.

8 year old

The most important thing is never to shake a baby and there is no such thing as a bad baby.

7 year old

Our visiting baby, Adam, has become such a part of the school family. People stop in the hallway to look in the door when he comes to visit. The children share feelings much more readily and I have witnessed for myself children who were 'not part of the group', become part of it, as the children bond with Adam and each other.

Roots of Empathy instructor

The children respond to his cues and ask a lot of questions about Jack's feelings and his needs. At our last visit, Jack fell over from his sitting position and began to cry and to watch the children trying to comfort him was a sight to see. Immediately, they offered comforting words or a toy and then sang him a song to make him feel better.

Visiting mother with baby in class

Teaching parenting skills and baby and child development to young children and giving them practice is the most powerful counterbalance to a culture of violence and materialism. It also helps children self-heal from their own poor parenting experiences. This effect is particularly noticeable among the boys.

Student teacher working with the Gonzaga Programme in Harlem

My students developed a close bond with the baby's family. We learned a lot about the care and love a baby needs and the importance of family. My students were so sensitive to the baby's needs and enjoyed watching her grow.

Teacher working with a Roots of Empathy instructor in a Toronto Elementary School

The children try immediately to apply the theory they are learning to their own lives, such as the effects of anxiety and anger. What they are learning is not just understood. It is deeply felt.

Chief Executive Office, Educating Children for Parenting in Philadelphia

It's the patient, firm, loving, and confident day-to-day handling of our youngest children at home and in the classroom that teaches children non-stop and indelibly about good human relationships. Add a mother and baby to enjoy and learn from and you are there!

Teacher in a UK primary school

Resources

Educating Children for Parenting, 211 North 13th Street, Suite 701, Philadelphia, PA 19107, USA
(Tel 215 496-9780); www.ecparenting.org
Details about Educating Children for Parenting can be accessed through their website.

National Childbirth Trust, Alexandra House, Oldham Terrace, Acton, London W3 6NH (Tel 0870 444 8707)
www.nctpregancyandbabycare.com
The National Childbirth Trust offers support in pregnancy, childbirth and early parenthood.

The Open University Worldwide, Walton Hall, Milton Keynes MK7 6AA
Courses information and advice: Tel 01908 858793. Details and purchase of course materials, videos and books: Tel 01908 858785; www.ouw.co.uk

Parenting Education and Support Forum, Unit 431, Highgate Studios, 53–79 Highgate Road, London NW5 1TL (Tel 020 7284 8370); www.parenthood.org.uk

The Parenting Project, 5776 Hamilton Way, Boca Raton. FL 33496, USA (Tel 561 620-0256)
www.parentingproject.org
The Parenting Project is a national organization dedicated to bringing parenting, nurturing and relationship skills education to all school age children and teens.

PIPPIN, Parents In Partnership Parent Infant Network, Birch Centre Annex, Highfield Park, Hill End Lane, St Albans, Herts (Tel 01727 899099); www.pippin.org.uk

Roots of Empathy, 215 Spadina Avenue, Suite 160, Toronto, ON, Canada M5T 2C7 (Tel 416 944-3001)
www.rootsofempathy.org
'Roots of Empathy' is a registered trademark and all programme content and materials are copyrighted.

Suggested further reading

Harris, R. H. (1996), *Happy Birth Day!* Walker Books, London
This picture book provides a loving account of a baby's birth and first day as seen through a mother's eyes.

Kitzinger, S. (1986), *Being Born*, Dorling Kindersley, London
This story documents the nine-month journey from conception to birth. The book is aimed at 7 to 11 year olds and is written very sensitively from the child's perspective. The photographs, by Lennart Nilsson, are exceptionally gentle and beautiful.

Manning, M. and Granstrom, B. (1999), *How did I Begin?* Watts, London
This book provides an introduction to human reproduction. It follows the first nine months of a child's life within its mother's womb. Suitable for national curriculum Key Stages 1 and 2.

References

Calouste Gulbenkian Foundation (1995), *Children and Violence: Report of the Commission on Children and Violence*, Calouste Gulbenkian Foundation, London
This report provides an overview of research on why children become violent and the incidence of violence by children. The report also includes recommendations for action.

Hope, P. with Sharland, P. (1997), *Tomorrow's Parents, Developing Parenthood Education in Schools*, Calouste Gulbenkian Foundation, London

Hope, P. with Sharland, P. (1998), *Education for Parenthood: A resource pack for young people* (revised edition), The Children's Society, London
This pack contains five photocopiable unit books covering: what it means to be a parent; what parents need; parent–child relationships; rights and responsibilities; health and development.

Smith, M. A. (1995), A community study of physical violence to children in the home and associated variables. Presented at Vth European Conference, International Society for the Prevention of Child Abuse and Neglect, Oslo, Norway
Research carried out by Dr Marjorie Smith of the Thomas Coram Research Unit and others, and commissioned by the Department of Health.

Working in partnership: Ashfield Nursery, Parents' Centre and community

Joan Lister

Ashfield Nursery School has created a partnership in which young children can develop a strong sense of feeling connected to their community. Joan Lister, the school's headteacher, describes the nursery school's attempt to establish and work in partnership with parents and the local community.

Although change occurs in all sorts of ways, the positive benefits that it sometimes brings are not always sustained. Ashfield Nursery School provides an example where the benefits of change have been maintained over a long period of time. The development of the school's partnership is traced back to an incident that occurred one morning about 30 years ago. Achievements of the partnership include the setting up of a parents' corner, a mother and toddler group, a parents' centre and the development of the nursery's garden.

Today, parent support and work with the local community continue to be important in the life of Ashfield Nursery School, which has also forged a successful link with a school in Italy.

Introduction

One wet October morning in 1974, one year after becoming the headteacher at Ashfield Nursery School, I discovered outside the school a huddle of very upset parents taking refuge from the weather and their misery of life in our area of Newcastle. The area was, and still is, designated as one of the most disadvantaged in the city, with a high unemployment rate and high crime rates. I approached them and suggested they might like to come inside and at least share their misery in the warmth of the school – they ran like scared rabbits.

With my firm belief in the education of young children in partnership with their families, I realized that we were going to have an uphill struggle if parents within our community could not even trust their nursery school staff to offer shelter and a listening ear. I discussed this issue with the staff and we decided to create a 'parents' corner' in our already cramped premises.

We chose a small room that was used, rarely, by the local chiropodist, who we suggested would be much happier working in the pristine conditions of the new health centre. Then I approached one of the more confident parents of our school community to help us reach out to the group who had been so distressed on that October morning. The first mother and toddler group to be formed in our city was the result.

Lily, the leading light from the community, helped us to prepare the room with whatever we could lay our hands on, to make it a warm, inviting drop-in area. She visited the families in their own homes and persuaded them that the nursery staff were not prying and were not ogres but only wanted to help them to help their children.

These were the halcyon days when we had a non-class-based teacher in the school – our deputy head, Norah Zvi – who was able to support the group from the word go. Norah was well known to the parents. She worked alongside them to create a haven in the ex-chiropodist's room and she looked after their children, while they had a 'ciggy', a moan and a laugh together. She gradually encouraged the parents to become involved with their children's play and it was obvious that we were going to need more space, as the group was growing and its needs were changing.

I then persuaded the staff to give up their staffroom and to use my office as a replacement. The staffroom adjoined the largest room in the school, which we euphemistically called our 'hall'. We were, therefore, able to create our 'haven' in the staffroom and our hall became a workshop area for parents and children.

We were extremely fortunate that the Primary Inspector at the time, Nancy Elliott, was very keen to support our method of working and she suggested that we should provide informal adult education within our parents' group. She then put us in touch with the newly appointed Education Community Worker, Pam Flynn, who attended our parents' group on a regular basis and then gradually began to introduce the concept that perhaps some form of informal adult learning could help to relieve some of their anxieties. Pam introduced 'Cooking on a budget', discussions on dealing with benefits agencies and social services, and creative arts sessions. As a result, we had a thriving community group who were sharing their expertise with the nursery staff and supporting their children both in school and at home. One problem: the group was still growing and we needed more space.

Ashfield Parents' Centre

Once again, fortune shone on us and the caretaker's house attached to the school became vacant. With the help of our Primary Inspector, we persuaded the local authority that rather than have it standing as a disused eyesore, it would make a marvellous centre for our parents. In 1982, Ashfield Parents' Centre was born. Parents, staff, the local community and the then Youth Training Service (YTS) worked side by side for one year, running courses on interior decoration, tiling, carpet-laying, plastering and so on. In May 1983, the Centre opened its doors to the community as a whole.

The Centre was initially managed by the school staff with parents co-opted, including Lily, our leading light from the early days, who had worked enthusiastically alongside us through our evolution. They offered similar courses to those of the original scheme and hosted a regular toddler group and advice session. One of the fathers who attended with his son eventually became chairperson of our governing body. He always said that involvement with the Centre gave him the confidence to change direction in life. Both he and his son came to us with bad stammers and by the time Michael left the nursery to go into 'big' school, both he and his father were talking freely and had the confidence to move

on accordingly. Michael's father gave up the chairmanship in 1995, but still remains on our governing body as a co-opted member. He now has a management role in the local authority, and Michael is in college.

The Centre is now managed by local parents, who undergo management training within the school and within the Centre, and staff and governors are co-opted onto the Parents' Centre Management Group. They offer a wide range of training courses: computing, accredited child-care training such as play worker/crèche/classroom assistant, first aid, healthy living and cookery, to name but a few. They employ two full-time workers, both of whom have done their training in the Centre, 15 sessional workers similarly trained in the Centre, and one group has set up a community business running an after-school club.

The following quotes from parents illustrate how they have benefited from their involvement with the Centre.

I first heard about the first aid course in the Parents' Centre from the admin worker. She encouraged me to go along. I felt a bit self-conscious, having been out of a learning setting for some time. However, there was no need to feel worried as the other people helped me. The knowledge I have gained has made me feel much more confident should I have to deal with a medical emergency inside or outside the home.

Anne Houchin (who is now doing her crèche-workers certificate and helps regularly in the classrooms)

The classroom assistant course started in October 2000. My friend encouraged me to do it. I was nervous at first, as I hadn't done anything like this before, but after the first hour I was fine as the tutor made us feel at ease. I found the course very interesting. Even if you did not intend to work as a classroom assistant, it gave you an insight into what your child does at school. We all had to do classroom placements. I done mine at Ashfield and the staff were very helpful and encouraging. The children

A volunteer with children

were great. Doing my placement in the classroom was the best bit of the course. The course was hard at times but we all got through it and I felt quite proud of myself when I received my certificate from the Director of Education.

Sharon Carr (now our playgroup leader)

I have been coming to the toddler group with my two children and enjoy it very much. Vanda, the leader, makes everyone very welcome and introduces us to new people. They do lots of different things and there is a lovely garden at the back of the nursery for the children to play in, which is smashing if you haven't got a garden at home.

Gurpreet Kaur

THE NURSERY GARDEN

One of the projects that the parents and local community took on board was the development of our nursery garden. Like our nursery building, the garden dates back to 1790 and, until the parents decided to take it over, was a traditional manor-house garden. The parents raised £35,000, in 1985 – no mean feat in the poorest part of the city – through applying for any grants available and persuading local dignitaries and businesses to help. Catherine Cookson donated the money for their first large piece of equipment, a huge see-saw, and they entered into a contract with Steetley Bricks, where I was on an industrial placement, to provide the materials for a peppercorn fee. The garden project progressed as a community project, with parents, children, staff and anyone else we could persuade involved in the design, building and maintenance. Our garden remains an oasis in the heart of Elswick, still maintained and loved by local families.

THE MEDITERRANEAN GARDEN

Recently our current parents group', led by their development worker Margaret Maughan and inspired by the work of their predecessors, decided to develop a Mediterranean garden in the disused backyard of the Parents' Centre. They sought sponsorship from local firms and were successful in obtaining a grant from Ringtons Tea. One particularly artistically talented mother designed the garden with a water feature, quiet arbour, paved areas and space for exotic potted plants. Then parents and grandparents proceeded to transform this derelict site into a haven for the parents and toddlers of our area. It was a proud day in July 2003 when the Director of Education was invited to present our parents' group with awards and certificates for their achievements throughout the year, and a doubly proud occasion as the presentations were made in their newly created garden area.

The parent, school and community project goes from strength to strength and, as a now very long-in-the-tooth headteacher, I get the same thrill from the achievements of our parents as I do from the achievements of our children. I am now receiving a third generation of children into our school/centre and know that our philosophy of family learning and family support will continue long after I am gone, as ownership belongs to the children and their families.

Newcastle/Turin initiative

In September 1999 our school became involved with the Scuola Materna Europea in Turin. This was the result of my attending a cross-phase training day, hosted by the middle school in Turin in which my son works, meeting with a group of like-minded early years practitioners, and realizing that cross-community links are as important as inter-community links.

Although we did not realize it at the time, this first contact was to provide the basis for a unique, exciting, long-term project that has just blossomed and blossomed. It has provided our school, our neighbouring primary schools and our city with the opportunity to develop a creative, educational and cultural partnership with a city very similar to our own – beautiful, historic, post-industrial and forward looking.

Our partnership has resulted in staff from the schools involved visiting one another to explore together how children acquire a second language and develop aesthetic and cultural awareness. It has resulted in children from the Scuola Materna visiting our school and having the opportunity to discover the delights of Newcastle and its surroundings. The children from the Scuola Materna are five or six years old when they visit us, but as our children are only three to four years old, and too young to travel abroad without their parents, they communicate with their Italian friends via the internet.

Our parent governor has visited Turin and one of our community governors, who is a teacher trainer, is now involved in in-service work with teachers from a group of primary schools in Turin who we have paired with primary schools in Newcastle.

Parent and children in Ashfield's tree house

Parents, trainees and children on Ashfield's 'trip-trap bridge'

Our shared interest in the creative and performing arts has enabled us to bring an exhibition of children's artwork from a nursery school in Turin (via National di Bologna) to a major museum in Newcastle. The exhibits came along with the Italian teacher and her colleague as translator who shared their expertise with young children in the West End of Newcastle in a series of workshops. We are currently working towards making this exchange of children's artwork an annual event to ensure our partnership continues to flourish through those who matter most – the children.

School linking: finding a partner school

The British Council Education and Training Group manage an extensive internet site (see Resources, page 73). Windows on the World is a free and easy-to-use database for schools and colleges that would like to develop links with other institutions worldwide. Using the database, teachers can:

- inform others that they would like to develop a link by registering their institutions on the site;
- browse the thousands of schools and colleges that have already registered on the site.

The Windows of the World site also contains case studies of international school and college linking projects and information on funding opportunities available to UK schools and colleges to support international partnerships.

Resources

Windows on the World, The British Council, 10 Spring Gardens, London SW1A 2BN (Tel 020 7389 4359)
www.wotw.org.uk
The Windows on the World database can be accessed from this website.

Suggested further reading

Leather, S. (1995), *School Linking across the World: A directory of agencies supporting north-south linking*, Central Bureau for Educational Visits and Exchanges, London

Teaching the heart:
the emotional value of play

3 Play and natural wonder

– developing a sense of wonder and excitement of the world

Play is the perfect bridge between self and the world of nature and the world of others. I know myself in relation to what is outside me.

Sally Jenkinson (*The Genius of Play: Celebrating the spirit of childhood*), author and founder member of the Alliance of Childhood

Teaching the heart:
the emotional value of play

Sally Jenkinson

The central role of play in enabling children to explore their feelings is the theme of Sally Jenkinson's contribution. Real-life accounts of children playing, drawn from several sources, are provided to illustrate the benefits of play in terms of emotional well-being. She argues the case, convincingly, for the way play touches the heart and helps children to explore their own feelings, to understand others and their sense of self in relation to the world.

Introduction

I sincerely believe that for the child, and for the parent seeking to guide him, it is not half so important to know as to feel. If facts are the seeds that later produce knowledge and wisdom, then the emotions and the impressions of the senses are the fertile soil in which the seeds must grow. The years of early childhood are the time to prepare the soil. Once emotions have been aroused – a sense of the beautiful, the excitement of the new and the unknown, a feeling of sympathy, pity, admiration or love – then we wish for knowledge about the object of our emotional response. Once found it has lasting meaning. It is more important to pave the way for the child to want to know than to put him on a diet of facts he is not ready to assimilate.

(Carson 1998, page 56)

The current emphasis on formal learning, and over-use of mediated experiences – television, video, computer games – can deprive children of immediate sensory encounters with the real world. Play provides the opportunity for a smorgasbord of wonderful first-hand experiences. Dry knowledge = bored learners.

In nature play, in which all the senses are active, a correspondence of feeling within the child, a symphony of responses to the world, is aroused. Our first feelings are educated by our senses, for it is the senses that begin the task of articulating and differentiating the feelings.

The immediacy of our childhood experiences offers a communion with the world and the opportunity for gaining wisdom and intuition unfettered by the intellect. Our early loves linger, as George Eliot poignantly observed:

Life did change for Tom and Maggie and yet they were not wrong in believing that the thoughts and loves of these first years would always make part of their lives. We could never have loved the earth so well if we had had no childhood in it...What novelty is worth that sweet monotony where everything is known and loved because it is known...Our delight in the sunshine on the deep bladed grass today, might be no more than the faint perception of wearied souls, if it were not for the sunshine and the grass in the far-off years, which still live in us and transform our perception into love.

(Eliot 1985, page 94; first published 1880)

This contribution is a slightly adapted version of a chapter from Sally Jenkinson's (2001) book, *The Genius of Play: Celebrating the spirit of childhood* (Hawthorn Press).

The threads of our childhood perceptions filter upwards and become integrated into our personalities. Our futures are built on our present perceptions, and the quality of our early encounters with the world have the greatest and most lasting influence over us. Deep knowledge, deep concentration, deep play bring deep satisfaction and contentment with life.

Can we imagine ourselves back into that place of discovery when the world was new, to that time when we were thrilled by our senses? Are we able to recapture the intense curiosity we had about the fascinating world in which we found ourselves, and can we empathize with those who inhabit that state of being now?

Whenever a child is physically doing – and much of young children's doing is bound up with their play – they are also feeling. Wet sand is not just a concept; it is an experience, causing an inner sensation, a *reaction*. Action and reaction. Sand between the fingers, sand in the mouth, rasping around, over and under the tongue, and cracking between the teeth, is different from sand in the shoes. Dry, warm, flowing sand is different from cold, wet, clumping sand. Yet these experiences are all sand. Sand *experienced*, as opposed to 'taught about or explained', is known, felt and understood. Sand is not reduced to a concept but a series of enlightening encounters; a conversation between the senses and the thing sensed. Life through feeling and doing becomes subtle and paradoxical: sand is hard *and* soft, lumpy *and* liquid. In all its mutability, there are many truths about sand.

Through healthy use of their senses, children first learn to understand oppositions between things. They learn subtlety and gradation and begin to build a personal feeling life: a sensory memory. A richly orchestrated sense life helps create a heterogeneous emotional life, which in turn creates a differentiated life of thought. This paves the way for a discerning adult response to the world.

Speaking at an Alliance for Childhood conference in Brussels in September 2000, Craig Kielberger, the 17-year-old founder of the international organization 'Free the Children', in which no officer is older than 18, said that the purpose of education should be 'to teach young people *to react to the world*'. He began his work after browsing through the weekend paper in search of the comic section and coming across an article on child slavery that made an overwhelming

impression upon him. He *reacted* by setting up an organization with his school friends to alleviate child suffering. Now leading a huge operation that has had great success in its work for children, Craig himself is an exemplar of what it means to react and respond to the world.

The slow acquisition of a language of feelings begins at birth. Watch the look on a baby's face when a new and unexpected taste is introduced for the first time. The reaction is total, the entire little body resonates with the experience. Our adult senses, in contrast, are easily dulled – the amount of beauty, suffering, noise to which we have become insensitive or immune is staggering. We need artists, poets and writers to help us feel again, to re-educate *emotions*, those moving feelings that have become stilled.

Daniel Goleman places great emphasis on the development of the feelings. In his valuable book *Emotional Intelligence* (1996), he suggests that our current view of intelligence is far too narrow, and that in fact emotional 'literacy' plays a far greater role in our success as adults than we realize. Our own rich life of feeling enables us to feel empathy for others (a fuller account comes later in this contribution).

Children explore their feelings through play

Play is the perfect stage for the theatre of feelings to find expression. Playing out the dramas resting on their own hearts can be a journey of understanding for children – about their own feelings and about those of others. The intensity of children's feelings, as many heart-rending autobiographies testify, should not be underestimated. Janusz Korczak (1992), author and friend to children, who died with the children in his care at the Treblinka concentration camp in 1942, wrote the following words:

> You say:
> – 'Dealings with children are tiresome.'
> You're right.
> You say:
> – 'Because we have to lower ourselves to their intellect.
>   Lower, stoop, bend, crouch down.'
> You are mistaken.
> It isn't that which is so tiring. But because we have to reach up to their feelings. Reach up, stretch, stand on our tip-toes.
> As not to offend.

If we impose other agendas upon our children, if we structure their lives so that the play agenda disappears entirely, the least we can expect from them is frustration and anxiety. A backlog of unresolved feelings will accumulate. Play helps children to explore and organize their feelings in a context that they can manage. Children do display a great need to replay the things that worry them. Play is not only an outlet for exuberance but is also a medium for dealing with emotional conflict and uncertainties about the world. Children's play can become a metaphor for their feelings.

Playing at divorce, birth, marriage, death – the determining moments in any individual's life – is essential. Children need to, and do, *think* about things through the medium of their play. How else can they express their grief, their joy? Children's thinking is not head-bound but is enacted in the willed landscapes of their play. Problems are played out in order to be understood. A play scene can settle turbulent feelings; deal with loss; make sense of confusion; and reorder the world for the child. Denial of this experience creates deep resentment. Play is 'thinking/feeling time' to a child in need. To be directed to play to an outer goal may constitute an emotional infringement against the child. As Margaret Lowenfeld (1935, page 17) has written, 'This necessity of the human mind to dramatize these elements of its environment that it perceives, in order to be able to emotionally assimilate them, is a characteristic that runs throughout the whole fabric of human life.'

A modern adaptation of a ring game reflects today's insecurities. The marriage game 'Poor Jenny is a-weeping' now has an extra verse. Jenny, a sad girl, weeps firstly for her sweetheart, then, in turn, for her bridesmaids, pageboys, vicar and a church. Eventually, her heart's desires are met, the weeping stops and she marries. In the last verse of the original song, Jenny dances with her husband on her wedding day. In the new version, there is an almost imperceptible pause and then Jenny starts weeping again. The refrain now goes: 'Poor Jenny is divorcing…' As a postscript to that sad little tale, Jenny often re-marries, so a happy ending is possible – alternatively, she might even learn to enjoy being single.

A woman whose father's recurrent illness was re-created in her play is quoted by Singer and Singer (1992, page 108). Her imaginary characters included Phena and Barbara Tall, as well as Ultra, Violet, and Ray. These pharmaceutical and therapeutic characters were often worked into a game-show quiz.

Many parents worry about their child's imaginary companions, but they have been positively correlated with less aggression in boys, greater happiness, more positive attitudes, less fear and anxiety during later play situations, and greater persistence in play. Girls with play companions were less prone to anger, fearfulness, and particularly sadness in their play (Singer and Singer 1992, page 103).

One man I met developed his own little world, or paracosm, over 40 years ago, and wrote to me about his childhood game. His name was Richardson, and when times were tough, he would call on his gang for help. Out of the wall they would come, 'a hierarchy of fellows': Semner and Demner and possibly Memnor and Temnor, led by the central character, the boy himself, splendidly titled 'The Richardson dipped in Gravy'. When alone in his bedroom he would enact, or rather 'become', these characters. In his words:

The characters were always involved in some heroic deeds against some injustices, defending the honour of some damsel in distress. There was many a rough and tumble on the bed between the Richardson D.I.G. and his men and the baddies. The greater the threat to the Richardson, the more 'disciples' were called upon. It is possible my teddy bear, Peter, got caught up in this too.

As a postscript, he added that, apart from his parents, he didn't think he had shared this with anyone before. In conclusion, Richardson, man and child, agreed: 'I'm happy for you to use this in any research material or book or whatever. (The Richardson nods his approval.)'

Too much directed play, with predetermined outcomes and learning objectives, will lead to frustration and unhappiness because what the child wants to explore through play will remain problematic. Unfortunately, much play in schools functions in this way, prioritizing only the intellectual/skill aspect of human nature and neglecting the affective side. This is demonstrably counterproductive, as a frustrated or unhappy child will have more difficulty in learning.

Spontaneous play, with adult interventions only when necessary, allows the development of an *integrated personality*. Respecting what Piaget describes as 'compensatory play' – in which a child replays events that may have been difficult or challenging – acknowledges the child's right to feel and express sad or happy moods. As a mother, I spent far too much time trying to cheer up my children, probably for my own benefit. I wanted happy children, and didn't appreciate their need sometimes to feel sad. Sad play can eventually help to promote well-being.

Play is invaluable where a child is anxious or worried. Good hospitals know this, and have successfully used play therapy for a number of years (see Russell Evans's book *Helping Children to Overcome Fear,* 2000). Research shows that children who play at hospitals – with doctors, operations, bandages and so on – show less resistance to medical procedures and recover more swiftly.

Adults reflect through discussion, through literature, through writing and meditation. Children reflect through concretely acting out past experiences, or concretely preparing for them.

(Bruce 1995, page 42)

In my time as a kindergarten teacher, I witnessed many little girls, and fewer boys, playing sick babies. Boys preferred to be dogs with wounded paws. Death and loss were intermittently recurring themes – as they are in life. The following anecdotes are examples of the importance of children's feelings and of the need, at times, to prioritize them over other educational outcomes.

During the inspection of a particular kindergarten, the children had behaved in an exemplary fashion and were beginning to get the hang of what it was their unusually inquisitive visitor wanted from them. On a walk across a field the inspector asked a spirited boy how many sheep he could see. Bemused at the question, the answer to which he knew was obvious to both of them, but now also canny about the way this inspection game worked, the boy responded: 'Two, but they have eight legs'. The inspector looked pleased and scribbled on her clipboard (evidence of arithmetical ability here). On their return, the same boy, eager to please, continued to inform her that his chair normally had four legs, six when he sat on it (ha!), but only two when he swung backwards. The world-view of this

intelligent child was rapidly contracting into a never-ending vision of legs – all expertly tailored to fit the anticipated frame of the inspector's questions. Later, the teacher brought some sparkling frozen winter leaves inside, and in a mood of silent fascination and amazement, the children watched the delicately frosted tracery disappear as the leaves slowly thawed in the warmth of the room. When the session was over, the inspector informed the teacher that the observation of the leaves had been a 'very good science lesson', but that she was keen to know where exactly the children had recorded their experiences. The teacher put her hands to her chest and answered with the exasperated passion of one who has little expectation of being understood: 'In their souls'. The inspector dutifully recorded it on her pad…

At a conference at Newcastle University ('Realizing Children's Potential', September 1997), counsellor and therapist Kathy Hunt gave a moving account of a small girl's overwhelming grief at losing her mother, who had died of cancer. The child needed to be held, would not tolerate change in the nursery, and was exhibiting 'all the identified behaviours associated with mourning – the panic, the crying out loud, searching in places over and over again. Wandering, unable to settle, very little ability to concentrate.' Slowly the child began to play. Hunt describes what happened.

> She began by selecting a plastic polar bear
> and its baby in the small world water play
> area of the nursery. She spent hours playing
> the same identically repeated game in the
> coloured-blue, cold water. Around the top of
> the water trough there was a small circular
> path. Sally would walk the adult and baby
> polar bear along the path circling the blue
> water. Every so often she would drop the baby
> into the water and let it sink to the bottom;
> then she would exclaim, with a deep intake of
> breath, 'Oh no!' – and with this the game
> would begin again.

Hunt describes this play as a metaphorical process. The child, she said, '…has created a metaphor that expresses the meaning she intends. She needs to play this game in order to make sense of her experience' (Hunt 1999, page 65).

Kathy Hunt sensed that she was driven to play and to repeat it, and that her own task was to respect and value this process by giving Sally the time, space and privacy to play. Kathy was the important adult in this child's life who was able to sanction play. Eventually, the little girl stopped. Her emotional readjustment had begun. The adults provided the room, the time and the space but, I would suggest, it was the *genius of play* that led the child to find the right metaphor for her feelings, and so to move on.

Jane Hislam cautions against the view that children are always 'playing things out', in either a conditioned or therapeutic sense, although she also acknowledges that '...at some level children's play acts as a kind of personal mirror and that through play children are coming to grips with their own realities' (Hislam 1996, page 42). When a child *has* exteriorized her inner reality in play– the better to get a clearer look at it – everyone else can see it too! Parents and teachers need sensitivity and respect when these open secrets are unwittingly shared.

Play embraces children's total experience. They use it to tell their stories; to be funny and silly; to challenge the world; to imitate it; to engage with it; to discover and understand it; and to be social. They also use play to explore their inmost feelings. In a single game – playing alone or with friends – the child can switch play modes, one minute imitating the television, the next making a discovery which leads to new thinking, then being reminded of something else and changing the play accordingly, and then suddenly being swamped by feelings, which require their own corresponding set of images, propelling the game in yet another direction. Like dreams, play is not ordered and rational. It does not give priority to one kind of experience or one kind of knowledge over another.

Rudolf Steiner likens playing to dreaming. In dreaming, he says, adults remain at play throughout their lives. Disconnected images from many levels of our experience rise up and fade away like great waves, sometimes leaving us with significant images and sometimes in total bewilderment. Like explorers, as image players we enter our dream world somehow to shift the events in our life, real and imagined, into a new shape – as children order and reorder their play. (Interestingly, dream-sleep deprivation results in hallucinatory experiences in waking life – indicating that dreaming [and play] are linked to well-being and mental stability.)

Playing out negative emotions can present a challenge to adults. There is no doubt that this kind of play is hard to handle. However, Margaret Lowenfeld (1935, page 324) suggests that *unmet* 'emotional satisfactions' from childhood, including

the forces of destruction, aggression and hostility – which can be safely displayed through play and then integrated into the personality – reappear unconsciously in adult life as negative drives, which seek outlets in industrial competition, anarchy and ultimately war. In her view, the pretend games of conflict in childhood, involving aspects of human behaviour such as destruction, aggression and hostile emotion, which 'form so powerful an element for good or evil in the human character', function as a kind of safety valve against potentially dangerous adult drives.

I remember a boy in my kindergarten staging a kick-boxing tournament – to my mind an aggressive and dangerous sport. He set up a ring, invited the girls and the more timid boys to buy tickets (which he made) to watch the spectacle, and began touting for sparring partners. A 'contestant' was found, his best friend, and they began to play together using a repertoire of largely imitated aggressive gestures: scowling, posturing, air punching, boxer's toe dancing and – yes – kicking. The protagonists went through the whole gamut of emotionally aggressive behaviour, and yet they were as gentle and controlled with each other, in their choreographed and mimed aggression, as two ballet dancers. I watched with bated breath, ready to intervene at any moment – a stance that in the event proved unnecessary. To claps and cheers, the winner received the vase of flowers sitting conveniently on a nearby window-sill, grasped in an inspired move by his partner; the boxing ring became a circus and the audience joined in.

At other times the boys, and less often the girls, would be fierce dogs, complete with studded collars and leads. These dogs needed to be mastered. There was always an interesting dynamic between dog and master: if the dog was too aggressive and wayward on its lead, the game would fail as the master would be pulled about willy-nilly. It was an exercise in control: the master needed to learn how to master the dog, and the dog to be ruled by the master. We need both behaviours in self-management and self-restraint, and there are times in life when we need to be ruled by the wisdom of others. (Playing at kings and queens and their subjects, especially when roles are interchangeable, is helpful in this sphere, as are games about parental/school discipline.)

Teachers learn that rough and tumble play is common and exists along a continuum commensurate with children's developmental ages (Klugman and Smilansky 1990, page 176). I believe

Young children absorbed in their play

bullying, intimidation and behaviour that really frightens or threatens other players is unacceptable. Pretend fear, however, is different and exciting. Following Lowenfeld, what I am arguing for is the understanding that a play context in which no one is hurt, and which stays at the level of fun, is a positive and enabling way of dealing with powerful feelings.

I also recognize that aggression, anger and intimidation constitute a major part of some children's lives. For those children who live in constant fear, one would expect, at some level, to see it reflected in their play. If this is handled sensitively it can be the safest arena for dealing with emotions that, as Lowenfeld suggests, in a different sphere might otherwise become destructive. We need to be tolerant and understanding as well as protective when we see this happening. Sadly, we live in a society in which violence is commonplace – violence that our children cannot help but imitate. It is not the child's imitation that is at fault – the fault lies with society. The teacher/parent needs great skill and understanding to deal with its inevitable appearance in children's play.

Empathy

Daniel Goleman (1996) believes that well-adjusted adults are people who have 'self-awareness, zeal and motivation'. They are empathic, socially deft and can exert impulse control. A well-adjusted adult is by definition an emotionally intelligent person. Quoting Martin Hoffman's research, Goleman describes the great capacity babies have to participate in the feelings of others through what he describes as 'motor mimicry'. Such a strong and immediate rapport do they have with others, he claims, that a baby hearing another child cry *will cry as if she herself were hurt*. There is an adjustment, an alignment with the other's feelings. A baby will put her own fingers in her mouth if she sees a baby with hurt fingers 'to see if she hurts too'. 'On seeing his mother cry, one baby wiped his own eyes, though they had no tears' (1996, page 98). Goleman again: 'Empathy stems from a sort of physical imitation of the distress of another, which then evokes the same feelings in oneself' (1996, page 98).

The Greeks felt that the experience of *mimesis* or imitation, especially in music, could arouse within the imitator ethical feelings of a positive or negative kind. Each of their musical modes had differing ethical significance, a different ethos. The Lydian mode, sadness; the flute, excitement (Huizinga 1955, page 162).

At about one year of age an infant will attempt to soothe another by offering a doll, or even her own mummy, to help. The older baby not only feels the other's pain reverberate in herself, but because of the intense experience of the other within, will also now try to find a more personal and appropriate solution to help. The altruistic nature of the human spirit in its germinal form is alive and well in the very earliest months of childhood.

Infant and childhood empathy create a foundation for later empathy, which leads to the ability to perceive the subjective experience of another person. Daniel Goleman argues that the empathic affect, the capacity for putting oneself in another's place, leads people to follow certain moral principles and to altruism. Living into the plight of the other can buttress moral convictions in adult life, and help us to be conscious of the need to alleviate misfortune or injustice against others. It also acts as a deterrent to prejudice and superficiality. In empathy play, through imitation, I put myself in your place – I play at being you.

A five-year-old girl in my kindergarten whose mother was working had spent some time being cared for by a woman with a new baby. One day she took one of the soft baby dolls, drew the curtains, made herself a cup of pretend tea and a biscuit (a conker), and sat down with her baby. She told everyone to ssshh! Then, she carefully placed her doll in one arm, lifted her jumper and began to breast-feed. So successful was her re-creation and so deep her absorption that a great peace descended on the room and the other children walked past her with care. Occasionally she lifted her small cup of tea and had a nibble of a biscuit – as nursing mothers do. In her imitation she had perfectly captured the qualities of a nursing mother with her child. This small girl had moulded her own frame to the precise contours of another. The moral forces imitated in her play appeared in the cast of her body rather than in her conscious mind; as Goethe says, 'Love does not rule but shapes and that is more'.

Tina Bruce (1999, page 117) gives a touching example of a child who begins to explore, through unsentimental imitation, the very different thoughts, feelings and experiences of someone else:

> A new girl called Jo joined a nursery class. Jo had an artificial arm and two girls, Nadia and Jody, were fascinated when she took it off at story time because she did not want to wear it all the time. That afternoon, the children played together and Nadia was Jo. Through her play, Nadia entered an alternative world to her own, in which she had no arms. She used all her knowledge of what arms are for and she came to know about Jo as she hadn't before.

In adults, this ability to enter an alternative world by 'empathizing' with someone else is the hallmark of a compassionate personality. Empathy play in childhood lays the foundation for this. What children do *physically* through their play, caring adults can later effect through the power of the imagination alone. A sympathetic listener often says: 'I can imagine how you must have felt – I wouldn't have liked to be in your shoes.'

Deep secrets are being revealed to the playing child through the initiations of the play ritual. Communion in its most pure and untutored form is being enacted, and intuition about the world of the other is at the centre of the ceremony. Like actors, children *re-create themselves in the mood of the other person*, reproducing every gesture, facial expression, tone of voice, effecting a 'magical transmission of emotion' (Goleman 1996, page 115). If I imitate you consciously in my play, I also begin to understand you, to attune myself to you, to unite my being with yours. Fluttering through my empathy play is my fledgling love…

> Sometimes I'm afraid, sometimes I don't know what to do, I don't know what the script is, but let me be you, I want to know how you feel, think and act. I want to know what responsibility feels like, although I can't sustain it. I want to look through the looking glass into your world in the only way I can, through my play. How will it be to be you? Can I climb inside your skin, transform myself into you?

'Human morality', says Rudolf Steiner, '…depends on the interest one man takes in another, upon the capability to see into the other man…Those who have the gift of understanding other human beings will receive from this understanding the impulses for a social life imbued with true morality' (1982, page 52).

Without empathy play, we may be doomed to live in a world lacking morality, looking only ever inwards. In her book *The Kindness of Children,* Vivian Gusin Paley (1999, page 61) makes a powerfully succinct statement about the importance of role play:

> If the need to know how someone else feels is the rock upon which the moral universe depends, then the ancient sages were right. For this is surely what happens when children give each other roles to play in their continual

inquiry into the nature of human connections. It is as schoolchildren that we begin life's investigations of those weighty matters.

Children sitting at desks doing worksheets or passively watching television are not engaging with these weighty matters. For young children to do is to understand and, in the case of role play, to do and to be. No swimmer ever learned to swim from an instruction sheet or from watching others alone.

'You can be the big schoolgirl.' (How do big schoolgirls feel, act?)
'I'm a spaceship man.' (How might a spaceship man behave? What fears might he have? How might he face up to challenges?)
'This is the door of my kindergarten.' (Now I can be as kind or as unpleasant as my own teacher.)
'Are you a mouse?'
'No, I'm a prince.' (So you need to treat me very differently.)
'What can I be?' (Whatever you wish!)

The questions 'Who am I in this game?' and 'How must I be as my new self?' are major preoccupations for most young players. Through imaginative play, and in particular through sociodramatic play, children are able to express and explore their own viewpoints and feelings, and those of others.

In his book *The Development of Play,* David Cohen (1993) refers to the work of Tower and Singer (1980), who catalogued the many benefits of imaginative play. In addition to 'improved emotional well-being and self-control', 'self-entertainment reducing fear and anxiety' and 'poise', the social benefits of imagination included 'becoming more sensitive to others' and 'increased empathy'. The researchers concluded that, 'the more a child imagines, the happier he, or she is' (Cohen 1993, page 144). Empathic imitation in play helps counteract alienation and enhances social awareness. Living imaginatively into the experience of 'the other' awakens the ability to 'read' the thoughts and feelings of others, and the journey towards emotional and social literacy begins. Social imagination, which first appears in germinal form in the imaginative games of early childhood, is the kernel around which all mature and tolerant societies are formed.

It is my belief that by trusting to the wise tutelage of the spirit of play, we parents and educators can be partners in the creation of a social future, and that in the 'Quick, now, here, now, always' of their play,

children are learning nothing less than what it means to be human (Eliot 1970).

Play and the sense of self

'Moon!' you cry suddenly, 'Moon! Moon!'
The moon has stepped back like an
*   artist gazing*
amazed at a work
That points at him amazed.

Ted Hughes (1982) 'Full Moon and Little Frieda' (2 years old)

Stuart Brown's work with animals led him to the belief that in spontaneous play something unique and individual is at work. Free from the laws of instinct and necessity, the genius of play, an independent spirit, nurtures in turn the spirit of those it inspires. To careful observers, a child's play reveals something of the innermost nature, both of the present child and of the future self. Mysteries of the future are both hidden and revealed in the open secret of children's play.

Friedrich Froebel and Rudolf Steiner, both spirited and sensitive educators themselves, demonstrated a remarkable convergence of thinking on this point.

FROEBEL AND STEINER ON PLAY
'Play', said Froebel,

> ...is the highest expression of human development in childhood, for it alone is the free expression of what is in the child's soul. It is the purest and most spiritual product of the child and at the same time it is a type and copy of human life at all stages and in all relations...For to one who has insight into human nature, the trend of the future life of the child is revealed in his freely chosen play.
> (Froebel cited in Lowenfeld 1935, page 30)

And Steiner tells us:

> Form inner pictures of these children and then think quite hypothetically: the individual gesture as revealed in the child's play up to the second dentition will emerge again in the characteristic way in which, after the age of twenty, he will form personal judgements. In other words after their twentieth year, different people vary with regard to their personal judgement in the same way in which, as children, they have differed in their play before the change of teeth.
> (Steiner 1981, page 169)

From Rudolf Steiner's description, one can visualize a child drawing towards herself certain toys and not others, selecting and structuring play opportunities specific to her need. Steiner links freedom in play and freedom in thought – pairing the child's ability to bring the right elements together to create her play with the way we cast around our mental landscape for arguments to support our judgements as adults. In adults the secret self works in private. In play the emergent self is revealed. Outer play becomes inner resource. The narrower the spectrum of choice, the more blinkered our thinking is likely to become. Playful adult thinkers are able to think 'out of the box'; free-range players make free-range thinkers.

What a human being acquires between birth and the change of teeth through the activity of playing, and what is enacted before our eyes in such a dreamlike manner, are the forces of the child's yet unborn spirituality.

(Steiner 1981, page 168)

Both Steiner and Froebel suggest that in the activities of *freely chosen play*, the child is telling us something about herself, about her own uniqueness. A playful prophet, she sits among her playthings – miniature auguries of her future – assembling the components of her intimated inner world.

It would be wrong to suggest that all play is either prognosis of the future or diagnosis of the past, but a wise eye may look for significances here and there, for glimpses of things that have been and might yet be. Anyone watching the play of the three sisters in the following story would not have been surprised at the future destinies of the girls.

As a child, the oldest sister loved to play 'Shops' – arranging and re-arranging small oddments for sale. The second sister played 'Schools' – giving expert instruction in the three Rs to all available dolls and siblings – willing or otherwise. The third sister played 'Nurse' to every needy being, including her devoted dog Mick who happily submitted himself to her tender ministrations – regularly sporting beautifully bandaged paws and a suitably sad expression. In adult life, the three sisters became a shop manager, a headmistress and a hospital theatre sister respectively.

These girls were indeed partners with their futures in their play.

Self and the world

Through imitation, reflection and self-determined action, we gradually learn to know ourselves: as individuals with a rich inner life (world in me) and as participating, creative world beings (myself in the world). 'Making the inner outer and the outer inner' was axiomatic to the educational philosophies of Pestalozzi and Froebel (see Lawrence 1970, page 244). It was also central to Rudolf Steiner.

The task of finding ourselves in the world, and the world in us, extends well beyond the confines of the narrow classroom, as Seamus Heaney illustrates so brilliantly in his poem 'Personal Helicon'. Heaney keenly recaptures the boyhood experience of peering into a dark well and seeing his own white face reflected back at him from the watery depths below. The child poet calling down the 'dark drop' of the well hears the echo of his voice which '…gave back your own call / With a clean new music in it'. Each interchange, each 'call' and 'answer' to and from the world, brings about a delicate unfolding of a new self.

In a wonderful inversion, Heaney links the vivid self-knowing of the engaged, playful, exploring, risk-taking child with the more distant self-knowledge of the rhyming, literate adult:

Now, to pry into roots, to finger slime,
To stare big-eyed Narcissus, into some
*   spring*
Is beneath all adult dignity. I rhyme
To see myself, to set the darkness
*   echoing.*

Seamus Heaney (1998) 'Opened Ground'

Children today still need the peace of a long, slow-paced, active and engaged childhood, with plenty of time to 'finger slime', peer into water, and make hosts of new discoveries that consolidate the process of knowing self and the world. As Joseph Chilton Pearce (1997, page 95), former humanities teacher and author of *The Magical Child*, puts it:

Structuring knowledge of the world takes at least six years because the world is filled with many things and its processes and principles are strict. The child is programmed to interact with the actual world: a place of rocks, trees, grass, bugs, sun, moon, wind, clouds, rain, snow, and a million things.

Play is the perfect bridge between self and the world of nature and the world of others. *I know myself in relation to what is outside me.*

Sociodramatic play is not only important for social development; it also promotes self-development. Herbert Mead (1863–1931) argued that children only develop a sense of self through role-playing at being the other. In the words of Meltzer,

> In referring to the human being as having a self, Mead simply means such an individual may act socially towards himself, just as towards others. He may praise, blame or encourage himself; he may become disgusted with himself, may seek to punish himself, and so forth. Thus the human being may become the object of his own actions. The self is formed in the same way as other objects – through the definitions of others.
>
> (Meltzer 1967 cited in Faulkner 1995, page 243)

Thus begins the development of consciousness and conscience. I know who I am through my social interactions with others, and through regarding myself also as 'an other'. By recognizing the other as a coherent self-entity, I also come to know myself as a self. And by adjusting to others' perceptions of me I understand myself further. By being Robin Hood, Princess Crystal, the wicked witch, the giant, the rabbit, the lion, I also know myself when I am me again. Me, is one of the people I am.

> We need to make it clear that today's main paradigm for understanding a human life, the interplay of genetics and environment, omits something essential – the particularity you feel to be you. By accepting the idea that I am the effect of a subtle buffeting between heredity and societal forces, I reduce myself to a result.
>
> (Hillman 1997, page 6)

James Hillman suggests that each life is formed by an image, an essence of life, which calls it to a destiny. This destiny is uniquely mine; it is distinct from my chromosomes or what my parents did or didn't do – it calls me to act. The call of that destiny is first heard in childhood. Our play helps us to reclaim the self. In our play, we assert our own-ness, follow our lodestar and meet our essence.

> When my cousin and I took our porridge of a morning, we had a device to enliven the course of the meal. He ate his with sugar, and explained it to be a country continually buried under snow. I took mine with milk and explained it to be a country suffering gradual inundation. You can imagine us exchanging bulletins; how here there was an island still unsubmerged, here a valley not yet covered with snow; what inventions were made; how his populations lived in cabins on perches and travelled on stilts, and how mine was always in boats; how the interest grew furious, as the last corner of safe ground was cut off on all sides and grew smaller every moment; and how…the food was of altogether secondary importance, and might have been nauseous, so long as we seasoned it with these dreams.
>
> (Robert Louis Stevenson, cited in Rosen 1994, page 97)

The wonderful milk-lapped treasure islands, spied by the eye of Stevenson's imagination in the breakfast bowl before him, have a unique quality, which prefigures what later appeared so vividly in the dramatic themes created by his literary genius. His play echoed the call of his destiny. In Stevenson's case, the imagination makes its first forays in the musings of childhood.

Resources

Alliance for Childhood, Kidbrooke Park, Forest Row, East Sussex RH18 5JA (Tel 01342 822115) www.allianceforchildhood.org.uk
Sally Jenkinson is a founder member of the Alliance for Childhood. The alliance is an international network of groups and individuals working together out of a shared respect for childhood.

Suggested further reading

Jenkinson, S. (2001), *The Genius of Play: Celebrating the spirit of childhood*, Hawthorn Press, Stroud
An important book examining play and how modern life endangers children's play.

References

Bruce, T. (1995), *Early Childhood Education*, Hodder and Stoughton, London

Bruce, T. (1999), *Time to Play in Early Childhood Education*, Hodder and Stoughton, London

Carson, R. (1998), *The Sense of Wonder*, HarperCollins, New York

Cohen, D. (1993), *The Development of Play*, Routledge, London

Eliot, G. (1985), *The Mill on the Floss*, Penguin Classics (originally published 1880), Penguin, Harmondsworth

Eliot, T. S. (1970), *The Complete Poems and Plays of T.S. Eliot*, Faber and Faber, London

Evans, R. (2000), *Helping Children to Overcome Fear: The Healing Power of Play*, Hawthorn Press, Stroud

Faulkner, D. (1995), Play, Self and the Social World. In Barnes, P. (ed.) *Personal, Social and Emotional Development of Children*, Blackwell/Open University, Oxford

Goleman, D. (1996), *Emotional Intelligence: Why it can matter more than IQ*, Bloomsbury, London

Heaney, S. (1998), *Opened Ground*, Faber and Faber, London

Hillman, J. (1997), *The Soul's Code: In search of character and calling*, Bantam, London

Hislam, J. (1996), Sex-differentiated play experiences and children's choices. In Moyles, J. (ed.) *The Excellence of Play*, Open University Press, Buckingham

Hughes, T. (1982), *Selected Poems 1957–1981*, Faber and Faber, London

Huizinga, J. (1955), *Homo Ludens: A study of the play element in culture*, Beacon Press, Boston, Mass

Hunt, K. (1999), Respecting the Wisdom of the Young Child in Grief. In *Realising Children's Potential: Excellence in the early years*, conference proceedings, University of Newcastle upon Tyne

Klugman, E. and Smilansky, S. (1990), *Children's Play and Learning: Perspectives and policy implications*, Teachers College Press, New York

Korczak, J. (1992), *When I Am Little Again* (originally published 1925), University Press of America, Maryland and London

Lawrence, E. (1970), *The Origins and Growth of Modern Education*, Pelican, Harmondsworth

Lowenfeld, M. (1935), *Play in Childhood*, Victor Gollancz, London

Paley, V. G. (1999), *The Kindness of Children*, Harvard University Press, Cambridge, Mass.

Pearce, J. C. (1997), *The Magical Child*, Plume, New York

Rosen, M. (ed.) (1994), *The Penguin Book of Childhood*, Viking, London

Singer, D. G. and Singer, J. L. (1992), *The House of Make Believe*, Harvard University Press, Cambridge, Mass. and London

Steiner, R. (1981), *The Renewal of Education through the Science of the Spirit* (from lectures given in 1920), Kolisko Archive Publications for the Steiner Waldorf Schools Fellowship, Forest Row

Steiner, R. (1982), *Man and the World of the Stars* (from lectures given in 1922), The Anthroposophic Press, New York

Tower, R. B. and Singer J. L. (1980), Imagination, Interest and Joy in Early Childhood: Some theoretical considerations and empirical findings. In McGee, P. E. and Chapman, A. J. (eds) *Children's Humour*, Wiley, Chichester

Charter for children's play

Sally Jenkinson and colleagues

Participants attending an international workshop on play held in Switzerland drew up the following charter. The intention of this international group – with participants from Canada, Finland, the USA, Denmark, Sweden, the UK and Switzerland – was to produce a charter for play that would be relevant to all cultures and all nations.

Children play best:

When adults are watchful but not intrusive, when safe ground lends courage to their discoveries and adventures.

When their trust in life is whole, when they welcome the unknown and the fearless.

When the world is shared with them. When there are places and spaces they can make their own.

When their games are free from adult agendas and when their transformations require no end product.

When they are directly engaged with nature and the elements.

When they are free to become gatherers, makers and world creators in their own time and in their own ways.

When they can play with others and make relationships.

When they can play alone, be solitary and private.

When they can become new selves through their play with others and in their own imaginings.

When they can reveal themselves, their joys, sufferings and concerns, without fear of ridicule, and when mystery and imagination are not denied by fact.

(Jenkinson 2001, page 129)

Resources

The International Association for the Child's Right to Play, www.ncsu.edu/ipa
The association is an international non-governmental organization. Its purpose is to protect, preserve and promote play as a fundamental right for all humans.

Suggested further reading

Moyles, J. (ed.) (1994), *The Excellence of Play*, Open University Press, Buckingham
This book gathers together authoritative contributors to examine the role of play in the early years. An essential resource for promoting rigorous, reflective practice.

Reference

Jenkinson, S. (2001), *The Genius of Play: Celebrating the spirit of childhood*, Hawthorn Press, Stroud
An important book examining play and how modern life endangers children's play.

Let the children play

Susan Piers-Mantell and Emma Craigie

Play within the educational environment has incredible value for promoting learning and well-being. Piers and Landau (1980, page 43), for example, argue that play 'develops creativity, intellectual competence, emotional strength and stability and…feelings of joy and pleasure: the habit of being happy'.

Susan Piers-Mantell and Emma Craigie's contribution reminds us of the need to protect children from the pressures of too early a formal education and to provide them with rich opportunities for play throughout childhood. The authors, drawing on their own teaching experience, provide practical suggestions for developing opportunities for play within the school environment.

Introduction

In the first seven years, children learn through doing what they do best – playing. Through play, children investigate their world and make sense of it. They learn to understand the people around them: by pretending to be other people, they learn empathy; by negotiating with them, they learn both to compromise and to assert themselves. They learn flexibility: when to take the initiative, when to watch and listen.

Through play, children digest life. They work through their fears and find security. They learn what it is to be human and what it is to be their unique self. Through play, children explore their potential and learn how to be a grown-up. Play is physical imagining, the spring of all creativity.

Play in nurseries and primary schools

The importance of play is recognized in the early years curriculum. However, for healthy development, children continue to need rich opportunities for play throughout childhood. What follows are ideas for encouraging play in both nursery and primary school settings. Our aim is to inspire, not to dictate. We hope our suggestions can be adapted to a wide range of situations.

In nurseries, lots of time is usually devoted to playing. For this age group our concern is that children be given free reign to their developing imaginations, unhampered and undisturbed by an adult agenda. Below are suggestions of how to let this happen.

In primary schools, there is usually little time available for child-led play because of the demands of the curriculum. It would take a brave teacher to include play in the busy weekly schedule, but what a hero he or she would be in the campaign for balanced, happy children. In these days of traffic, televisions, computers and Game Boys, children do less and less playing outside school. How enriching it would be, and how popular, if on Friday afternoons, or at least one Friday afternoon a month, everything was cleared away and the computers switched off. Then the tables and chairs could become the scaffolding of dens and the children let loose on the dressing-up box. We include lots of ideas on materials, which will inspire imaginative play.

The longer lunchtime break can provide a good opportunity for playing but, unfortunately, playgrounds rarely have suitable props for imaginative play. Our section on Gardens and playgrounds below offers ideas to stimulate imaginative outdoor play.

Materials to inspire play

THE DRESSING-UP BOX

Go for a variety of rich colours and textures: silks, chiffons, fake furs, feathers, velvets, satins, hats, belts, cords, strings of beads, small cushions. Collecting your materials should not be expensive. Raid secondhand shops and jumble sales. Avoid designed dressing-up clothes, or even shaped garments, which restrict the children's imaginations. Best of all are cloths, and it is useful to have a range of sizes as these can become the roofs of dens as well as cloaks or skirts or whatever the children need.

Children come to nursery or school with their own experiences and concerns, which direct what they need to play. Our job is to provide them with simple resources, which they can adapt to those needs.

They can be a pregnant mummy with a cushion on her tummy; a brave firefighter with a cushion helmet on his or her head; a scary witch with a wooden spoon wand; a heroic knight with a wooden spoon sword; a shy dog on a cord lead with a feather tail; a mischievous fairy with chiffon wings held in each hand. The inventiveness of children is beyond our imaginings. All they need are the raw materials. Between the ages of five and seven children become more self-conscious and may enjoy performing dramas which have developed from their play.

TOYS

Conkers and shells and pine cones and buttons and corks and pegs and glass stones and slices of wooden logs, saucepans, an enamel teapot, eggcups, wooden spoons, little wooden or cardboard boxes (with or without lids), baskets, chopping boards, bowls, wooden blocks, wool, cord, bean bags. With these magical materials, a den can be transformed into a kitchen with saucepans full of shell pasta and wool sauce; a café with conker buns on log plates, and eggcups of tea; a shop selling baskets of cork sweets for button money; a wizard's castle where potions of glass beads are stirred in cauldrons.

The baskets of shells, stones and other props that can furnish all these games of make-believe will be enjoyed by the younger nursery children for the sheer pleasure of packing and unpacking. For the older children, these materials can be transformed into the landscape of miniature imaginary worlds. Now the child can become the creator and controller of a fantasy scene: it might be a cosy village with cottages bordering a village green; it might be a

tower block reaching to the clouds; or a river racing over rocks; trains passing fields of grazing animals; ships on a choppy sea. Muslin cloths are particularly versatile and can easily be smoothed into fields or wrinkled to resemble water.

Again, the older, more self-conscious children often enjoy planning and producing shows to be watched. Peopled by simple dolls, these scenes become the sets for puppet shows.

DOLLS

We are all used to dolls with lots of detail, but for your children to have complete imaginative freedom, you might like to have available some much simpler 'dolls', which can allow greater scope for make-believe. A doll with a fixed smile can never suit every mood. It has become very hard to buy simple dolls, and there is something very special and homely for children to be able to play with dolls that someone has made. You do not need advanced needlework skills to make rag dolls for the children. Older children can themselves make peg dolls with old-fashioned pegs and scraps of fabric, or they can make knot dolls.

Places to play in

DENS

Again, all that children need are the raw materials; and, again, cloths are the key. At its most simple, a big tablecloth can be draped over a table. But the most magnificent dens can be made when the children are free to create more complex structures. It is wonderful if you have a few clothes horses, planks of wood, lots of cloths, and even upturned chairs and tables can be incorporated into the children's building. Dens can be the catalyst for all sorts of imaginings: shops, houses, rockets, boats, cars.

It might be that the den needs to be a hospital, because someone has had an ill grandparent. Fears might be faced through the creation of a dungeon. Or a den can be a refuge, a place to escape and hide.

Any group of children will soon need ground rules about who is and who isn't allowed in. In general, we would recommend that no one can be excluded from large dens, but that children who want to retreat on their own are allowed to make little private dens.

GARDENS AND PLAYGROUNDS

If you have a garden or playground with trees or bushes, or benches, or a clothes line, you can drape

Prince and princesses

cloths in all sorts of ways. Large pieces of light muslin thrown over the branches of a tree can make a palace for a fairy queen; some heavier cotton could make a dark cave or be hung over a clothes line and pegged down on either side to become a tent on a camping holiday. As indoors, planks can make bridges or seats, and logs can become balancing walkways between settlements.

If you want to introduce this sort of play into a setting, then to begin with you might need to prepare a simple structure, perhaps before the children arrive. There is no need to say what it is. Let the children make of it what they will, and ensure that they have access to more cloths, more planks or chairs, so that they can adapt and develop the structure as their imagination takes them. After a while, the children will be able to initiate den building, although they may need your help in reaching the heights, tying the cloths to the upper branches or throwing on the roof.

Sand and water are of course age-old ingredients of play. This wonderfully messy and malleable combination can be adapted to any play need. Break away from buckets and spades. Furnish your sandpit with spoons of all shapes and sizes – from mustard to wooden – and a range of different-sized containers from eggcup to flowerpot.

Materials – the natural and the beautiful

Why the emphasis on natural resources as playthings? In this day and age, when children are constantly bombarded by so much that is not natural, it is great to offer opportunities to feel, touch and revel in such pleasures as the shiny beauty of a conker, or the slipperiness of a shell or the resinous scent of a pine cone. They are also fun for the children to collect for their own play if you have countryside or a park to walk in near you. Materials that delight for their sensuous qualities can add another layer of inspiration to children's play and also connect them to the world of nature and its rich pattern of seasons.

The bubble of play

Whatever the setting, play needs respect. Self-consciousness kills play. We need to take care not to burst the bubble. As adults, we should intrude only when invited, or to prevent accidents. When we are invited – maybe to taste food, to visit a shop or to adjust a costume or a roof – we need to enter the world of play as if it were real. Our language should reflect this. Objects should be described as they are in the game: not cloths, but roofs; not conkers, but coins; not a doll, but a baby. If we take their play seriously, the deeper the children's experience can become. In most situations what a child needs is the security of an adult nearby, who is too absorbed by his or her own tasks to interfere, but who is available when things become unstuck.

Sometimes, for many different reasons, individual children are unable to play. They may just need a little encouragement. Try talking to them in the terms of an imaginary world, for example: 'Can I have a cup of tea' or 'Here's a basket, could you do the shopping? I'd like some...' Or play might come from finding something in the dressing-up box that particularly appeals to that child.

Play can be encouraged, but it cannot be forced. If a child is really unable to play at nursery or school, find a little job that he or she will feel comfortable doing. This could be sanding a piece of wood, doing the washing-up, making a little wax or plasticine animal for a tabletop scene, but try to avoid those activities that tend to close down imaginative play, such as playing on a computer.

There is a vital difference between children losing themselves in front of a screen and losing themselves in play. In front of a screen, children can switch off. In imaginative play they lose self-consciousness but unconsciously face themselves and their needs. Children need to play. As educators it is our responsibility to ensure that they get the chance.

Resources

The International Association for the Child's Right to Play, www.ncsu.edu/ipa
The association is an international non-governmental organization. Its purpose is to protect, preserve and promote play as a fundamental right for all humans.

'Too Much, Too Young' – A *Despatches* programme available as a video from Mill Productions Ltd, 45 Loftus Road, London W12 7EH (Tel 0208 743 2544)
An overview of the different attitudes towards early years education in the UK and on the continent where the child's need to play is fully recognized and upheld.

Suggested further reading

Jaffke, F. (1988), *Toy Making with Children*, Floris Books, Edinburgh
This book contains numerous suggestions for making wooden boats, log trains, puppets, and much more.

Moyles, J. R. (1989), *Just Playing? The role and status of play in early childhood education*, Open University Press, Buckingham
Explores why we should encourage, promote, value and initiate play in our classrooms.

Reference

Piers, M. W. and Landau, G. M. (1980), *The Gift of Play and Why Children Cannot Thrive Without It*, Walker and Co, New York
This book provides psychological insights into the significance of play for children. The authors explore the biological roots of play and stress that play and learning are inseparable.

Gardening with children: natural wonder

Elspeth Thompson

Elspeth Thompson describes how to develop creative gardening projects with primary school children. Drawing on her own work with an infant school in south London, she provides practical advice and suggestions for promoting young children's interest in plants.

Her contribution offers practical support, so that even teachers with limited gardening experience will feel able to make a start in their own school. Planning considerations are discussed, including the choice of area to be developed and the selection of plants to create a cultivated garden. Helpful suggestions are given for working with children in the garden and for encouraging children to use their senses in the garden.

Elspeth Thompson also demonstrates the value of creating a wildlife garden. At first hand, children can learn about a particular habitat; for example, the inclusion of a pond provides opportunities for pond-dipping activities. Finally, some novel ideas are suggested for involving children in particular design projects that will enhance the functional elements within the school grounds.

Introduction

Think of a sunflower unfurling from its seed: in a few days it is a young seedling, in a few weeks a sturdy young plant – a couple of months on and it is a great towering giant with a sunshine yellow face. Gardening really is the closest thing to magic, and so children are already well disposed to joining in. In these days of instant effects and computers, though, they will need to use their patience. Gardening is about preparing and waiting and connecting with the changing seasons – as well as reaping the rewards. In a city setting, where there may not even be trees in the streets to provide signposts of the seasons, the connection will be particularly powerful.

Some schools will already have a patch of ground that can be used for growing flowers and vegetables; others may need to liberate a piece of tarmac. Involve the children in this right from the first stages. For city-born children it can be a mesmerizing experience to watch the lifting of tarmac and see that there is soil underneath – to realize that this is the same all over, beneath the roads, beneath their houses, under the train tracks and tower blocks. The 'asphalt desert' can become a fertile leafy garden, providing food to eat, flowers, and exciting opportunities for play and learning. In a domestic setting, it is usually easier – children can be given their own 'patch' in a larger garden, or particular pots in which they can sow seeds and grow things. Even if all you have is a sunny window-sill, there is still room for the best magic of all: your name in mustard and cress seeds on blotting paper – just add water and wait.

School project

I became involved through a friend with the creation of a kitchen garden at Bonneville Infants School in Clapham, south London, in spring 2002. A Victorian building surrounded by the usual asphalt playgrounds, the school also had a 'secret garden' in one corner of the grounds that was much loved but had become seriously overgrown. A gardening group of interested teachers and parents began to clear the site and I was asked to give advice on building raised beds and preparing and improving the soil for vegetable growing.

A planting session

one preparing the hole and the other taking care of the plant, and then filling in the holes together. They did about six plants per pair, and I kept an eye over the work, making sure everyone got a go at all the different tasks. We watered well, put in bamboo cane stakes for the broad beans and made a teepee of taller canes for the runner beans to grow up. Seeds of nasturtiums and other flowers were sown around the edges – not only does this look pretty, it also attracts beneficial insects that can help with pest control and pollination. It is a nice idea afterwards for the children all to join hands around the beds they have been working on, close their eyes and imagine the plants growing strongly and well.

The children followed up by watering every other day and making drawings of the work they had done. In a couple of months' time they were harvesting the beans – eating the broad beans raw and cooking the runner beans to taste in the classroom. Then the children planted overwintering onions and garlic, and planned for lots of salad and soft fruit for the following year. The garden was awarded a prize and £3,000 grant.

Working with children in the garden

Do not worry if you are not an experienced gardener – it will be all the easier for you to convey and share the excitement and magic of gardening as you see your plants grow together. Sometimes, more experienced gardeners forget how little most children know about plants – how fragile the stems of young seedlings can be, for instance, or how fine seed can blow about in even the slightest breeze. Try to think yourself back to a time when you knew none of this yourself. When I was gardening with my group of five year olds, they were intrigued by what I thought were the simplest things – such as how was I going to get the bean seedlings out of the pot. And when planting the seedlings out into the beds there were quite a few casualties, as I had not stressed quite how careful the children needed to be when handling young plants.

In springtime I came along to do a planting session with the children. Two classes of 30 five year olds had grown runner and broad beans in pots in the classroom. The teacher had explained the concept of 'hardening off' or acclimatizing the plants to the change of environment and temperature by leaving them outside during the day and taking them in again before going-home time. They had done this for a couple of weeks, so the plants were ready and raring to go. The children had prepared questions to ask me and we had a quick session all together inside, passing round the pots so they could look closely and identify the differences between broad and runner bean plants. We talked about how the plants would grow and what the beans would look and taste like.

When we went outside the children were divided into groups of ten to work in rotation with me planting out the beans. We watered the beans first in their pots, and I explained that this helps them settle into their new homes more easily. I then showed the children how to scoop a hole with a trowel, pour some more water in the bottom, tap the plant out of its pot and place it in the hole, and then fill in around it with soil, keeping the level of the soil on the stem the same, or a little higher, than it had been in the pot. Then they got on with it themselves in pairs –

Getting children to 'think like a plant' can be a good way to begin. Ask them to close their eyes and imagine they are a plant growing in the soil, that roots are stretching down from their feet into the soil and their hands are leaves or branches waving in the air. What do they need? Space to grow bigger, water, food, sunshine, maybe a stick to support them when they get too tall – play with these different notions, asking the children to imagine what it feels like for the plant when it is raining, windy, sunny, too hot or

Watching and learning

too crowded. Get them to do what the plant might do in these circumstances. This can help to get even quite boisterous children into the right sort of mood for gardening.

For fiddly practical jobs, work in the smallest groups you can, so that everybody can be given proper attention, and then swap over. If there is only one available adult who feels confident about gardening, perhaps another could supervise the children in some other related activity, such as watering, digging over new ground, or drawing or writing about their activities.

Make a pictorial record of the garden throughout the year using photographs, drawings and paintings by the children. You could measure the sunflowers every week and weigh the produce from a single broad bean or potato plant.

Getting started

All you need is enthusiasm and a sunny space (preferably not too windy) with access to water. You may want to grow food crops in special raised beds, but they can also be mixed in with flowers or shrubs in a border. If the soil is poor you may need to get some compost or well-rotted manure delivered; get

as much as you can afford, as good soil grows good plants and you will not regret this initial investment.

When it comes to choosing what to grow, it is best to start with easy things, as you do not want to begin with disappointment when fussy plants or tricky varieties fail to deliver. The following are more or less foolproof and should give quick and reliable results from seed: sunflowers, radishes, nasturtiums, rocket, broad and runner beans, peas. These all grow pretty much where they are sown, though you may get better results (and less damage by slugs and snails) if you raise peas and beans and sunflowers in small pots inside and then plant out when they are 5–8cm (2–3in) high. Lettuce and other salad leaves are also very easy – you can sow them in the ground and thin out the rows when the plants are 2–3cm (an inch or so) high; the thinnings can be eaten as 'baby salad leaves' while the rest are left to grow larger. 'Cut-and-come-again' seed mixes of a variety of different types of salad can be sown in patches and the individual leaves picked as needed; the plant will re-sprout in no time.

If you are planning a school garden, you also want to choose things that fruit or flower during the school year. For instance, choose autumn-fruiting raspberries that begin bearing fruit in late August, rather than the summer-fruiting ones. Autumn-sown onions, beetroot, broad beans, carrots, courgettes, early potatoes, peas, spring onions, turnips and winter spinach are all things that will help to spread the produce through the times of the year when children are at school.

Raised beds are the best way to grow vegetables with children – long narrow plots that can be worked from both sides. The beds can be built up using bricks, timber or stone. They must be able to drain, so if you are building on tarmac it needs to be broken up first. As the children can crouch in the pathways between beds, the soil will not get compacted and there will be less danger of feet trampling young plants. For children's use, the beds should not be wider than 1.2m (4ft) so that they can reach into the centre to sow, weed or pick from either side.

Many flowers, fruit and vegetables can be grown in containers, but they need much more watering, so choose the largest size that you can. Some herbs, such as mint, which have a habit of spreading, are best confined in a container.

A compost heap will help the children think about what happens to waste. For schools, check with local authorities. Can kitchen waste, as well as garden waste and leftover paper from the classrooms be added to the compost heap rather than thrown away?

Working with the senses in the garden

Children can be encouraged to use their senses in a variety of ways:

SIGHT

Invest in a few hand lenses or magnifying glasses and spend time with children looking at flowers and leaves in close-up. The centre of a passion flower looks like some extraordinary underwater creature; a magnolia becomes a fairytale castle.

SOUND

Sit and listen to all the sounds in the garden. At first you may just hear traffic roaring past or aircraft overhead, but as you listen for longer and more attentively, you will start to hear the wind in the trees or rustling the leaves of smaller plants, birds singing or insects buzzing about the flowers. What other sounds might it be nice to hear in a garden? The sound of water? The tinkling of a wind chime?

TOUCH

Collect ten or so things from the garden that have different textures – bark, a blade of grass, a soft fuzzy leaf, a handful of soil – and spend time feeling each with eyes closed. Blind people can still garden; where we see colours they feel these wonderfully distinct textures. Grass and gravel feel different underfoot. Some plants are prickly, others soft and smooth.

SMELL

Lead each other around the garden, stopping to smell a rose, a handful of earth, the wet grass, a tomato leaf, aromatic herbs such as mint, sage and lemon balm. Can you guess what each is? What is your favourite smell in the garden? Are there nasty smells, too?

TASTE

It is not only fruit and vegetables that you can eat. Herbs and some flowers are also edible, but you need to be careful here. Pick and taste nasturtium flowers, which look pretty in salads, and starry blue borage flowers, which can be floated in drinks. Rose and violet petals can be picked and dipped in a sugar and water mixture to make cake decorations. Some plants are poisonous, so raise awareness of toxic berries, leaves and mushrooms (which should not form part of a children's garden).

Wildlife gardening

When you create a garden, you are creating a potential new home for animals, insects and other wildlife as well as plants. The plants provide food, shelter and breeding grounds for all sorts of creatures – just wait for them to arrive. If you have made a pond, it will be teeming with new life in just a few days. Birds may take a bit longer, but you can encourage them by putting out food and setting nesting boxes on trees or walls. A wildflower meadow attracts butterflies, or you could even make a special butterfly garden by choosing plants where they can feed and breed. A compost heap attracts worms that help to break down waste material and make it into new soil. This side of gardening can open up the educational potential into other areas.

Other activities in the garden

All sorts of functional elements in the garden can be made beautiful by involving the children in art and design projects outside:

- Make a living willow bower using wands of cut willow that re-sprout when set in the soil as uprights, woven together with horizontal basketweaving round the base. This can provide shade in summer when the leaves sprout to make a green canopy, and a cosy enclosed space for games and stories.

- Make a stage area for story-telling or other performances and ceremonies outside – a maypole to celebrate May Day, for instance.

- Plant trees that are dedicated to particular people or events in the school year. They can be commemorated by a special plaque on the ground or a decorative label hanging from the branches.

- Seats can be sculptural – there are kits to make turf seats, but you could just shape earth into sculptural shapes and sow seed or cover in strips of turf, watering well in the early stages. Alternatively, you could carve or paint old tree stumps. The website www.allotmentforestry.com has some ideas and easy-to-follow instructions. How about creating a 'friendship stop' where children who feel like company can go to find a friend?

- Think about covering a wall with a mural or mosaic to depict things grown in the garden.

- In a school setting, think about including something, a plant or a found object or piece of artwork, that refers to the school's name or the local area. (Common Ground's leaflet on Local Distinctiveness has lots of ideas here. See Resources, below)

Key ideas and practice pointers

- Gardening is interesting all the year round. Keep a diary and make a pictorial record of the garden throughout the year using photographs, drawings and paintings by the children.

- Involve the children in the design and development of the garden area. Ask the children what they would like and why. Could they help to design a new garden or transform an existing one?

- Consider how the functional elements in the garden can be made beautiful.

- Garden for short periods of time until children's enthusiasm grows. Start with easy plants to grow.

- Encourage the children to use all their senses in the garden.

- Encourage wildlife by devoting an area of the school grounds to wildlife gardening. Plant native trees, shrubs and wildflowers. Include nest boxes and a bird table.

Resources

Common Ground, Gold Hill House, 21 High Street, Shaftesbury, Dorset SP7 8JE (Tel 01747 850820)
www.commonground.org.uk
Internationally recognized for its role in the arts and environmental fields.

Eco Schools, ENCAMS, Elizabeth House, The Pier, Wigan WN3 4EX (Tel 01942 612639)
www.eco-schools.org.uk
An international programme for environmental education for sustainability.

Growing Schools, Department for Education and Skills, Westminster Suite, Caxton House, 6-12 Tothill Street, London SW1H 9NA; www.dfes.gov.uk
The key aim of this initiative is to increase pupils' interest and involvement in the natural environment through first-hand experience of outdoor resources including the school grounds.

Learning Through Landscapes, Third Floor, Southside Offices, The Law Courts, Winchester SO23 9DL (Tel 01962 846258); www.ltl.org.uk
A national charity dedicated to promoting the effective use of school grounds to support the full development of every child and for the benefit of the wider community.

Suggested further reading

Carson, R. (1998), *The Sense of Wonder*, HarperCollins, New York
Rachel Carson's award-winning classic provides an intimate account of adventures with her young nephew as they enjoy walking through dense forests and open fields, observing wildlife, strange plants, moonlight and storm clouds and more. Features stunning photographs.

Cornell, J. (1979), *Sharing Nature with Children*, Exley, Watford
A collection of games and activities to enthuse and inspire children in the beauty and wonder of the natural world. A classic book written by one of the most highly regarded nature educators.

Horsfall, J. (1997), *Play Lightly on the Earth: Nature activities for children 3 to 9 years old*, Dawn Publications, Nevada City, Calif.
A collection of original games and activities to encourage children to experience and enjoy the natural world. This book weaves scientific concepts into imaginative outdoor play.

Lovejoy, S. (1999), *Roots, Shoots, Buckets and Boots: Gardening together with children*, Workman Publishing Company, New York
In addition to information about planning, planting and caring for a garden, this book contains 12 easy-to-implement ideas for creating theme gardens such as a garden for giants, a flowery maze and a Moon garden.

4 Peace and conflict resolution

– developing positive relationships

We have flown the air like birds, and swum the sea like fishes but we have not yet learnt the simple act of walking the earth like brothers.

Martin Luther King

*He drew a circle that shut me out...
Heretic, rebel a thing to flout,
But love and I had the wit to win...
We drew a circle that took him in.*

Source unknown

Disputes may be inevitable, but violence is not. To prevent continual cycles of conflict, education must seek to provoke peace and tolerance, not fuel hatred and suspicion.

UNICEF 1996 State of the World's Children: Anti-war Agenda

The old law of an eye for an eye leaves everyone blind. Violence ends by defeating itself. It creates bitterness in the survivors and brutality in the destroyers.

Martin Luther King Jnr

Talking out: an approach of an inner city first school

Joan Webster

This contribution demonstrates how even very young children are capable of peaceful conflict-solving if they are taught appropriate peacekeeping strategies. Talking out is a strategy to help children understand each other's problems and feelings.

The more children each have their own sense of self-worth, the less they can become victims. The more we can help every dominant child to understand and empathize with the quieter children and be tolerant of different people, the less they will name-call and bully. These successes can only grow out of a school ethos that celebrates individuality, respect and responsibility.

Joan Webster describes the use of talking out and other whole-school strategies at Cavell First and Nursery School to create a positive school ethos. This involved embarking upon a policy of child autonomy, independence and a programme of personal and social development that became the heart of their curriculum.

Introduction

Cavell First and Nursery School lies within walking distance of the city of Norwich. In the mid-1980s it was an area of mainly local authority housing with high unemployment and a high number of single-parent families. Most families were struggling financially. At that time numbers of pupils at the school had fallen to 118 and were forecast to continue doing so. Most parents were dissatisfied, suspicious and sometimes aggressive. They were not involved in the day-to-day life of the school.

The behaviour of the children was appalling and academic achievement very low. Staff were caring and concerned, but struggling. Expectations were low. We realized that changes were needed urgently; so what did we want for our school? We wanted a school:

- where parents, children and teachers worked together in harmony;
- where individuals mattered;
- without hierarchy;
- where being different was welcome and celebrated;
- to which we would send our own children.

To begin with, we focused on parents. Long before any government regulation, we put into writing our commitment to working with parents. The policy document was displayed on the school notice board. The major aim was 'to enable parents to believe that they are a vital part of the school community and that together we are partners in a shared task'. We welcomed everyone into the building by unlocking doors and inviting them to come inside at the beginning and end of each day. As head, I made sure that I was a visible presence by walking around the school welcoming the children and parents as they entered. It was not until I retired that I discovered how much parents appreciated this small act.

At the close of each day I joined the groups of mothers as they waited for their children. They were then able to share any problems informally with me and could feel supported by the friends around them. Sometimes they would approach in a group to give added weight to their problem. In this atmosphere there was less need to resort to aggression.

At the same time, I paid particular attention to the 'tone' of any letters and news items I sent out. In those days, the secretary typed them and it was not unknown for her to return them with 'Bossy Boots!' scrawled across.

Notices were placed outside each classroom door saying: 'Welcome! Please come in' and 'Have you any time to spare? We need your help'. 'HELP! We need it! Mums, Dads, Grans, Uncles, Aunts – ALL welcome to come in anytime!'

There was a positive policy of no school uniform, as this would have contradicted our commitment to celebrating differences.

The door of my office remained permanently open so that children, parents and teachers could just walk in. If the door was closed then the meaning was clear – confidential matters. At eight years old Emily wrote, 'When I first came to Cavell I was terrified. I kept going to Mrs Webster so I knew she was still there…Mrs Webster was like my mum to me. She's got an open door for all the children.'

I made sure I learned the names of all the children as they started school. For them this is very important. It gives a sense of security and belonging. I spent all break times with the children, talking, reading, circulating so that I was aware of difficulties and problems as, if not before, they arose.

There was no appointment system to see me. I made sure I was always available at any time so that any problems could be dealt with and the outcome reported back to parents immediately.

Gradually, a feeling of mutual trust and respect began to grow. There was a feeling of warmth and friendship between staff, children and parents. Children could witness the friendship between their teachers and their parents. They knew we were working together.

At the same time, expectations in the classroom were rising. There was a marked improvement in standards of presentation, literacy and numeracy, and parents were noticing the changes. However, in common with most schools, there remained a persistent problem. The behaviour of a number of children during break times was wild and aggressive, and resulted in quarrels and arguments and even physical fights.

Then, in 1986, following a discussion meeting set up by the Centre for Applied Research in Education (CARE) at the University of East Anglia, we embarked upon an experiment in an attempt to solve this problem. Little did we realize the impact this would have on the entire learning process in our school. Briefly, we decided that any children who were quarrelling would be told to go to the library area or head's office to talk together about their problem. (I should point out that my office was not a punishment area, as many children would choose to visit my room at break times to read if they did not want to go outside.) Any problem, whether verbal or physical, would be resolved by talking out and I would leave the room while they did so. The children accepted the idea in a matter-of-fact way and so we embarked on 'talking out'. Initially this was used for any form of conflict on the playground but such was its impact that we very soon realized the potential for use in the classroom. Within a short while we adopted the same system throughout the school for all disputes, whether physical or verbal, in class as well as outside, and the entire staff became fully committed to it. No more 'There, there, I'm sure he didn't mean it'. We embarked upon a policy of child autonomy, independence and a programme of personal and social development, which became the heart of our curriculum.

What is 'talking out'?

Talking out means teaching children to listen to each other, express their feelings and agree a solution. For small children this is very hard until we give them the words and phrases they need, and use them often enough in front of the children so that they can understand the meaning thoroughly. We tried to build their vocabulary and their ability to empathize with others by using every occasion of sadness, ruction, dispute, confrontation or hurt. We would talk with small groups and often the whole class about how they were feeling and particularly about tone of voice. Often, it was not merely what was said but the manner of saying that caused hurt. We became very aware of our own voices and manner when dealing with problems. Throughout the process it was made very clear to all children that no physical aggression would be tolerated, whatever the provocation. This was an absolute rule.

In the classroom, we exploited all opportunities for children to make choices so that, for instance, they could decide where to spend playtime, where to sit in assembly, when to go to the toilet. We abandoned lining up, whistles, bells, shouting by adults or children for attention. We used a raised hand at all times for attention, even on our very large playing field. There was no punishment of the whole class or group because of the behaviour of a few.

We tried to give children a sense of self-worth so that they did not become victims; they were not afraid to put their point of view and we tried to encourage the more dominant ones to understand and empathize. The children were learning how to accept and be tolerant of others.

Team teaching plus lots of discussion meant that expectations, strategies for handling behaviour and attitudes were the same in every class, and new staff and children could be easily assimilated into the programme. Thus, a whole-school approach was established and maintained. In practical terms, we needed to teach the children to negotiate and to provide them with the appropriate language. Certain phrases rapidly became part of the culture: 'Can I rely on that?' 'It's not appropriate...you are not listening to me.' There were many more. Statements such as 'Wayne hit me' or 'Emma has taken my pencil' were discouraged. Instead, we would encourage the children to say something like 'I have a problem with ... please will you help?' or we would say, 'What are you going to do about it?'

WHAT DID THE CHILDREN UNDERSTAND BY 'TALKING OUT'?
These are their words:

> You talk out when someone's being nasty to you...calling you names.

> We talk out. We have to make a decision about what we are going to do – whether to make friends.

> You say why did you do that to me? I feel upset, sad. You talk politely...you really try to sort it out.

> You really try to listen and you try to sort it out quickly and straight away...not leave it.

> You don't tell the teacher...you just sort it out.

> If you take a long time, it gets muddled up again.

> You say please don't do it...and at the end you say sorry and make up, shake hands, hug each other...and then you be friends. Me and Natasha did and then we loved each other very much and kept bringing each other cards and things.

> It makes you feel better.

Acknowledging each other's feelings

> If we never talked out it would just carry on forever, just fighting.

> If you can't sort it out then you can stand in front of the class and sort it out with everybody...other children help. They make suggestions.

At this point I thanked the children for their help. I said that they had done really well, to which Amie replied, 'We put our thinking caps on...we've got too much brain!' The parting shot, with a reassuring pat on my arm, was...' There you are...now you know how to sort out, don't you.'

OUR EXPERIENCES OF 'TALKING OUT'

Talking out is handy when somebody is very unkind to you but if talking out does not work you tell a teacher and they tell you to find a friend to help you talk it out. You feel much better if you talk it out and make friends. Talking out works and I use talk out at home sometimes when Samantha is unkind to me.

Rebecca (aged 7)

Before you sort out your problems you find the people you have to talk out with. First you tell them how you feel then you ask them why they did it. Then you keep talking again until you feel happy with each other.

Brendan (aged 8)

We found that children needed sufficient time to resolve conflict; sometimes they would need support from another child or children or occasionally, usually in more serious cases, an adult. Sometimes I would ask what had been decided. More often I would say, 'Do I need to know?' Usually the children would say, 'No, we've sorted it.'

We found we needed to provide spaces, physical as well as emotional, to talk out. Back-up support was essential for a few children who found resolution difficult. Some children, particularly those new to the school, found talking out difficult and expected an adult to solve the problem.

We frequently shared difficulties, particularly serious ones involving aggression with the whole class. We discussed disputes and listened to others' suggestions. The children could always be relied upon to find a way of helping someone to change his or her behaviour to everyone's satisfaction. Their solutions were usually kinder and more forgiving than mine.

We spent a lot of time talking about and exploring feelings, adults and children together; we talked and wrote about each other positively and regularly. Physical contact in the form of hugs became a natural part of every day. Cuddly toys were available in all classrooms for anyone feeling 'wobbly'. Circle time provided opportunities to express our feelings, particularly at the end of the day. It provided children with the chance to express any negative feelings so that any worries could be resolved before going home. Circle time was an activity enjoyed by the children.

We start off by making a circle. Then we put our heads down and think about what we have been doing. Then we put our heads up and we pass the teddy along. When we've got the teddy we can talk about what we have been doing, what you've enjoyed and what you've learned. I feel happy when we do circle time because we get a teacher to listen to us all by our selves.

Lorna (aged 7)

I feel peaceful but a little bit scared as well. I am feeling happy too. I enjoy it when we share things. I hope I get brave.

Sarah (aged 6)

It is quiet and it makes me feel loved.

Chelsea (aged 6)

We insisted that each person should take responsibility for his or her own actions and his or her own behaviour, something even adults find hard to do. The overall aim was to move away from a discipline imposed by authority towards a sense of responsibility for oneself and one's own behaviour so that, in a child's own words 'you can't just blame someone else'. What a breakthrough when Daniel says 'Yes I did it!' and even better when he adds 'I wish I hadn't'. Frequently, we would give whole-class affirmation of a child, particularly of those who had previously found co-operation difficult. Joseph once said vehemently, 'It's much harder for me. I'm so used to being bad it's hard to be good all the time!'

Within the classroom we used a wide range of activities that demanded co-operation so that there were constant opportunities to share and negotiate. We saw a marked change in behaviours, especially at playtime, with fewer children upset and asking for adult intervention. The ritual of talking out proved invaluable. Everyone knew that you could talk out if you had a problem. A pattern was established of sitting on the carpet in a quiet place and listening to each other, agreeing what to do and asking for help if needed. The process became ritualized and a belief system evolved: children and adults came to believe that children could sort out their own and each other's difficulties. Children developed their own quick rituals, particularly in minor upsets, for talking out, usually on the lines of: 'I'm sorry, Let's make up.' 'Okay, you can sit by me in story then.' At first, they would report back to the teacher that they had 'made up' but later that often became unnecessary. It was as if they felt that such disputes were not worth wasting time over. They settled it quickly by behaving like negotiators without actually needing to negotiate. When there were several children involved they would take it in turns to speak. I would hear comments like: 'No, you have had your turn – it's my turn now.'

In such a situation the children responded positively, with maturity, to the trust, belief and high regard shown to them. Matthew, aged six, wrote: 'I can use the library at playtime and dinner time because teachers trust me to be sensible.' They learned in an atmosphere free from fear. Children and teachers grew to realize that making mistakes was part of learning and growing. Mistakes were expected and accepted because you could have another chance.

Self-respect and self-esteem for adults and children grew higher and higher. Spending time in school became a pleasure and absenteeism was minimal.

PROBLEMS AND DIFFICULTIES ENCOUNTERED

All adults had to learn not to try to solve children's arguments but instead to comment in such a way as to enable children to help themselves. We explained that 'John hit me' is telling a tale but saying, 'Please could you help. John and I have got a problem?' means that you are not making the angry feelings greater and that you are willing to sort out the problem together. We had to say, 'What are you going to do about it?' and help them to become independent.

If a child was unwilling to go to a quiet place, through being too angry or incoherent to manage discussion, then time was allowed for the child to calm down and another child or adult was on hand to help a short time later. This was a very rare occurrence. Most children preferred immediate negotiation.

We watched and noted the various patterns and styles of negotiation that developed, to see for which children talking out was failing and why. Those children whose behaviour was frequently difficult needed to be closely monitored and strategies for handling were agreed with all staff so that we could ensure a consistent approach. We had regular discussions to maintain consistency.

- Occasionally, there might be a child who thought that talking out had no implications for changes in behaviour and continued to show a high level of aggression or meanness.
- There were sometimes children who were not popular, so no one seemed to want to play or sit with them.
- Some children were too nervous to speak out.
- There were 'attention seekers' who used talking out as an activity to bring them to the centre of attention rather than to solve a conflict (usually non-existent).
- Occasionally, a particularly dominant child could manipulate the situation to suit himself or herself and an unconfident child would collude with him or her for the sake of approval.

At the beginning of each new school year the youngest entrants who had not attended our own nursery were either very frightened of the older children or saw them as potential sparring partners. It was they whose behaviour challenged the older children for the first few weeks, so we had two playtimes for a while: five year olds and eight year olds together, leaving the middle years alone. In this way the youngest learned from the example of the oldest. They learned much about relationships as well as becoming familiar with the language needed. The older children, in turn, grew in maturity and responsibility.

We constantly reiterated 'talking out' so as to remind children what it was all about. Sometimes we would ask those involved separately if they were happy with the outcome. We might suggest that another child or grown-up should help. We might say, 'This is really important. Let's talk about this together', and the whole class would be consulted.

The expectation was that children would help sort out a difficult problem by suggesting positive and not punishing solutions. They could always be relied upon to produce an answer. They never ceased to amaze me. The emphasis in their discussions always rested on truthfulness, honesty, gentleness, kindness, respect, friendship and consideration for others.

It was this that seemed to have the greatest impact on two or three children who had been expelled from previous schools for disruptive behaviour. The rest of the children seemed to be saying, 'No, we don't like the way you behave but we like you and we can help you to change'. Certainly, the miscreants became happier children and consequently achieved more while they were with us. For them, working and playing harmoniously, with minimal conflict between children and teachers, was a new experience and one they came to enjoy. For very aggressive children the other effective strategy was the 'bolt hole'. We gave them a 'way out' when they felt on the verge of losing control. Whatever the situation, they knew they could come immediately to my room, no questions asked until they felt calm enough to speak. I would sometimes leave the room but remain on hand nearby or I would just nod and carry on with my work. This avoided confrontation until we could speak calmly.

Every day we emphasized positive behaviour rather than negative. We gave praise, encouragement and a wide range of rewards, certificates, stickers and so on for acts of thoughtfulness, kindness or consideration. We saw ourselves as role models and had the same expectations of ourselves as the children.

WIDER IMPLICATIONS

As the children grew in maturity they were able to discuss the wider implications of talking out and to apply the same principles to conflict situations around the world. During the early 1990s many interesting debates arose at the time of the wars in Bosnia, which resulted in the following letter written by seven-year-old Jamie.

To all the people fighting in Bosnia,

When I watch the news I feel that the world is turning into a horrible place instead of a nice calm place. So I think I have a way to solve your problems. This is what we do at my school instead of fighting. We do talking out. This is how to do it. If someone does something horrible to you say please would you come with me and sit down in a special quiet place. It could be sitting on a riverbank.

When we talk out we talk calmly and try to understand what the other person is feeling. This is a very hard thing to do but everyone in my school can do it. The secret is to throw away the thing you want to do and think about the other person. We talk and talk and talk until we agree on what to do. Why don't you try it?

Keeping 'talking out' alive

Keeping 'talking out' alive and active was a never-ending process. New children, teachers, parents and ancillary workers had to be inducted and convinced. We found it hard to accept that we could not be one hundred per cent successful. However, the following comments from parents make it all seem worth the struggle:

Children learning respect for each other and adults...values so thoroughly and effectively built in...being kind, loving, considerate and knowledgeable human beings.

Cavell has found a perfect balance...wonderful atmosphere...all children strive to the best of their abilities...

Cavell has a family atmosphere...Parents feel at ease in the friendly, helpful, happy and relaxed atmosphere.

Danielle has never lost the basics that she got taught at Cavell. One of her specialities is to try and 'talk it out'.

We appreciate your concern for the individual...

Cavell celebrates individuality, respect and responsibility.

It was the children who created the atmosphere; their warmth, empathy, respect for each other, capacity for forgiveness, sense of fun and joy in life made going to school a pleasure for us all.

What of the future? Does talking out continue? We do not know, but Melissa, aged ten, says, 'I am now at middle school. I still use the things I have learned. I'll always use them. They'll help me every step I go.'

Talking out is a strategy that enables children to resolve problems by:

- defining the problem from their viewpoint;
- identifying and expressing their feelings and needs;
- hearing the feelings and needs of the other child or children;
- finding and agreeing a positive solution;
- following through the agreed solution.

Suggested further reading

Highfield Junior School (1997), *Changing our School: Promoting positive behaviour*, Highfield Junior School and the Institute of Education, Plymouth
A detailed, practical and inspirational book telling the story of how a school beset with problems changed to a high-achieving, peaceful and happy community.

Melicharova, M. (1998), *Working Together: A handbook for co-operation*, Peace Pledge Union, London.
This handbook provides practical suggestions for developing skills in working together and is supplemented with more theoretical material to provoke thought and discussion.

Mosley, J. (1993), *Turn Your School Round: A circle-time approach to the development of self-esteem and positive behaviour in the primary staffroom, classroom and playground*, Learning Development Aids, Cambridge
This book draws on Jenny Mosley's 20 years' experience of using regular circle time sessions to involve all adults and children in the school community to develop, implement and review a self-esteem and positive behaviour policy.

Mosley, J. and Thorp, G. (2002), *All Year Round: Exciting ideas for peaceful playtimes*, Learning Development Aids, Cambridge
Playtimes can be a source of tension and anxiety for children that can cause unhappiness and underachievement. This accessible and practical book offers a systematic model for producing an emotionally healthy school based upon calm and happy playtimes.

Circle of Friends

Gill Taylor

The Circle of Friends approach is becoming an increasingly popular means of fostering and supporting inclusion of children with emotional and social needs in mainstream schools. Gill Taylor summarizes the Circle of Friends approach, which originated in parts of Canada and the USA. This is followed by case studies illustrating the nature of the Circle of Friends approach and the potential benefits for all those involved.

Introduction

The Circle of Friends approach is a highly effective strategy for enabling the inclusion of children with challenging behaviour and relationship difficulties within schools. The values underpinning this approach include respect and empathy for vulnerable and troubled children, who are at risk of exclusion from school. This is a way of working that seeks to empower children within the school environment and mobilize peer support in a positive and enriching manner.

Children develop skills of citizenship, talking and listening skills, problem solving and emotional intelligence. Teachers report positive changes in relationships and behaviour and an improved climate for learning. The approach is highly effective across the whole school age-range.

A Circle of Friends is created and meets regularly to support a particular child at risk of exclusion, and develops so that all members of the Circle are supported in their relationships and learning. A Circle consists typically of eight children and a teacher, and is formed from within the focus child's class.

Two examples of Circle of Friends

The following two case studies from the research of Gill Taylor and Professor Bob Burden (2000) illustrate the nature of the Circle of Friends. Names provided are fictitious.

Friendships provide emotional support – helping us to feel safe and secure

Case study:
Emma

BACKGROUND

Five-year-old Emma found making friends in her reception class very difficult. Both her mother and her class teacher were very concerned about this.

> Because of her problems relating to other children, she finds it difficult to be engaged in things that involved co-operating. Often, imaginative play will end with a dispute. Emma will walk off and be on her own because she hasn't been able to negotiate with other children what she wants…she rejects them and often tells them, 'I want to play with somebody else'.
>
> Emma's teacher

> Emma says, 'At school nobody plays with me, I've got no friends', and she starts crying.
>
> Emma's mother

Emma's teacher decided that the Circle of Friends would be supportive, as Emma was relatively isolated within her class.

CREATING AND DEVELOPING THE CIRCLE OF FRIENDS

The Circle of Friends was planned to be facilitated by Emma's teacher. However, once established, the school's special educational needs co-ordinator (SENCO) became the facilitator.

> I think this group had quite a good balance of children; there was a variety of confidence and friendships, so that worked. I think it worked that it was me taking the group because they had a certain sense that something special was happening.
>
> School SENCO

OUTCOMES

Emma, the Circle of Friends (the Friendly Fish Group), Emma's mother, the class teacher and the Circle's facilitator (SENCO) all reported positive outcomes for Emma during the four months of the Circle of Friends. Some of these are indicated below.

Emma played with other children in the playground:

> It's given her some friends and now, in the playground, she approaches those children in the Circle of Friends, whereas before she was quite limited in the children that she would approach. So that's positive.
>
> Emma's teacher

> My friends play with me in the playground.
>
> Emma

There was more co-operative play and work in the classroom:

> People are nice and they're kind to people.

> We play together.
>
> Members of the Friendly Fish Group

Emma had an increased awareness of the effects on others of her own behaviour:

> I think Emma is aware now of how people feel when she acts in certain ways. And it doesn't mean she can necessarily stop herself doing that, but I think she is aware.
>
> Emma's teacher

Emma developed an increased awareness of her self and ability to express her thoughts and feelings:

> She seems more confident in herself and she just goes and plays with other children rather than clinging to the teacher all the time…I think it's helped her a lot.
>
> Emma's mother

Friendship developed out of school:

> They [Emma and Julie] go to each other's houses, which is something nice which has happened.
>
> Emma's teacher

Emma seemed happy:

> It's been a help.
> They play with me more…we play things a lot.
>
> Emma

There was also evidence of a significant positive effect on the group as a whole and upon aspects of the behaviour of other children within it:

> There's a lot more discussion about friendship and playground things in our class circle times.
>
> Emma's teacher

> People are kinder.
>
> Members of the Friendly Fish Group

> Julie and Marianne are more able to ask other people to play with them. And I think Marianne's found it easier to talk to people when she's upset.
>
> Emma's teacher

Case study:

Sylvester

BACKGROUND

Sylvester, a nine-year-old boy, was causing concern to his mother and teacher because of his aggressive and disruptive behaviour, which had made him a social isolate.

> At registration he sits there and shouts out a lot…makes very silly noises, like whistles to himself or sings, but so loudly it's heard…[The other children] tell him to be quiet or have a go at him. At which point, he starts having a go back, and it can get very spiteful at times.
>
> Sylvester's teacher

> …he definitely feels excluded most of the time from his class…He says he's got no friends…he's never invited to birthday parties, and he never goes to people's houses, so I've been trying to explain to him that people are afraid of his reaction…
>
> Sylvester's mother

CREATING AND DEVELOPING THE CIRCLE OF FRIENDS

The Circle of Friends was initially facilitated by Sylvester's teacher and then by a support teacher who took over the running of the Circle.

OUTCOMES

During the six months of the Circle, Sylvester, his mother, his teacher and members of his Circle of Friends all reported positive outcomes. Some of these are indicated below.

Sylvester gradually began to take control of his temper, calming down much more quickly when he became upset:

> He seems to be able to take in the situation much better than before; even if he blows up, it would take him longer to do that. I still see him, if he's being pushed really hard, I mean, I can see him really 'going' but he's trying at least not to lash out. I'm not saying it works every time, but he's trying…
>
> Sylvester's mother

The members of the Circle made a genuine effort to befriend Sylvester and help him to control his behaviour by chanting their mantra 'Forget it; it's not worth it':

> [We had this] catchphrase 'Forget it; it's not worth it'…[it was] boring at the beginning, but we got used to it. We kept on saying it when somebody got into trouble…People tried it mostly to help me.
>
> Sylvester

Friends came for the first time to Sylvester's birthday party and made it a great success:

> Last Sunday it was his birthday, so we did like a school party at home…he was really worried that no one would turn up…he didn't say 'Oh, I'm worried' but I could see he was really nervous… He was really excited, but at the same time so nervous that no one would come…because he's always been the one left out…I must admit only three people came, but I was so happy…It was lovely; they really had a good time.
>
> Sylvester's mother

The whole class began to calm down and support each other:

> We try to help other people.
>
> Members of the Circle of Friends group

There was an increased awareness on Sylvester's part of his own responsibility for how he behaved:

> At least he accepts now that it's his own behaviour that's the problem…Before, it used to be other people's fault and I don't think he can understand, still, that if he didn't start it, why he's getting into trouble.
>
> Sylvester's mother

> I had some problems with other people sometimes. I stopped it. Sometimes I do have little fights, but most other things have changed…[Now when there's trouble] I just walk away…It's easier now [because the other children] kept out of trouble as well [and] they did help each other.
>
> Sylvester

A more positive relationship developed between Sylvester and his mother:

> …it's definitely feeling more positive.
>
> Sylvester's mother

A more positive relationship developed between Sylvester and his teacher:

> If I can see him going through a process of getting angry, I can diffuse it. And I think, and I don't tell him [but] I'll question him. Then, because of that, he'll start thinking and can calm himself down.
>
> Sylvester's teacher

Resources

A video and a handbook describing the Circle of Friends process in detail are available from Gill Taylor (gilltaylorcircle@btopenworld.com). These resources show all the steps involved in creating and maintaining a Circle and describe key issues and roles, including the role of Circle facilitator (the teacher). Workshop conferences are planned, which will enable teachers and support staff to learn and develop their skills and understanding of this approach.

Suggested further reading

Taylor, G. (1996), Creating a Circle of Friends: A case study. In Cowie, H. and Sharp, S. (eds) *Peer Counselling*, David Fulton, London
This chapter provides a full description of the procedures required for establishing a Circle of Friends for a child with emotional and behavioural needs.

Taylor, G. (1997), Community Building in Schools: Developing a circle of friends, *Educational and Child Psychology*, 14 (3), pages 45–50
This paper describes all the stages of creating a Circle of Friends and emphasizes the importance of community and empowering children in school.

Reference

Taylor, G. and Burden, B. (2000), *The Positive Power of Friendship: An illuminative evaluation of the Circle of Friends approach within the primary and secondary phases*, Exeter University Research Papers, Exeter
This report describes the process and outcomes of a small-scale evaluation project into the effectiveness of a Circle of Friends.

Emotions are at the centre of children's relationships and well-being. Children at Coombes School use the prayer walk

What's normal?
Using drama to challenge the culture of violence in which children are reared

John Airs

Since 1994, Liverpool LEA has pioneered the Challenging Attitudes to Violence Project in a number of its schools. This is a remarkable education project that challenges present-day attitudes to violence in the most positive ways. The project has been an unqualified success in changing the whole ethos of those primary and secondary schools that have taken it up as a whole-school strategy.

Challenging Attitudes to Violence is a drama initiative that addresses the broad issue of violence but with a focus on domestic violence. Drama is an extremely powerful, safe and effective mechanism for examining this issue within a non-threatening context in that it fictionalizes characters and scenarios.

John Airs, a drama consultant and member of the Challenging Attitudes to Violence team, describes several classroom exercises that form the drama Earthwatch.

Introduction

Violence is normal. It is normal – indeed, natural – to use violence to get what you want. Violence pays.

My father beats me up
Just like his father did
And grandad he was beaten
By greatgrandad as a kid

From generation to generation
A poisoned apple passed along
Domestic daily cruelty
No one thinking it was wrong.

And it was:

Not the cursing and the bruising
The frustration and the fear
A normal child can cope with that
It grows easier by the year

But the ignorance, believing
That the child is somehow owned
Property paid for
Violence condoned.

Roger McGough 'Beatings'

Research indicates that in our culture one in every four women at some time in her life suffers violence in her own home. Children witness this violence, may be brought up with it, may be the victims of it. Children can watch violence on TV and video, play violent computer games, watch violent sports, buy violent toys. Little boys, in particular, have for long played exhilarating, make-believe, violent games. Recently, girls have discovered the thrill of forming threatening and violent gangs for real; until now, this was more of a boys' thing. The news we see, hear and read is steeped in violence, to the point that a story is hardly deemed newsworthy unless it is violent. Who takes much notice of a peaceful

This contribution is a slightly rewritten version of a chapter which appeared in *The Invisible Dimension: Violence Prevention Education*, published by Liverpool LEA.

demonstration? We can hardly blame our children for seeing violence as a natural feature of life.

McGough's poem, however, does add after 'No one thinking it was wrong'...'And it was...'

And the dramatist, Bertholt Brecht, in the introduction to his play, *The Measures Taken*, asks us through his play...

...expressly to discover
That what happens all the time
Is not natural.

Just because violence seems to happen all the time in our culture does not mean that it is natural. Can our children uncover this truth through their own play? Can they come to realize through drama that domestic violence, for example, is wrong? Domestic violence is a crime.

Why drama?

Drama as a medium for learning has several advantages when you want to teach about something as sensitive and significant as violence and, in particular, domestic violence.

BEGIN WITH WHAT THEY KNOW

Drama offers pupils, of whatever age, a means of investigating something important in a way that asks for their full engagement, takes their knowledge and their opinions seriously but challenges them to think and feel and make judgements beyond initial, unreflective responses. In drama, we start with what they know and build on that.

SAFETY OF FICTION

Drama allows us to approach this challenge in the relative safety of a fiction. Students may be drawing on their own experience or on what they have seen on film and television, but the characters and the stories they invent are, and must be, fictitious. They are not being asked to reveal intimate details of their own lives or merely to replicate episodes of a television soap.

THERAPY OR EDUCATION?

This is not therapy, although on occasions there are clearly therapeutic effects, side effects as it were. The object of this work is quite specifically educational. We are studying a culture, which appears in many ways to accept violence as normal. What are the reasons, the feelings, the values, the attitudes implicit in this culture? What are the consequences and the

cost of living with violence? And how could things be different?

LAYER UPON LAYER

The following example of a drama, Earthwatch, demonstrates a careful building up of involvement and information. The momentum that is created by the drama, over a period of weeks, generates commitment and allows students to develop their skills and their understanding in depth.

Earthwatch

First, negotiate with the class some simple ground rules for drama work:

- it is to be taken seriously, though it will be good fun;
- everyone has to respect each other's work at all times;
- everyone, as far as he or she can, should be willing to co-operate and respond to whatever comes out of the work as it develops;
- but no one should be forced to do anything they do not want to do.

The purpose of the drama is to discover things about our lives that really matter to us.

Explain to the class that you and they are going to go into role. You are going to become characters other than yourselves. With the class sitting in a circle (their stage), say something along the lines of the following:

Thank you for your brilliant research work. It looks as though you may have found, at last, a planet on which we can settle. Your research informs us that some of the inhabitants of this planet – who are incredibly like us in every respect – speak a language they call 'English'. Is that correct?

Stop the role play at this point and check that everyone understands the game, who we are and what our function on the spaceship is – research scientists from another planet, studying the planet Earth with a view to settling. You are in role as a co-ordinator, not one of the researchers. The distinction is significant because the 'research data' should come from them, not you. Then explain that you are going back into role.

VIOLENCE ON THE PLANET EARTH

There is only one major concern that the ship's parliament has and they have asked the research scientists to address it. After the disaster to our own planet, we have all sworn never to resort to violence again and we have managed to keep that oath. Some of the research findings indicate that the Earth beings can be quite violent. Is that the case?

Ask the scientists to list, with you, a range of the different sorts of violence they have observed on Earth. Record the list and display it as a reminder.

IMAGES OF VIOLENCE

Report to the scientists that the ship's parliament is quite shocked at their findings and has asked for further research on this issue. Could the scientists beam up some precise examples of human violence as observed in the homes, the streets, the playgrounds?

Demonstrate, using volunteers, the making of a tableau or still image. Choose one of the violent behaviours from their list and, adding children one or two at a time, build the picture of a particular instance of it. There will be no movement, no words, but the precise nature of the violent moment must be agreed on. Who are these people? Where are they? What relation are they to each other? Why are they doing what the picture shows? What does each think about what is happening? Can you see that from the way they look?

When it is clear that the children know what this image work involves – it must tell a precise and detailed story – then divide the class into working parties with four or five scientists in each. Each group sits down together and decides on the details of a different violent incident, and then carefully builds an image of it. These images will be the scientists' holograms beamed up from the planet Earth to the hologram chamber within the circle of chairs.

READING THE IMAGES

Study each 'hologram' in turn. Ask the holograms to remain perfectly still until you have heard as many interpretations or readings of each as seems helpful or until a generally agreed reading has been reached. It is important not to rush the reading of the images. Invite the observing scientists to look very carefully and to interpret such things as body language and expression, proximity or distance between the humans, where each is looking. When each hologram has been studied by the observing scientists, invite the scientists from the image to relax, sit back in the circle and explain what they 'saw' in their own image. It may or may not be what

the other scientists saw. That does not matter. The purpose of this task is for the class to explore and reveal to you and to each other what violence means to them.

As each study is completed ask for and record an appropriate title under which to file the hologram. The working parties will be able to reproduce these holograms at a moment's notice any time within the next few weeks.

ROLE ON THE WALL

Draw a gingerbread figure on a flip chart. Select one violent character from one of the holograms. Explain that you would like the research scientists to focus on this man (since most domestic violence is perpetrated by men, though you do not need to say this at this stage) and uncover more data.

As a whole class, build up a fictional dossier for this character, whom we have so far seen only in a still image. It is essential that this human is fictional and that several scientists contribute at least one 'fact' about him. We need such things as names, age, occupation (if he has one), character, likes, dislikes, appearance, values, attitudes…

Once this process is under way and clearly understood by the class, stop the brainstorming and explain that the working party that first showed the character in their hologram will go on to complete his details in a moment or two. They will be responsible for research into this particular human being.

From each of the other holograms select one character – agent or victim of violence, witness or intervener – who could be a member of the first character's family (though, of course, the original images were not designed with this in mind). Select a wife or partner and a range of children. Each working party now has a human subject to 'research'. They will draw up, with felt-tips and flip chart or sugar paper, a dossier in the same manner as was demonstrated for the dossier of the original character. Each working party now has one member of the same family for which they will be responsible.

After 10 or 15 minutes, call the working parties together again and invite each to report back its 'findings'.

GETTING INSIDE THE HEADS OF OUR SUBJECTS

Explain that you, as co-ordinator, are now going to ask them to undertake an experiment that will involve getting inside the heads of these human subjects. Draw an imaginary line across your working space. At one end of the line is a statement such as 'This human hates violence, believes it is never justifiable'. At the other end would be the statement, 'This human thinks violence is normal, nothing wrong with it at all'. Ask all of the scientists to think, privately, where on the continuum between these two poles would they place their subject. Stress that the chances are that most humans would be somewhere in between the two poles, though someone might have a total commitment to violence or be completely against it. Then, without any communication with their colleagues, without even looking to see where their colleagues go, each scientist places herself or himself on the imaginary line at that chosen spot.

Go through each 'character' or human subject in turn, asking the scientists responsible for her or him to raise a hand. Observe whatever spread along the continuum there is (generally there is some spread, which makes things more interesting, but if there is not that does not matter).

Ask each working party to reconvene. For five minutes or so let them discuss why they chose to stand where they did and then attempt to negotiate an agreed position. Ask one volunteer from each group to take up that position with a prepared brief statement (one sentence would do), explaining their group's choice. If, as sometimes happens, a group simply cannot come to an agreement at all, then, as a last resort, it might send two representatives with varying views. Humans are, after all, sometimes complex and contradictory.

HOT SEATING

You now have the scientists representing the family expressing the family's individual views on the subject of domestic violence. Would they be willing to allow the remaining scientists to question them further on these views and how they come to hold them? If they agree (and, as volunteers to come out from their working party in the first place, they probably will) then encourage the hot seating or interrogating to go on for as long as is productive. Then, all as researchers again, discuss what has been learned from this experiment about humans and violence. At this juncture, you might consider it appropriate to submit an interim report, drafted by the whole group or by working parties, to the ship's parliament.

DRAMATIC DEVELOPMENTS

Your class now has a substantial basis on which to build its drama. Where might it take its research? It might want to look at the family in action. How does it function? What do they imagine are the costs of domestic violence?

Set up new working parties based on one representative from each of the original working parties – giving you family groups. Ask these groups to prepare a brief episode from the life of the family, which we, as researchers, can examine and reflect on. Suggest that they start and finish their episode with a still image. It would be useful to identify each character at the outset, before going into action. Explain carefully that we, as researchers, are now concerned with why the violence happens, not with the violence itself. Their episode must show a moment that might lead to an outburst of violence and should freeze just before the violence sets in. Stress this point.

If your class is not yet up to working in this way (it is quite a challenging task) then model an example with one group in the centre of the circle, asking them to move the scene on step by step, slowly and carefully. Take advice from the rest of the class as to what each character might do and say.

At any appropriate stage in this process you might tell the characters to freeze and then ask the outer circle of observers to say what one or other of the characters might be thinking at this precise moment. This is called thought tracking and can be an enlightening strategy. If you consider the class ready for it, allow the working parties to prepare and present their own brief examples of episodes from the family's life.

The focus of the work must be fixed on the question, 'Why?' What triggers that violence? And why do humans, in particular male humans, think that it is not only acceptable but also even desirable that they should be violent? If that is the case...

(Beneath this question hides another. Do male humans in fact think violence is acceptable, even desirable? Or do they think that they ought to think that? Do many of them actually not think that at all? Our culture, and cultures around the world, have quite explicitly taught men that it is their responsibility, their duty, to be violent. They have been, they are, the noble warriors. They are the masters of their wives and children, 'property paid for, violence condoned'. Until very recently it was a man's duty to control his wife and children if they were not behaving themselves, if necessary with a stick. This taught culture is residual. In some parts of our society – and that is not limited to any one class

– it even remains the dominant culture. But for many boys, and certainly for many girls, the emergent culture knows that it is wrong. Their drama may permit them to acknowledge that. Through the drama they may present an alternative culture that others in their class will recognize as more acceptable than the culture of violence.)

WHERE NEXT?

As a development of the episodic presentations of family life, or as an alternative to them, other dramatic strategies may be useful in exploring the nature, the causes and the cost of human, or inhuman, violence:

- In pairs, the scientists may devise a telephone conversation between two members of the family or between a member of the family and a significant other.
- They may devise text messages or emails.
- They may devise a message left on an answer phone.
- They may write a brief entry in a diary.
- They may write a few lines of a letter, perhaps never sent.

The research scientists will then study this data and reflect on what they are learning about human behaviour, attitudes and values. Your task, as co-ordinator, is not to tell them what they ought to be thinking, but to encourage them to think for themselves.

TEACHER IN ROLE

You may feel it appropriate to ask if you can represent a member of the family, perhaps the abusive parent, and place yourself in the hot seat for the research scientists to interrogate and challenge. If you do this, and they are challenging your violent attitude, it can be productive to play devil's advocate as convincingly as possible to start with and then gradually, even reluctantly, allow yourself to take their emerging values seriously. Acknowledge that you hadn't thought of things their way. They might have a point. Allow them to enlighten you, but not too easily. So, what do they suggest that you do to change?

WHAT PRICE CHANGE?

There is no point pretending that stopping violence will ever be easy, but it is important to look for the seeds of change. Ask the scientists to create a final set of images – holograms – of moments that hold the potential for change. Read and analyse these images together. Can the poisoned apple be arrested? What cultural changes are necessary to halt the domestic daily violence, no one thinking it is wrong?

FINAL REPORTS

To conclude the drama you might suggest a final report on violence and the scientists' hopes for the planet Earth. Can we recommend that our spaceship approaches the humans and asks if we might settle there? The report will, of course, be submitted to the ship's parliament, which will act on our advice.

DEBRIEFING

When the drama is over, discuss it with the class. What, if anything, have they gained from working in this way? Is what they have done serious? Have they discovered anything useful? Schiller claimed that 'Man is only truly human when he plays'. Have these aliens been truly human?

The aims of the Challenging Attitudes to Violence Project are

- to focus on the prevention of violence before it happens by attempting to alter attitudes, values and behaviour;
- to help pupils learn the skills that build healthy relationships, which are based on sharing with others as opposed to exerting power over others;
- to promote emotional well-being for all;
- to develop strategies, via the curriculum, that help to reduce aggressive behaviour.

Resources

John Airs Educational Drama Consultancy, 42 Woodlands, Liverpool, L17 OAP (Tel 0151 727 2398)
Conducts drama sessions on violence prevention, bullying and challenging macho culture.

Thames Valley District School Board, Ontario, Canada, www.tvdsb.on.ca (find 'Safe Schools' section under Search.)
This website provides resource information about safe schools policy and procedures for parents, teachers and support staff. Ensures a consistent, co-ordinated approach to violence prevention and handling of violent incidents that occur in schools.

Suggested further reading

Brown, S. (2001), *The Invisible Dimension: Violence prevention education – A teachers' handbook*, Liverpool Education and Lifelong Service, Liverpool
This handbook is based on and extends the work of the Challenging Attitudes to Violence Project. It contains over 80 classroom exercises for Key Stages 1–4 providing valuable support for PSE and citizenship within the national curriculum.

Calouste Gulbenkian Foundation (1995), *Children and Violence: Report of the Commission on Children and Violence*, Calouste Gulbenkian Foundation, London
This report provides an overview of research on why children become violent and the incidence of violence by children. The report also includes recommendations for action.

Towards a non-violent society: Checkpoints

George Varnava

George Varnava provides a very direct summary about a series of publications designed to promote non-violence in society. These publications, known as Checkpoints, have attracted attention both nationally and internationally.

In his contribution, George Varnava explains how the Checkpoints publications work and how the programme is developing and spreading across Europe. Schools are well placed to promote non-violence. They can draw attention to the problems of violent behaviour. Checkpoints guides enable schools to add a specific violence-prevention perspective to all aspects of their work and to evaluate their progress.

Introduction

In 1983, the Inner London Education Authority began a major investigation into student underachievement, with particular regard to race, sex and class. Since then, it is argued that the enormous efforts and resources deployed to address this problem have succeeded in raising standards of educational achievement. By contrast, however, there is little evidence that behaviour has improved. Indeed, in Britain, there has developed a culture of aggressive behaviour, conflict and violence that permeates society, highlighted by incidents attracting national media coverage; but the undercurrent of so-called 'low-level violence' that commonly occurs is seen and allowed to go unchallenged. The causes for this antisocial shift are many and complex: poverty, consumerism, competitiveness, media influence and social instability are among the most apparent.

Violence is difficult to deal with, particularly among the impressionable young, who learn that violence works. Violent people need victims; they target the vulnerable. One feature common to a significant proportion of victims of bullying or other violence is that they are, in some way, different from their peers – they stand out and easily attract unwanted attention. The continuing use of taunts and attacks against black and other ethnic groups demonstrates that, in spite of all efforts, prejudice and discrimination in respect of race, sex and class have not been eliminated or significantly reduced.

We don't need to sit here talking about it, chatting about it. We need to get action now! And if we don't this is going to carry on and if it carries on this world is not going to be a nice place.

(Seven-year-old girl in Student Council discussing bullying – BBC TV programme *Fighting Aggression*).

The Checkpoints project was commissioned by the Forum on Children and Violence and funded by the Calouste Gulbenkian Foundation. This was in response to the Gulbenkian report on Children and Violence and the news media coverage of incidents that shocked the nation. The first publication, *Towards a Non-violent Society – Checkpoints for schools* (Varnava 2000), was launched by Charles Clarke, then government Minister for Schools. It was followed by an adaptation for the pre-school sector (Finch 2000) and then by *Checkpoints for Young People* (Varnava 2002). For the purposes of this work, violence is defined as 'behaviour which causes physical or psychological harm'.

Violence and the consequences of violence can be explored through drama and role play

Checkpoints is a series of publications designed to facilitate a process of intervention. The process has three main functions: to raise awareness, to serve as an institutional self-audit and to provide guidance towards non-violence. The process works through the main aspects of school life. In Checkpoints these are defined as Home/School/Community; Values (see box, page 119); Organization; the Environment; the Curriculum and Training.

The guide includes a diagram – or web – which, when completed, illustrates a school's strengths in violence-prevention and suggests areas where further action may be taken.

Checkpoints has attracted attention both nationally and internationally. It was selected for the European Commission's 'Connect' project, which researched violence in schools across all member states with a view to considering the adaptability of schemes to different school systems. A presentation to an international seminar hosted by Finland took place in September 2002. The project has aroused keen interest from a number of organizations outside education, for example the National Society for the Prevention of Cruelty to Children, Sport England and the Royal Society of Medicine. Sport England and the NSPCC have collaborated to produce major guidance documents for their respective members nationwide, in which Checkpoints is central. The dissemination of Checkpoints is helping to bring into closer collaboration the education service and the voluntary sector and it has contributed to the debate in England on parental smacking.

Feedback confirms that schools are finding Checkpoints useful in addressing the problems of violent behaviour, including bullying, verbal aggression and physical assault. To quote from one of the pilot schools: 'We have lowered the incidence of confrontation and established a quiet, secure environment where everyone can learn and feel safe.

The following chart, reproduced from the Checkpoints Series, illustrates the nature of the audit.

Checkpoint 2. Values

Every school decides what its values are. Values apply to self, relationships, society and the environment. These values support the general principles of equality. It is made clear that disrespect based, for example, on gender, ethnic origin, religion, culture, disability, sexual orientation or other attribute is unacceptable and will be challenged. Formulating values is important to the personal development of each individual and to the health of the school as a community.

All violence is unacceptable. The right of all members of the school to a safe, violence-free experience is acknowledged as fundamental to the school's ethos.

a in place **b** proposed **c** not in place

	a	b	c
1 Creating a happy, non-violent, positive atmosphere is accepted by all as an important aim.	☐	☐	☐
2 All members of the school participate in the development of a Code of Conduct which specifies non-violence and is prominent throughout the school.	☐	☐	☐
3 It is understood that the school's values apply both inside and outside school.	☐	☐	☐
4 The school ensures that its rules do not contradict external regulations or laws relating to violence-prevention.	☐	☐	☐
5 Good relationships are consistently fostered, and all adults model non-violent behaviour.	☐	☐	☐
6 Mutual respect is consistently promoted and expected of everyone.	☐	☐	☐
7 The school helps everyone to adopt a sense of responsibility for one another and for the school.	☐	☐	☐
8 Violent language, the violent use of language and name-calling are consistently discouraged.	☐	☐	☐
9 All disciplinary measures are non-violent and appropriate to the individual's stage of development.	☐	☐	☐
10 Positive non-violent behaviour is noted and commended and the school assembly is used as an opportunity to promote the values of the school to all its members.	☐	☐	☐

Source: Varnava 2000, page 4

Even our tough boys now admit to and talk about their problem.'

Checkpoints is evolving in the light of experience, giving clear indications of how it can develop further. Evidence on its use and effectiveness is being gathered from schools, trainee teachers, classroom assistants and, most usefully, from young people. For example, discussions with 11-year-old pupils reveal their apprehensions about transferring to secondary school: 'bigger children, too many people, bullying and queuing for food.' Checkpoints has been used as the agenda for a Student Council conference, putting the issues and the solutions firmly in the hands of young people themselves. A gratifying outcome from all the schools reporting has been the involvement of pupils.

Checkpoints for Schools (Varnava 2000) has been presented at a variety of professional conferences and distribution continues by request to the National Children's Bureau. Plans are currently being laid for training courses in its application. Checkpoints is designed as a support to schools addressing their own individual and different needs; it is not imposed and there is no obligation on the school to accept any of its advice. It is neither judgemental nor critical and, for the moment, there are no prizes or penalties. It can usefully be aligned to the national curriculum against PHSE, citizenship and parenting education. Where Checkpoints succeeds, the satisfaction and the credit go entirely to the school community itself. Nevertheless, an evaluation of its effectiveness being conducted jointly by the Roehampton University of Surrey and the City of Birmingham LEA will provide validated data on its effectiveness as an intervention strategy.

The companion to *Checkpoints for Schools* (Varnava 2000), entitled *Checkpoints for Young People* (Varnava 2002), is being given to pupils in Year 6 as part of their preparation for transfer and, in some schools, in Year 7 as part of their secondary school induction. It is pocket-size, for use at school, at home and in student councils. The main aim is to employ a two-pronged approach to the problems of violence by providing the stimulus for dialogue between children and adults – to mutual benefit. The booklet is also a device to get the messages of non-violence into the home.

Increasing interest in Checkpoints is encouraging. This is likely to be further stimulated as *Checkpoints for Young People* demonstrates that, although young people are the most vulnerable, violence-prevention cannot be the business only of adults.

Resources

National Children's Bureau, 8 Wakley Street, London EC1V 7QE (Tel 020 7843 6000) www.ncb.org.uk
The Forum on Children and Violence commissioned 'Checkpoints' and is a membership organization based at the National Children's Bureau.

Suggested further reading

Varnava, G. (2002), *How to Stop Bullying in Your School: A guide for teachers*, David Fulton, London
This book provides teachers with a practical intervention programme to prevent bullying in their schools. It identifies common characteristics of schools that have successfully reduced bullying and recognizes the involvement of young people as being a key element in tackling bullying.

References

Finch, S. (2000), *Towards a Non-violent Society: Checkpoints for early years*, National Children's Bureau, London
A slim publication designed for early years educators. It aims to raise awareness, to help nurseries and pre-schools add a violence-prevention perspective to all aspects of their work, and to evaluate their progress.

Varnava, G. (2000), *Towards a Non-violent Society: Checkpoints for schools*, National Children's Bureau, London
This publication is designed to promote non-violence in schools. It is an auditing tool to raise awareness and to establish a commitment to a strategy for violence-prevention.

Varnava, G. (2002), *Towards a Non-violent Society: Checkpoints for young people*, National Children's Bureau, London
This publication is intended for young people moving from primary to secondary school.

5 Reflection and contemplation

– developing inner strength, self-belief and understanding

Within you there is a stillness and sanctuary to which you can retreat at any time and be yourself.

Hermann Hesse

One of the most valuable things we can do to heal one another is to listen to each other's stories.

Rebecca Falls

Tai chi in the playground before the school day starts

Anne D'Souza

Tai chi is an ancient Chinese martial art and system of self-development that uses sequences of slow, graceful movements and breathing to relax the mind and body. Through posture training and exercising all parts of the body, tai chi improves physical and mental health.

Using tai chi exercises, children can enjoy exploring the movement potential of concepts such as large and small, and loud and quiet. Tai chi movements can give children an inner stability, which can help them to grow up with the changes that form part of their everyday experience.

Anne D'Souza briefly describes how she has introduced this ancient Eastern practice into her primary school teaching.

I started teaching at Broad Town School in 2000. During my first term of teaching, my father suggested that I introduce tai chi as a form of morning exercise. I was dubious and did not think such a choice of activity would engage much interest in a rural village environment. However, I was mistaken. The temporary head at the time gave me the all clear; morning exercises began and continued through to the following academic year.

Before registration, the whole school assembled in the playground. The children formed lines standing opposite me, from Year 6 at the back to Reception at the front. Members of staff and parents stood outside the lines of children.

The exercises started with our hands relaxed by our sides and then the children copied my movements, co-ordinating every aspect of their bodies in completing one action at a time, which was to be slow and soft. They had to listen very carefully to my instructions as to when they should breathe in and out.

An example of an action is one called 'Dancing like the Rainbow'. The children would raise their hands, with palms facing down, first in front of their chests and then up to their heads, at the same time slowly straightening their knees and breathing in. This is only a part of the whole action, but needless to say the children grasped these multiple movements quite quickly. Eventually, some children became competent enough to teach and assist their older or younger friends.

Tai chi became part of the regular school day and benefited the school by allowing everybody to join in, calming the children down in readiness for their work, as well as helping to instil a sense of community spirit.

One child's parent said, 'He loves it. He knows all the moves and he is teaching them to his granny. I have been trying it, too – it gets oxygen to your brain in the morning and wakes you up.'

Children practise their tai chi before lessons

Comments from some of the children also reflected enthusiasm:

It's quite easy and it's really good for us. It makes us feel all relaxed.

It calms us all down and it's a lot of fun. I really look forward to it.

It is good fun, and it makes your hands feel tingly, but it makes you do your work better.

Suggested further reading

McFarlane, S. (1999), *The Complete Book of Tai Chi*, Dorling Kindersley, London
A detailed practical guide to the techniques of this ancient martial art. Illustrated with full colour, step-by-step photographs.

Olson, S. A. (2001), *Tai Chi for Kids: Move with the animals*, Bear and Company, Santa Fe, New Mexico
This book introduces children to tai chi in a novel and enjoyable way as all the moves are related to the movements of animals (for example, a swooping bird and a playful monkey). Clear step-by-step instructions and illustrations ensure that the moves are easy to follow.

Parry, R. (1997), *The Tai Chi Manual: A step-by-step guide to the short yang form*, Piatkus, London
Written for adults, this book contains over 250 colour photographs illustrating various movements.

Meditation for young people from the age of ten

Laura Hyde

St James Independent School for Senior Girls in west London has at its cornerstone philosophy and meditation. The latter is practised daily on a voluntary basis. Laura Hyde, headteacher of the school, describes the benefits of meditation and how its initiation and teaching is a very special and traditional event within the school.

The practice of meditation is a way of focusing, being quiet and still. The benefits for pupils include the ability to focus attention, inner strength and purpose, courage, sensitivity to words, and an understanding of themselves and all their relationships. This contribution includes children's own descriptions of how meditation has helped them.

The St James philosophy and practice

The St James philosophy is very simple. It proceeds on the basis that the essence of every human being is perfect, pure and complete consciousness, which shines through the heart. This is the reflection of God's divinity, described as that 'true light which lighteth every man that cometh into the world' (St John 1:9). This divine essence is the very self of the person and is the same in all creatures. This unity of spirit is love made manifest, God made manifest through form. Around this perfection, which is not subject to change, play the causes and effects of human nature that manifest through the mind, heart and body of the person during the course of life. The 'play' involves good and bad, right and wrong, desire and aversion, pleasure and pain, and the laws that proceed from these pairs of opposites. The ultimate purpose of life is to come to fully appreciate the divinity of one's self and the self of all creatures. Alongside this, the proper function of the human birth needs to be fulfilled; according to the potentialities in nature, each individual needs to find her way to use her talents to enhance the general good.

The job of the parent or teacher is to lend a helping hand, so far as it is needed, to guide the person on the way towards this understanding and fulfilment. Parent and teacher have to discover how that particular individual needs to travel on her journey and respect the route she must take. It is absolutely essential to the well-being of the young person that the teacher or parent remains firm in the knowledge of the true essence of the person they are caring for, while dealing lovingly and reasonably with all that nature presents. Clear boundaries of discipline are necessary to healthy upbringing, but there need never be violence nor hatred in any of its forms. The guardian must keep his or her attention on all that is best in the child in order to allow it to be fully manifested in the course of time. Trust between pupil and teacher, parent and child, should never be broken.

The young person needs to be provided with a strong foundation from which to start her journey of adult responsibility. She needs to be given a rich education spiritually, academically and creatively so that she becomes strong – emotionally, mentally and physically. Emotional well-being is akin to spiritual well-being. The human being could be described as a spiritual being undergoing a human experience. Young people need to be introduced to this well-being. Firstly, they need to have been introduced to clear moral principles so that they can, to a greater extent, live by them and thus enjoy a certain level of happiness. Immoral or amoral conduct causes emotional pain. Secondly, they could be introduced to a simple practice of enjoying brief interludes of stillness between activities. At St James we call this 'a pause' between activities and it is introduced to the youngest children from the age of four.

'THE PAUSE'

The purpose of the pause is to allow freedom from the accumulation of agitation. Anxiety, elation, distress or simple over-excitement may cause agitation. In any case, agitation acts as an impediment to the clear and free state of attention upon which the efficiency of any action entirely depends. So, in simple terms, well-being and success in any activity depend upon attention. The opposite is also true, and all educationists recognize only too well that a fractured or dissipated state of attention is a fundamental cause of poor comprehension, communication or retention of information. Only too often, children enter school in the morning carrying the burden or pain of emotional distress from the home. A practice that offers the mind and heart the opportunity to drink of the balm of peace is extremely restorative and comforting.

At St James we engage in a regular practice of offering a couple of minutes' pause between the end of one lesson and the start of the next. The pupils are asked to sit upright and balanced in their chairs. This disciplined posture, in which the spine is straight and the body evenly balanced on the chair, is important. It is the first step in the physical world to allowing the release of tensions and achieving a state of balance. The children are asked to close their eyes. This reduces physical distractions and causes of agitation; eyes are particularly active sense organs and tend to 'run' after their objects – form and colour. Mental quietude is encouraged by letting the attention concentrate on the sense of listening and expanding that listening to the furthest sounds. Beyond the furthest sounds there is a great quiet that embraces all sound. The children are encouraged to rest in this quiet and to allow all impressions of the past activity and anticipations of the future activity to be let go.

In this peace, the children are asked to offer the action that is to come to the service of God, or to the service of all. The depth of sincerity or lack of it with which this offering takes place is not something over which any external agent can have any control. However, at the very least, it engenders a spirit of generosity in which the action is offered rather than undertaken for selfish purposes alone. The capacity to attend to any task is a very great attribute and the practice of the pause strengthens it. The ability to direct the attention or to choose where it is to go and where it is not to go is a great freedom indeed. The significance of this is great, in relation to the activities of the mind and what is attended to there, as well as to the force of any particular emotion, and what is permitted to receive the support of one's attention and what is not. Spiritually, this is tantamount to realizing that we have a real choice as to what we subject our minds and hearts to and therefore whether we experience the bondage of emotional pain, mental distress, anxiety, fear, or a simple state of freedom. The practice of meditation is most relevant in this respect.

MEDITATION

Like many words, the word 'meditation' is understood variously. To some, it means contemplation, to others it means prayer, consideration or thought. There are also many methods or systems of meditation. Therefore it is necessary to state which of these possibilities we mean here. Meditation is essentially understood to be a practice of concentration of mind, of attention. The question then arises, 'on what?' Again, people meditate or concentrate on all kinds of objects; some concentrate on physical forms, some on mental images, some on physical sounds and some on mental sounds. Obviously what then takes place depends very much on what is being concentrated upon. In this case, we offer a traditional method of mantra meditation, which has been made available to us in the West from the ancient spiritual tradition of the East. A mantra is simply a special combination of extremely simple sounds that, when concentrated upon in the mind, is designed to bring about a state of inner quietude, a cessation of all mental or emotional movements. This reveals a deep and extensive peace that finds its origin in pure being. This enjoyment of pure being is a state of unlimited happiness. The mantra does not have any particular religious connotation; one of its important attributes is just this, that it is good for anyone, regardless of their religious conviction or spiritual leanings. This was the intention of the tradition that formulated it.

Meditation is the practice of withdrawing the attention from other objects of attraction and letting it remain with the sound of the mantra. The tendency of the mind to be very active and present all sorts of images of one kind or another is natural, but in meditation these are abandoned through the practice of simple concentration. This regular placing of the attention strengthens the capacity in the young person to direct where her attention goes. For many, there is little cognition of where the attention is at all.

Stilling the mind

The practice of stillness and meditation teaches one to realize that, as the conscious being, one is witnessing all that comes into view in the mind and heart. As such, 'I' am not involved with whatever is presented there, however attractive or repulsive, pleasurable or painful. Furthermore, as described above, 'I' am therefore free from what takes place in the domain of mind and emotions, because 'I' am clearly witnessing them. This is liberating wisdom and of enormous spiritual significance. As a young person of 15 years of age, when I chose to learn to meditate, this knowledge was immediate and awe-inspiring. Having experienced the customary 'slings and arrows' of adolescence, this was a revelation, and the light of its wisdom has never gone out.

On the whole, young people between the ages of 10 and 16 do not experience a strong spiritual hunger in the way in which some adults do. The world of creative activity, play and work is a young person's spiritual world; it is their natural field of satisfaction. Nature tends not to initiate any extra yearning or dissatisfaction. Nevertheless, children of this age group are very interested in the benefits of meditation and also attracted to the possibility of finding peace.

The tradition from which the mantra method of meditation comes advises that children should be ten years of age and above before being offered meditation. There is great wisdom in this. The child

of ten enters a new stage of development. There is an expansion of interest in the world and, with this increased awareness, the child finds that her perceptions deliver a more powerful impact, mentally and emotionally. This opens the doors to a variety of changes and disturbances in her condition. In addition, the mental and emotional worlds begin to experience a greater level of energy; there is more movement. A child of this age often wonders why her mind is moving away from the present moment; mental agitation and the tendency to daydream are new experiences. Some children are disconcerted by this new phenomenon and need guidance on how to learn to keep their attention where it needs to be.

The regular practice of meditation is a wonderful aid in this matter. Most young people are very desirous of being successful in their activities, regard a state of steadiness rather than emotional turbulence as something to be sought after and would like to think it possible to have access to undisturbed happiness within themselves. These great benefits of meditation are certainly attractive to the young. Younger children recognize the advantage in being able to sit still, free of physical agitation. They also recognize that the ability to sustain and direct the attention enhances their chances of success in their studies and activities; and adolescents yearn for emotional equilibrium. We all know only too well that the degree of emotional distress experienced by many of our young people is growing daily and, particularly in these pressing circumstances, the healing power of meditation has a very significant role to play. It falls to those responsible for guiding the young people's practice of mediation to discover how to inspire them and how to open up the vast potential that the practice offers, so that it becomes a part of personal experience.

After the age of 16, the child becomes a young adult and begins to assume responsibility for her worldly and spiritual welfare. This beckons a more mature relationship to the practice of meditation and, for some, a spiritual search may begin to open up.

HOW IS THE METHOD OF MEDITATION PASSED ON?

The method of meditation is passed on through the School of Meditation in London. St James Schools have links with the School of Meditation in so far as it introduces meditation to those children who express a desire to practise it. Thereafter, some guidance for the children's meditation is provided during their years at school through a 'tutorial' offered to each child, once a term. These tutorials take place within the school day, at school. The 'tutors' are not teachers but women who have been meditating for a number of years, are mature in its practice and, most importantly, love to meditate. Some of them are past pupils of St James and, of course, this works particularly well because they can remember all the stages through which the children tend to travel in their experience of meditation. The need for meditation to be properly introduced and subsequently cared for by really experienced people cannot be overstated.

OFFERING MEDITATION TO TEN YEAR OLDS
Firstly, one ensures that the offer of meditation is described to the children on the same day as it is explained to the parents, so that there are no misunderstandings. As headteacher, I handle this myself and hold a parents' meeting on the evening of the day meditation has been introduced to the children. Both parties seem to respond very enthusiastically and most children opt to meditate; invariably, they come from a cross-section of cultures and religions. It has often been the case that after the parents' meeting one or two people ask to be introduced to the practice themselves. It is rather nice when parent and child decide to do so at the same time. I am always pleasantly surprised at how keen parents are for their children to meditate. When one describes the potential benefits of the practice the common response is, 'I think this is just what my child needs!'

There is one very important principle to observe in all of this. The decision to meditate is a personal one and must never be subject to compulsion of any kind. However enthusiastic a parent might be for their child to meditate, if the child is not keen, she should not be coerced. In addition, it is important that the decision to meditate is taken seriously as far as the child is concerned; it should not be regarded as a passing 'fad' or hobby, like roller-blading, which is picked up with zest one week and dropped the next. Children should have it explained that meditation is very special; it is a universal activity that, in varying ways, humanity has engaged in throughout history, and in choosing to learn to meditate you enter an ancient tradition that is available to you for life. Children and parents often ask, 'What happens if, after time, she stops enjoying meditation and wants to give it up?' The answer has to be that no one can compel someone to meditate. However, every encouragement and guidance should be given to help people over arid or difficult periods with the practice, if they occur. Certainly, as young people develop we all know that they go

through huge changes in a relatively short time. It is preferable to take the attitude that one keeps going; conditions fluctuate greatly throughout these years of development.

Often, as parents or guardians, we can see the beneficial effects of meditation on our children very clearly, even if these benefits are not so obvious to the children themselves. Nevertheless, after the age of 16, the condition of a young person who has been meditating in her earlier years is very different from that of a child who has never meditated. There is a sense of a depth of being, an inner quietude that is accompanied by the obvious availability of a steady power of attention.

In general, there is a very important principle to observe in guiding young people's meditation. They should feel that meditation is their responsibility. They should also be encouraged to assume responsibility for the 'progress' of the practice. It is a process of discovery that depends upon their own interest, initiative and sense of purpose.

Finally, if a family has already received a method of meditation through their own 'guru' or if a child already has a mantra, she should not take on another method of meditation. One is enough.

WHEN AND FOR HOW LONG SHOULD CHILDREN MEDITATE?
Meditation is a special gift available to the individual to use as fully as she or he is able. All that is required is the simple discipline of sitting on a chair with a straight spine and attending to the mantra twice a day, once in the early morning and again at the onset of the evening. Dawn and dusk are particularly propitious times to meditate because there is a gentle quiet throughout nature at these times. Obviously, it is not always possible to meditate at these times. Children's lives are always packed full of activities, in and out of school. To help them find the space to meditate we offer a short period at the beginning and end of every school day. Those who do not meditate use this same period for quiet reflection or scripture study of their choice. There is a simple rule for everyone that no individual should interfere with another person's freedom to meditate.

It is not easy for children to turn their attention away from the thrust of outward activity and to withdraw their sense organs from the variety of experience that they offer. Five minutes is all one would require of ten year olds, increasing gradually to ten minutes for 11 year olds and so on to 15 to 20 minutes for older children. Experience should guide this. Although meditation is 'timetabled' into the school day, it is important that children realize that this is for their convenience only. It is very easy for them to assume that meditation is something that belongs to 'school' and we do it there. Emphasis should be made on the prerogative of the individual who has availed herself of the tradition of meditation – 'it is yours to use wherever and whenever you like, especially at home.'

As far as location is concerned, it is best if the room in which one meditates is quiet. External noises are unhelpful. If possible, it is good to provide plenty of physical space and, if many people are meditating in one room, they should not be sitting too close to each other. Ideally, one should meditate alone or with one's family members, if desired.

WHAT CHILDREN SAY ABOUT MEDITATION PRACTICE

Meditation, for me, is a good way to start and end the day. It gives me the opportunity to draw my energy together so as to start the day fresh, and at the end of the day, let go of all the hassles of the day. I have found that meditation has been a thread running through my life, and a comfort during difficult times.

Lucy (age 16)

I find meditation clears the mind. It settles and calms you, and in some circumstances comforts you. I use meditation when I am sick or feeling lonely, because it helps to know that there is someone there. At the beginning of a day or event and at the end, it helps you focus throughout the day. I also use it to settle my nerves before an exam or test. My introduction to meditation was a wonderful experience, and I feel it has made me see the world in a different way.

Laura (age 11)

Meditation is always there as a simple route back to stillness, allowing agitation or stress to fall away. Even when there's no specific need, it keeps you calm and alert without you realizing its benefit.

Alix (age 15)

Meditation is good in that it helps you come to rest at the end of a long day. It is useful to have just a moment of stillness after all the activity. Saying the mantra gives you time to get away from the thoughts that are filling your mind, even if only for a while, it still helps. Meditation gives you both physical and mental rest and has a calming effect.

Alice (age 15)

I find meditation very good when I'm angry or annoyed. It helps me calm down. It isn't always easy to meditate, but it really does help and I'm glad I was introduced to it.

It really helps me to start and end the day at school. In the morning we meditate, and it's like I've started my day, I've got plenty to be done, and then at the end of the day we meditate again, and that's like I've done everything, it's the end now, time to go home. So our meditations are real signs through the day.

Also, a lot of the time at school I'm walking to different classes, talking, getting out books and, of course, working. So it's nice to have a few minutes of stillness before and after all this.

So, all in all, I get a lot out of meditation, and I give it all I can.

Charlotte (age 11)

Resources

The Right from the Start book *Stillness, Imagination and Meditation for Children* (in preparation) provides a further range of ideas and information.

Appendix 3 contains a list of classical and contemporary music for peaceful activities, imagination and meditation.

School of Meditation, 158 Holland Park Avenue, London W11 4UH (Tel 020 7603 6116)
www.schoolofmeditation.org

Suggested further reading

The following four texts focus on guided imagery and fantasy work in schools.

Beesley, M. (1990), *Stilling: A pathway for spiritual learning in the national curriculum*, Salisbury Diocesan Board of Education, Salisbury
This booklet contains sample scripts for guided imagery and guided fantasy.

Hall, E., Hall, C. and Leech, A. (1990), *Scripted Fantasy in the Classroom*, Routledge, London
A step-by-step practical guide for teachers interested in introducing imagery and fantasy work in schools. It contains over 50 sample scripts for use in the classroom.

Viegas, M. (2004), *Relax Kids: Aladdin's Magic Carpet and other fairytale meditations for children*, O Books, Winchester
An inspiring book in which the author has transformed traditional well-loved fairy stories into simple visualizations. See also the Relax Kids website (www.relaxkids.com).

Weatherhead, Y. (2004), *Enriching Circle Time: Dream journeys and positive thoughts*, Lucky Duck, Bristol
This resource (book and CD-ROM) provides 20 positive thought scripts and eight dream journeys with teacher notes on how to prepare children for these powerful visualization techniques and ideas for follow-up work.

A Quiet Place

Penelope Moon

A Quiet Place is a specialized 'within schools' programme of therapeutic care that was set up to address the needs of children in danger of exclusion from school, as well as to prevent the development of socially unacceptable behaviour and later mental health problems. It is a very specific programme, characterized by the supervised practice of therapists trained to a professional level through nationally recognized training programmes. Each school sets aside a room that is used to run a holistic programme offering counselling, massage, therapeutic play, story-telling, and art and music workshops.

The child smiled up from the chair, eyes luminous in the softly lit room. She was tiny and undernourished, blonde hair tied back harshly, but her smile warmed you deep inside. The chair, a big relaxer, seemed somehow to enfold her safe at last. She was playing quietly with some fuzzy felts, her feet contained in the hands of the reflexologist. Quiet music played in the background to the accompaniment of the water fountain. The room was filled by a lovely fragrance and was an Aladdin's cave of treasure to delight children of all ages.

'Hello, do you mind if I come in and look at Quiet Place?'
'No, come in,' she replied.
'What is happening to you?' I asked.
'I am having my feet massaged,' she said. 'It's lovely.'
'I can see, you lucky girl. I wish it was me. What else happens here?'
'Well, Kathy lets me take a smelly tissue back to class and I have got one for my friend and the teacher, too. Oh, yes, and one for my mum.'
'And what is that?' I asked.
'Kathy lets me choose a smell from her box and put the oil in the foot spa. Then I can have the same oil to take with me in case I feel sad in the day, and it will make me feel like I am back in the Quiet Place again, happy.'

'Ah, I see. And what are the rest of the things in here for? I can see that Kathy has finished now, so would you mind showing me around?'
She put on her shoes and socks, still smiling and relaxed, and took my hand innocently.
'This is where I can go and hide and listen to one of the stories.'
She took me into a tent made of many colours and filled with soft cushions, sparkling lights and soft toys.
'Mmm,' I thought, 'I could just stay here myself.'
She invited me to sit down and showed me some of her favourite books, all full of spirit and hope and fun. Then we came out of the tent and went to the musical instruments; a huge gong hung on a beautiful carved wooden hanger.
'What is that?' I asked.
'I can only bang the gong on the way out.'
She looked up shyly at Kathy, who nodded permission.
'But I can show you now if you like.'
'Yes, please.'
She picked up a blue, padded hammer and, shockingly for one so fragile, gave it an almighty thwack. The whole room vibrated with a beautiful but hardly quiet sound.
'Wow,' I said, for there was nothing else to be said.

A Quiet Place – a calming influence

She laughed mischievously at my surprise and took my hand to show me the other instruments: lovely sounding bells, a rain stick, ocean drums and wooden xylophones. 'What do you use these for?' I asked.

'Well, I see Fran as well as Kathy and if I am feeling a bit too sad to talk, Fran talks with me through the drums and we have musical conversations. I usually feel better then and perhaps do a drawing or play with the sand or the clay.'

'But come and look at these, this is my favourite toy, she is a mummy polar bear with her baby.' She picked them up and started to play without any self-consciousness. Mummy bear speaking to baby bear, having a little tea party and being tucked up in bed. Little things that go on in most children's lives as the norm, but not with this little one.

'What is that?' I asked.

'It's a trampoline which Fran lets me jump on when I come in. It helps me keep fit.'

Keep fit, I thought. This fragile girl?

'Yes, I go to ballet.' She smiled up at Kathy, who nodded for her to continue.

'I was on stage yesterday and everybody clapped.' She looked down shyly. 'I have asthma and cannot always do my practice and so Fran and Kathy have helped me to do this show.'

I raised my eyebrows. 'Tell me more.'

Kathy said, 'When N first came she was very shy and often felt unwell. Her little brother comes as well and he used to be a bit grumpy with you N, didn't he.'

'Yes, he used to kick and punch me very hard all the time but now he has stopped and we are good friends. I don't seem to be so sick all the time and have been able to practise and won my prize and that is what I wanted to do when Fran first asked me.'

'Yes,' said Kathy, 'N is on her second six-week programme because we are making good progress and wanted to support her through this show, and there we are. Now it is time to go back to class, N.'

'Thank you for showing me around.'

She smiled sweetly and, taking Kathy's hand, went happily back to class. I picked up her case notes, for I already knew of her case through giving supervision to Fran.

I stood in the room enjoying the atmosphere, the sense of stillness and peace I had hoped would be here when the idea first came to me: to be able to share this peace with others who did not want to sit and meditate, whose lives were noisy and chaotic simply because that is how they were, with no privacy just to think and be still. Then there are those whose circumstances are more nightmarish, living with trauma and violence, who need to learn how to trust an adult again, to touch and be touched with care and nurture, to be listened to and respected. To feel love and experience compassion for others – that is what a Quiet Place is all about. It encompasses the whole family, because we are not islands floating in the ocean unattached to our families, environment, communities and society. Each of us is a unique flower blooming in the soil of our genetics and nurtured by our experiences. Because of the connections rippling between body and mind, these experiences inform our behaviour – affecting the immune system and the body's ability to fight infections, and therefore our ability to respond and learn to the best of our potential.

The creation of a Quiet Place is based on this premise that experience and behaviour are connected. It has various criteria that roll out into the unique form of a school or whatever environment within which it exists.

I spoke to one of the teachers who had sent a number of children through the programme and made good use of it herself. This woman, whom I knew to be one of the best and most dedicated teachers I had come across, had been having her own family problems. So difficult had things become at home with health problems that she had taken time off for stress-related illness. We had been able to offer her aromatherapy and psychotherapy, which had maintained her in school with her 11 year olds at a crucial transitional phase for the last half term of the year. For her self-esteem this had been a wonderful achievement; for the children, the least disruption to their learning; and for the school, hundreds of pounds of supply cover costs have been saved.

A Quiet Place aims to:

- provide children with a beautiful and peaceful space where someone will listen to them in moments of crisis and stress;

- help children to benefit from education by assisting in the removal of blocks resulting from stress;

- assist in the process of preventing the build-up of mental health problems by addressing issues at an early stage;

- deliver effective interventions via the holistic and creative use of innovative person-centred approaches;

- provide therapeutic support to children and their families within the host school;

- provide training and support for the staff of that school;

- provide innovative and targeted interventions that support the child to remain in mainstream provision.

Resources

The Cheiron Trust – A Quiet Place, University of Liverpool, Room 303, 19 Abercromby Square, Liverpool L69 7ZG (Tel 0151 794 2431); www.cheiron-quietplace.com
The Cheiron Trust provides consultancy and training in a variety of settings. The trust's approach is both holistic and innovative and aims to develop the full potential of individuals within the context of their environment.

Suggested further reading

Moon, P. (2001), A Quiet Place, *Positive Health,* April 2001, pages 9–11
Penelope Moon, founder member of Cheiron – A Quiet Place, provides her own account of the setting up of the Quiet Place project.

Spalding, B. (2000), The contribution of a 'Quiet Place' to early intervention strategies for children with emotional and behavioural difficulties, *British Journal of Special Education,* 27 (3), pages 129–134
This article outlines the nature of this holistically oriented therapeutic intervention. It includes an evaluation of the first cohort of children to complete the programme, which is analysed in comparison with a control group. Key factors in the success of the provision are identified.

Spalding, B. (2001), A Quiet Place: A healing environment, *Support for Learning,* 16 (2), pages 69–73
Bob Spalding describes the practical detail involved in establishing a Quiet Place in schools. His article also draws attention to the benefits of a Quiet Place to the whole school and also for parents.

Quiet Place:
a school's experience

Phil Doyle

Phil Doyle, headteacher of St Margaret Mary's Catholic Junior School in Liverpool, describes how a Quiet Place was introduced into his school. There are many Quiet Places in Liverpool and others are developing all over the country, with interest overseas.

Background – November 2000

Our Chair of Governors, Reverend Father Gerry Proctor, heard a programme on Radio Merseyside talking about a Quiet Place at Hope Valley School in Everton, Liverpool. He was really enthusiastic about the project and we decided to visit.

At Hope Valley we met Penny Moon, one of the founder members of the Cheiron Trust that provides consultancy and training for the setting up of Quiet Places, and we could see the potential for good in our school. I came back to the school and told the senior management team about what we had seen, and we decided to pursue the idea. I also invited Penny Moon to come and explain the philosophy to all the staff. At all times there was only ever a positive response.

Finance

The main difficulty was finding the money for the project. Father Gerry wrote to several Catholic trusts and received responses totalling approximately £9,000 – we were on our way. Penny Moon brought out some representatives from the Tudor Trust (see Resources on page 136). They must have been impressed because they gave the Cheiron Project £60,000 and we received £30,000. We now had the opportunity to establish the room, employ a therapist and a body worker, and we had enough money for 12 months.

Quiet Place room

For some reason we settled on a rainforest theme. Penny Moon arranged a designer, we provided the artist, one of our parents, Ronnie Smith, whose day job was at the fruit market. Ronnie did a magnificent job. Pat Charnock was appointed as our administrator/therapist and set about furnishing the room. We received donations from parents and spent quite a lot at IKEA.

Parents

At every opportunity, we asked parents to come and see what we had created, Open Evening was very successful, and we also used our weekly newsletter to publicize the initiative.

Staff and governors

As I have already said, staff were very supportive (I think the idea of the chance of a lunchtime massage was an attraction). We appointed a member of staff to oversee Quiet Place and she gave governors a presentation on the room, which they were able to visit.

Getting started

We asked staff to nominate children who exhibited introvert/extrovert behaviour. In a school of over 500 children it did not take too long to identify 12 pupils to begin working with on a one-to-one basis. On 6 June 2001 we held an official opening with Peter Kilfoyle MP (an ex-pupil) and the actor Michael Starke, who made his name on the television programme *Brookside*.

Response

The following responses of children and adults to their experiences of Quiet Place indicate its beneficial impact:

Quiet Place is the best thing that happened to me.

Year 4 pupil

An oasis of peace and calm for the community, in a world of stress and pressure.

Father Gerry Proctor, Parish Priest and Chair of Governors

Quiet Place is an amazing, exciting initiative that had a dramatic effect on our school.

Phil Doyle, headteacher

My child's experience in Quiet Place helped me as she was able to teach me how to relax.

Parent

A Quiet Place room is designed to promote a sense of peace and relaxation and is serviced by a number of therapists. Each room has its own theme (for example, fairy-tale castle, dolphin cave, rainforest) to foster creative imagination.

The following are important features of the room:

- **Lighting** – This is soft and masked to enhance the feeling of mystery or wonder. Dim areas within the room allow the child to retreat and find comfort.

- **Colours** – Mostly pastel shades are used, which are soft and relaxing. These colours enhance the overall feeling of stillness. A magical effect is created through the use of fairy lights.

- **Kinesthetics** – Soft furnishings help to counteract the child's experience of harshness in the outside world. Opportunities exist for physical activities to let off steam.

- **Auditory effects** – The room is quiet with a prevailing 'sound of stillness'. Background music is sometimes used (for example, works by Mozart) and water features provide subtle background sounds.

- **Aromatherapy and massage** – Essential oils are used for their calming and uplifting effect and children receive the benefits of therapeutic touch.

Resources

The Cheiron Trust – A Quiet Place, University of Liverpool, Room 303, 19 Abercromby Square, Liverpool L69 7ZG (Tel 0151 794 2431); www.cheiron-quietplace.com
The Cheiron Trust provides consultancy and training in a variety of settings. The trust's approach is both holistic and innovative and aims to develop the full potential of individuals within the context of their environment.

The Tudor Trust, 7 Ladbroke Grove, London W11 3BD (Tel 020 7727 8522); www.tudortrust.org.uk
Tudor is an independent grant-making charitable trust. They focus their grants on projects in England, Scotland, Wales and Northern Ireland, particularly where there is significant deprivation in urban, rural and coastal areas. Promoting people's well-being and enabling them to make positive choices about their future is central to the trust's current work.

Suggested further reading

Spalding, B. (2001), A Quiet Place: A healing environment, *Support for Learning*, 16 (2), pages 69–73
Bob Spalding describes the practical detail involved in establishing a Quiet Place in schools. His article also draws attention to the benefits of a Quiet Place to the whole school and also to parents.

Tell me a story

Martyn Rawson

In this contribution, Martyn Rawson examines the important role story-telling has in children's development. Through telling and listening to stories children are able, for example, to form bonds, resolve difficulties and share experiences with each other. Story-telling provides children with a way of dealing with fear, crisis and uncertainty. Furthermore, stories also help children to construct their identities.

Martyn Rawson identifies particular phases of story-telling, such as the use of stories as speech acts for pre-school children engaged in play. Suggestions are given on how teachers can successfully foster narrative development.

The meaning of the story

It was Gordon Wells, in his seminal book *The Meaning Makers* (Wells 1987), who identified the importance of story-telling not only for language but also for cognitive development. Based on the now famous Bristol study 'Language at Home and at School', a longitudinal study of children from the earliest acquisition of language through until they left primary school, Wells' research highlighted the importance of stories as a preparation for literacy.

Stories, he concluded, were better than other methods for several reasons. Firstly, in listening to stories children can 'gain an experience of the sustained meaning-building organization of written language and its characteristic rhythms and structures' (Wells 1987, pages 152–153). Secondly, stories extend the range of the child's experience beyond his or her actual life circumstances. Thirdly, stories provide an excellent opportunity for the kind of collaborative talk between adult and child that helps children to understand the world, and also stimulate the child's inner dialogues with itself, which form a key stage in the development of independent thinking.

What Wells said concerning written stories also goes for oral stories that are either told from memory or made up spontaneously. The difference, I feel, is that the child's perception of the thought processes involved in telling, rather than reading, a story are more direct. Of course, the story written in a book may have a far more consciously structured form, it may even have high intrinsic artistic merit, but the thought processes involved are at one stage, at least, removed. Unprepared reading may even cloud the inherent literary structure through wrong emphasis on sentence structure. At a more advanced stage of literacy children will be able to re-create the vivid pictures of the story by reading on their own. In the young child, then, the perception of the story-telling activity is a complex one involving the observation of gesture, facial expression, hearing and recognizing words, and the perception of an individual's thought and imaginative processes at work. All these elements are inseparable from the content of the story itself.

At an early stage, perhaps stories should also be told from memory. Parents have no doubt also noticed how with very young children the telling of even the most mundane of stories, in effect merely recounting the events of the day, will be listened to with rapt attention. The reason for this is perhaps the intense interest the child has in how the adult organizes sequential events in narrative form. The child's naive and unreflected attention may perceive cognitive processes in what the adult says from which the child can learn – through assimilation and imitation –

perceptions to which older children or adults need no longer pay any attention.

It is the symbolic value of language that the child has to learn in order to be able eventually to grasp the abstraction of reading and writing the letters of the alphabet, comprehending the qualities symbolized by numbers and so on throughout the curriculum. Meaning is communicated by context on the one hand and by imitation on the other. If something has meaning for an adult, the child will adopt the assumption that the word or symbol in question is meaningful. A story gives both context and is imbued with personal meaning by the teller. Thus, hearing stories enables the young child to grasp the symbolic value of language before having to cope with the added abstraction of writing.

Understanding through narrative helps children organize their experiences, describe events and follow instructions. Most importantly, children who have become used to hearing and expressing themselves in narrative form can more easily understand adults' language, particularly when they talk about things not present in the room and perhaps quite outside the children's life experience, which is what teachers tend increasingly to do in talking about other lands, other times and other peoples (Wells 1987, page 157).

In order to direct their own thought processes, children must be able to use symbols and relate them to their own direct experience. As Gordon Wells (1987, page 194) put it:

> Stories have a role in education that goes far beyond their contribution to the acquisition of literacy. Constructing stories in the mind – or storying, as it has been called – is one of the most fundamental means of making meaning; as such, it is an activity that pervades all aspects of learning.

Story-telling is probably as old as human culture and certainly as old as language in the form we know it today. The heritage of each culture, including the sum of its knowledge about the world, its technical achievements as well as its world view, has traditionally been preserved in its oral story traditions. To a large extent cultures define themselves through the sacred stories they tell in ritual circumstances. A fine example of this are the Songlines of the Aborigines, which relate the narrative biography of the landscape and its relationship to the 'People'.

Literate cultures have incorporated their most important values in sacred texts that are read from at significant moments in the calendar of the annual cycle. Most of such texts are in narrative form, describing the journey of the soul, as in the Egyptian or Tibetan Books of the Dead, or recording the history of the 'People', their heroes and kings.

Modern cultures continue to record what society deems as valuable, using books and now electronic information technology. The basic principles remain the same. Even scientific facts are told in narrative form, otherwise they would be largely incomprehensible. The underlying need for stories has always been essentially the same: to provide a meaningful interpretation of those aspects of human experience deemed to be fundamental and of abiding concern. What is it, then, about narrative that makes it so essential? What makes narrative? What is in a story?

Narrative structure

Jerome Bruner (1990) has characterized narrative as follows:

- Narrative must have sequence.
- Narrative must have a plot, a sequence that conveys meaning.
- Narrative must have a high point, a tension that meets some kind of resolution.
- A narrative may be a narrative whether it is true or not. It is indifferent to facts.
- A narrative distinguishes between the usual and the unusual.
- A narrative directs attention to personal or subjective experience.

Implicit in this characterization is the fact that narrative uses formal, even ritualized forms for describing the world. It also implies a speaker–listener relationship that is dynamic rather than passive. The meaning is enhanced by context – including background information assumed to be known to both story-teller and listener. For that reason, a mere list of events does not constitute a narrative because it has not been constructed with a particular listener in mind, nor has the list been constructed with any particular meaning in mind, other than one of face value. It is often the sequence that imbues the events with a particular meaning, as does what is left out of the account.

According to speech-act theory (Searle 1969), telling stories is a kind of doing, an action that has three components: the story as it is told; what the speaker intended to achieve with the story; and the effect the story has on the listener. This framework enables us to see how story-telling by and for children can involve active social and conceptual interaction. A story can provide the pretext for establishing, clarifying or changing relationships. Stories can help to form bonds, resolve conflicts and share experience as well as provoke, annoy or simply attract attention. What is told can often be quite secondary to how and to whom.

Stories as speech acts are particularly important for pre-school children in play. Narrative structure can provide a basic plot, which enables the children to take roles in a play situation. If they are playing doctors, one child can be the doctor, the other the mother with the sick child ('...and then let's say the mummy goes to the doctor and the little girl says, "I feel really sick", I'll be the little girl and you be the doctor, OK?'). This plot generates sequences of play with dialogue but also includes narrative parts ('...then she gives the mummy some pills and writes in a book').

Young children spend a lot of time and energy in collaborative story-telling in which role-playing is highly varied and complex. Through such stories they not only learn to socially interact, they learn to organize their experience and what they know, and also learn how to communicate that knowledge to others.

We are the stories we tell

Stories not only help children give meaning to their worlds, improve their listening, verbal and literacy skills, they also, as Susan Engel has shown evocatively in her study of children's narrative, help children construct their identities. Children are the stories they tell. Stories not only reconstruct and communicate experience, they are experience. As Engel (1995, page 185) puts it: 'a central reason it is so important to understand all these whats and hows of story-telling is that the stories play a vital role in shaping children's sense of themselves and their presentation of that self to others.' Susan Engel has pointed out that a developmental line runs through the stories children tell, from the simplest, 'I did this...' kind, to the elaborate 'fiction' stories that children of eight or nine years old make up.

Through the stories children tell about themselves in the past or the future ('I'm going to make a sword and chop up that monster...') emerges a sense of extended self, which includes both enduring and transient aspects of their personality. The stories map out a region – the child's inner home base and its surrounding areas – that the child has explored. The details may be imaginary or real. In fact, in young children the imagination may even be more compelling than objective outer reality. The world of 'I want to be' is as important in defining a sense of self as 'this is what I am'. Of course, for an adult to have a sense of self that was largely defined by the imagination could indicate a psychologically risky state of mind. The healthy transformation of this would be a set of ideals one strove to realize. Adults may appropriately define themselves by the ideals and sense of truth they bear within them.

In both children and adults it is the 'I' as core of the individual's being that clothes itself in the garments of the extended self. The 'I' itself remains invisible – in the sense that a person's self becomes visible to us when we get to know them – though we can recognize it through its activity (Engel 1995).

The content of such narratives helps to define and give expression to something of the child's being. What is vitally important to the child is the child's own perception of that being, a perception of self. Children gain this perception in and through their relationships to the world and to other people. 'I went in the shop with Daddy and this big dog was there!' It is essential for the child to tell her story to a listening person who can respond in an affirmative, even participatory way. The story will need to be told several times until the encounter with the big frightening dog has become a shared and assimilated experience. Throughout this whole process the child is able to gain a perception of herself in relation to a specific experience and through the eyes of another person.

STORIES AND DRAWINGS

Just as young children's drawings unconsciously reveal something of the dynamic process of the inner being of the child coming to terms with and mastering the physical organism, so too in a similar way do stories. Children's drawings express the sense of bodily well-being, balance, orientation and co-ordination of the body in space, and this is true whatever a child's professed intentions may be. In this sense, their linear quality expresses the unconscious forces of the will and their use of colour is the soul's response to bodily experience. In a nutshell, one could say that the child's drawing shows to what extent the child feels at home in his or her body.

Stories, however, draw on another realm of the child's whole being, less that of the motor–will activity and more of the linguistic–cognitive part of the soul. Stories express how children understand the circumstances of their lives and relationships. It is, of course, artificial to separate the cognitive from the motor and will side of the child, especially in the young child. The two realms are far more closely integrated at that age. It is the middle, the feeling realm of the soul, that is the source of both drawing and storying. Nevertheless, I suggest that the child's feeling of life responds to the bodily organic sense of being through the expression of movement and drawing, whereas storying and speech generally are more conscious and therefore a reflection of the cognitive pole. What is fascinating is when a child first draws a picture, which is a much more self-contained activity, and then engages a convenient adult to relate the story of it. The educator must use both drawing and storying as diagnostic tools.

COLLABORATIVE LEARNING

It is through the process of narrative construction that children can reflect on themselves in the present, in relation to themselves in the past or future. This involves dialogue and exchange. A child needs to hear, and that often, the adult's own version of events: 'Do you remember we went down the garden and peeped into the little birdy's nest?' Following this, children need to construct the narrative themselves on the basis of the adult's 'scaffolding'. This way, children gain a two-way perspective on themselves in and through the story. In fact, it is usually three-way, since there is an adult's version, the child's version and the collective 'we' in the form of a dialogue, with both parent and child taking turns to recount the event, possibly to a third party.

Many psychologists have used storying with adult patients in therapy to recast the story of their lives. In telling the story from a slightly different perspective, patients can change the way they see themselves or their relationships to others. This points to the fact that when we tell a story about ourselves we become an object that we can relate to, or simply contemplate from another point of view. This gives a certain inner perspective. The way we represent ourselves in stories, and the way stories shape us, varies over the course of development.

Susan Engel has identified five phases in childhood. The first phase involves children gaining an initial sense of self by participating in the stories their parents tell about them. They learn that they can be both subject and object of events in the world. The second phase begins around the age of three, when children have begun to develop sufficient personal memory to describe their own past experiences, though they are still dependent on adults and older siblings. As Engel (1995, page 192) puts it: 'Parents... have become vital partners in describing past experiences to fill out their children's sense of themselves over time.' Parents not only provide support, they influence the process in other important ways.

When children tell stories about their past to and with their parents, not only do the parents' specific contributions help to shape the content of those stories, but their role as audience affects what children put into the story. The child may include details that will please a parent, attract his attention, or provoke him. The child's sense of his listener will end up influencing what goes into the story and how it gets told. Ultimately, that story will contribute to the child's inner sense of self.

The third phase sees children between four and five expanding their circle of conversation partners to include friends of the same age. These kindergarten-age children increasingly learn through feedback from their playmates. Initially, three and four year olds tend to talk to each other while playing, by the age of five they tend to talk more about what they are going to play. Between the ages of six and seven they spend most of their time telling each other about what they like and dislike and exchanging stories, especially common experiences: 'Remember when we made that hideaway...' This helps to form social bonds and strengthens the sense of identity. Not to share in the memory is to challenge a child's sense of personalized past.

The fourth phase Engel describes as the increasing ability to hold different ideas in the mind at the same time and the ability to return again at intervals to certain topics and themes. In earlier phases, the child has been far more bound to present experience and the circumstances of the immediate environment. Engel (1995, page 200) writes:

> Whereas two year olds use stories to understand the social world contained in their immediate family life, children [of] seven, eight and nine years old use collections of stories and ongoing sagas to penetrate the complexities of the expanded world in which they are now active.

The fifth phase sees a dwindling of the act of story-telling. It is less observed in the home or at school. Susan Engel suggests that what is retained is the repertoire of stories/memories that we use to give friends and new acquaintances a certain picture of ourselves. What does seem clear to my observation of adolescents is that the story-telling becomes internalized. Children speak to themselves when they are engaged in some concentrated activity in order to remember the sequences or stages in a complex process that they have not quite mastered, and they later internalize this in the form of thought. A similar situation occurs with the identity reinforcement of story-telling. Speech becomes internalized thought, and story-telling withdraws inner memories, dreams and reflections (to paraphrase the title of C. G. Jung's autobiography). The other outcome of the story-telling development of childhood is, of course, literature. One assumes that Dostoevsky, Dickens, Ben Okri and Kate Atkinson all started off as infant story-tellers. As Ben Okri (1998) puts it in *The Joys of Storytelling*:

> It is in the creation of story, the lifting of story into the realms of art, it is in this that the higher realms of creativity reside.

And:

> It is easy to forget how mysterious and mighty stories are. They do their work in silence, invisible. They work with all the internal materials of the mind and self. They become part of you while changing you. Beware the stories you read or tell: subtly, at night, beneath the waters of consciousness, they are altering your world.

Perhaps the most significant aspect of memory and language development in children is that it benefits from social or interpersonal exchange. It has been long recognized that societies and communities build up their cultural identity by telling and re-telling their common tales. It is the same with children. Through the dialogue of telling and re-telling commonly shared (or imaginative) experiences, parents and young children together not only build up a family identity but the child begins to be able to place herself in an ever-expanding context. Taking turns to tell parts of the story, parent and child re-create all manner of situations from which the child gradually gets a clear picture along the lines of:

> I'm the girl with the Terry shoes who goes to playgroup in the morning and says hello to Helen my playgroup teacher and goodbye to my mummy. And after we have played and made buns and done circle time Mummy comes and gets me and we go in the car to our house. At our house Tabby [the cat] is sleeping on his chair and we have our dinner…

This narrative (which is authentic, though names have been changed to protect the innocent) is constructed out of conversations between child and slightly anxious child about going to playgroup.

What holds true within the family is obviously also true in the community of the classroom. Collaborative story-telling (which may seem more like a conversational exchange between adult and child) is very important not only for children's language development but for their whole social, emotional and psychological development as well. Through story-telling they learn to define who they are in relation to the rest of us. Stories provide young children with the scaffolding to help them to attain the next stage of their development, to proceed from being babies to toddlers, from toddlers to young children and so on.

Furthermore, story-telling provides children with a way of dealing with crisis, fear, anxiety and uncertainty. It enables them to digest and relate to their experiences in a healthy way. It helps them to extend and feel secure in their social environment. It helps them to become whole people.

Stories are the secret reservoir of values: change the stories individuals or nations live by and tell themselves and you change the individuals and nations.

Ben Okri

The phases of story-telling in school-age children

By the age of five children spend as much time talking to each other as they spend playing and often the two activities go hand in hand. The planning of the game may take up the whole time and the carrying out of the plan may have to be put off. By six or seven the children tell each other long stories about what they like and what they do not like. They also greatly enjoy recalling shared experiences, which strengthens their intimacy and this in turn strengthens their sense of self. Stories begin to feel like personal possessions. When an older brother challenges your version of the story this is taken as an affront to your very existence, often with tears and anger. If your version of the story is confirmed, the sense of pride is profound. It is like someone confirming your existence.

That is why daily news time is so important. Children should have the opportunity to sit around together and tell what they think is important, what has happened to them, what they saw, heard, thought or felt. It is important that this is done in an atmosphere of total acceptance. We do not challenge each other's news stories. We may give another version but news is not debated, it is allowed to stand in its own right.

I know school classes in which this has been practised (ten minutes news time) every day over seven or eight years. The preoccupations, topics and style, and the main contributors change over the months and years. But by the age of 13 these children have the most astonishing ability to freely describe even the most intimate experiences in the knowledge that they will be listened to but not judged (at least, not unjustifiably). And this at an age when most 13 year olds become increasingly inarticulate and secretive about their innermost feelings. The power of talk is immense but the situation has to be right and the rules must always be adhered to.

There are many adults who cannot articulate their thoughts and feelings – in other words they cannot share their story with anyone. Instead their emotions bottle up and come out as anger, frustration, depression, self-denial, illusions, an inability to face the truth.

By the time children are six they have a wide repertoire of stories about themselves. This can extend from oral to written versions. By now they have heard all manner of other story-telling genres, told by parents, friends and teachers. They can choose the story-lines, themes and plots that suit them and adopt them in their play (which also means in their inner life). The identifications can be strong. Powerful stories with real archetypes can nourish the inner life of an individual in ways we as adults can barely imagine.

The children will now increasingly seek and respond to stories that reflect the inner developmental challenges they are going through. Thought is obviously individual but there are general themes that appeal to each developmental stage.

Collaborative story-telling tends to dwindle during the school years, which is a shame. There is a phase when children talk to themselves, especially when they are trying to master complex matters. This self-talk often consists of repeating instructions: 'I have to do this, then I do that, then I look out for those…' Gradually, this becomes internalized and we continue these dialogues with ourselves in thought.

The story-telling mode transforms gradually into, on the one hand, the ability to reflect on one's life and relationships and, on the other hand, into creativity, not least into literature itself, the ability to create a story within a range of aesthetic rules we call style.

The desire to hear and read stories, of course, does not fade. In fact, those who have developed an ear for a good story, those who, perhaps unconsciously, recognize the stages of narrative development, will be the most avid readers, those most interested in going to the theatre.

What are these stages of narrative development? In most stories a situation is presented, the main players introduced, something happens, crisis ensues, perhaps followed by more crisis and some kind of ultimate resolution. In classical drama the plot unfolds in the following stages:

Act 1: Exposition: the problem is portrayed

Act 2: Intensification: the main tension, the drama becomes apparent

Act 3: Reversal: something happens to worsen the crisis

Act 4: Retardation: a reflective element delays the resolution

Act 5: Resolution: transformation occurs

Even the simplest parent–child stories have something of this classic structure. It is a universal theme and something that has a deeply therapeutic (perhaps even cathartic) effect.

People are as healthy and confident as the stories they tell themselves.

Ben Okri

How to foster narrative development

1. Listen. It is often said that children need to be watched to grow. They need to be listened to as if what they say is meaningful, interesting and informative. Listening means reacting and responding with smiles, frowns, looks of

surprise, disbelief, astonishment and so on. The active listener participates in the story and helps the teller to be more motivated and supported. Children soon sense if adults are not really listening. Of course, this does not mean dropping everything to listen at any given moment in the day. There is a time and place for everything, just make sure there really is a time and place.

2. Respond. Do not listen to children's stories with a view to correcting them. Accept them as they come and ask questions that lead them to elaborate or clarify. A good way to respond is to tell them a story.

3. Collaborate. Enter into the world of the story and participate accordingly. That means adopting the same story conventions as the child. Do not ask logical questions if the story is not at the logical level (for example, the child tells us a fairy flew down the chimney; we don't say, she couldn't, we have a gas fire). Teachers especially run the danger of having specific outcomes in mind when they ask children questions. If the answers come from a different perspective or consciousness, do not be pedantic.

4. When telling children stories, choose stories from a wide range of different sources. Children are very receptive to interesting phrases, new words, different styles, unusual sounds. They do not have to understand everything they hear. Even if a story is beyond them they will appreciate the structure and what little they can visualize. This generates an interest in and respect for the as-yet-unknown and stimulates the desire to learn. Children are quite open to all styles. You do not need to say which are better, their own instinct will judge whether the story has nourishment for them.

5. Choose the best stories you can find. The main benefit of traditional tales is that they have stood the test of time and probably stem from cultures that contained far more wisdom in their story-telling traditions than we do. Authentic traditional stories (as opposed to modern or Victorian sentimental versions) contain archetypes in both the characters and plots. Many traditional folk and fairy tales were once teaching stories that have come 'down' to the level of children's tales. They contain great wisdom that we can no longer access with our intellect. We do not need to fully understand the stories ourselves but rather trust that a good tale can carry itself.

Obviously, many traditional folk tales contain sexist or racist stereotypes, usually acquired in more recent historical times. Feel free to change heroes to heroines or get rid of little nigger boys and so on. Replace them with more appropriate characters but try to stay true to the plot and the situation. Let the princess wake up the prince – the important thing is that one of them stayed awake and cut through the vegetation to wake up their sleeping partner. There are many excellent collections of tales. The more scholarly collections are probably more authentic, even if the illustrations are not as good.

Summary

Given the importance of story-telling for child development, I wish to suggest a few points worth remembering (see Rawson and Rose 2002, chapter 16):

1. Certain features of linguistic development appear to be universal. These include the tendency of children by the age of three to sequence their experience when describing it. They talk about what happened and then what happened next. This is the first prerequisite for narrative. By the age of five, most children have mastered the other prerequisites of narrative, place and time. They can say when and where it happened. When children recall events it usually has an opening, a high point and an ending.

2. Children adopt the story-telling characteristics of their culture. In all cultures children 'learn to tell stories in order to become full participants in their community and to develop relationships with other people, as much as they do to formulate experience for themselves' (Engel 1995, page 206).

3. Stories are crucial to cognitive development and in the child's developing relationship to self and the world.

4. Children's capacity to tell stories becomes increasingly individual.

5. Story-telling may be an inborn predisposition but it requires from the very beginning willing, enthusiastic and skilled partners. Parents and educators need to value children's stories by responding to them in appropriate ways. We need a phenomenology of stories and we need to train our observational skills in recognizing their qualities.

6. Teachers in kindergarten and in school (though this is far more likely in school) need

to avoid stifling the story-telling habits of children through formal and informal instruction and correction. Schoolteachers need to find ways of encouraging rather than hindering the story-telling process. Gordon Wells (1987, pages 116–117) has written that many school situations limit the development of linguistic development and learning generally because of what he terms the 'transmissional' concept of teaching. He wrote:

> …knowledge cannot be transmitted to students in a prepackaged form in the hope that it will be assimilated in the form in which it is transmitted. Knowledge has to be constructed afresh by each individual knower, through an interaction between the evidence…and what the learner can bring to bear on it.

Bearing this in mind and taking account of the need for an interactive relationship to learning, a number of factors limit learning opportunities. These include:

- too much frontal teaching in which the teacher does most of the talking;
- groups that are too large for individual children to have the opportunity of interactive conversation of the kind needed to develop skills and further understanding;
- too little allowance is made for individual children's abilities and experiences.

Learning becomes passive when there is too much emphasis on the teacher's plan for the lesson and too little emphasis is placed on 'where the individual child is at' – that is, building lessons on what the children know in a given situation. Wells' main point is to stress the active involvement of children in their own learning. He points out that, under stress, too many teachers fall back on the 'being talked-at' style they themselves have been educated by. What Wells terms 'collaborative' methods of teaching activate the child's own learning activity. In anthroposophical terms, one speaks of engaging the child's 'I' or ego.

The engagement of the 'I' is at risk where outcomes are too rigidly defined in the curriculum and teaching methods are used that deliver these outcomes as 'efficiently' as possible. In education, the journey is always as important and often more so than the goal.

This method of teaching does not imply that the teacher becomes redundant or relinquishes responsibility for guiding learning situations – far from it. In fact, a collaborative partnership between child and teacher is a great art, requiring considerable professional expertise. In a Steiner Waldorf school most teachers would see the partnership with the young child as being with the 'I' of the child, the child's higher being. The teacher, of course, converses with the child but the collaboration as such consists in 'hearing' what the 'I' of the child is communicating. As the child becomes more mature that dialogue increasingly needs to be direct and verbal.

7. Susan Engel identifies two ways teachers neglect or stifle the developmental potential of story-telling. The first is an overemphasis on 'correctness' and logic at the expense of the child's impulse to convey personal meaning. The other is the effect of simply not taking what children have to tell us seriously, of seeing the child's inventions as 'childish'.

8. The role of the listener is an active, creative one. This means not only encouragement but appropriate responses. Story-telling is a collaborative process. In order to collaborate we have to enter into the story. It is no good asking questions outside of the framework of the story or introducing your own, different story.

9. Children need to experience a variety of styles of story-telling, different genres. Susan Engel (1995, page 215) gives a very revealing piece of advice:

> We tend to reserve great stories and poems until we think children are old enough to appreciate them. Instead, assume that if they start hearing beautiful language, well-constructed narratives and different genres early in life, they will acquire a vocabulary of narrative in the same way that they seem so easily to acquire a vocabulary of words. This accords with basic practice in Steiner Waldorf schools.

10. Allow children to read, hear and write stories about the things that concern them. This includes things we usually try to shield children from. It is better that they retell the story of some TV crime series than that they simply repress the experience. The beauty of stories is that we can change them in the retelling and in so doing we can change our relationship to them. It may be a cliché, but it is good to talk and even better to listen.

Resources

A list of children's books for exploring human values and issues concerned with spiritual and emotional well-being can be found at the back of this book (see Appendix 2).

References

Bruner, J. (1990), *Acts of Meaning*, Harvard University Press, Cambridge, Massachusetts; London, England
Bruner examines the role of culture in shaping our thoughts and the language we use to express them.

Engel, S. (1995), *The Stories Children Tell: Making sense of the narrative of childhood*, W. H. Freeman, London
This book, written by a developmental psychologist, examines the methods and meanings of children's narrative and how the story-telling process changes as the child grows older.

Okri, B. (1998), *The Joys of Storytelling*. In Okri, B. *A Way of Being Free*, Phoenix, London
Ben Okri examines the power of narrative in this essay.

Rawson, M. and Rose, M. (2002), *Ready to Learn: From birth to school readiness*, Hawthorn Press, Stroud
This book considers the transition from kindergarten to school. Chapter 16 examines the meaning of the spoken word.

Searle, J. R. (1969), *Speech Acts: An essay in the philosophy of language*, Cambridge University Press, Cambridge
This book has made an important contribution to the philosophy of language.

Wells, G. (1987), *The Meaning Makers: Children learning language and using language to learn*, Hodder and Stoughton, London
A very readable book based on the Bristol research study 'Language at Home and at School'.

Group story-telling

Virginia Gordon

Virginia Gordon was a systematic family therapist. For several years she worked with children in primary schools, day care centres, children living with disability and children living in care. She devised the MISST (Moral Intervention in Systematic Story-telling Therapy) model following an extended research trip to South America, New Zealand and Mexico in the mid-1990s.

The context of referral for her clients had a common theme: dysfunction and trauma following exclusion from their peers. Some children were referred because of disruptive behaviour that could lead to temporary or permanent exclusion from school. Others were experiencing learning difficulties, which could result in low self-worth aided by the bullying they may have experienced, which may have encouraged them to become bullies in return.

Using the MISST approach, Virginia Gordon found that within the umbrella of a shared story, children heard their thoughts and feelings echoed by the words of others. The methods used to externalize these stories are described and examples provided from three groups of story-tellers who have used this approach.

Introduction

Some 20 years ago, I was asked to run an adult education story-telling class for students with Down's syndrome and severe learning difficulties. I was already teaching sculpture, so this did not seem an impossible task at first but as the day approached for the first class I began to see the difficulties of running a story-telling class with students who did not read or write. I decided to read a story from *Aesop's Fables*, including the moral at the end of the tale, then ask each person in turn to say something about the story, with particular reference to the illustration of each fable and the moral at the end. The ten sentences up on the board at the end of the session had produced an alternative story to Aesop's, but it was just as coherent and reflected the position of my students, so often perceived as 'idiots'. We were all excited, and for myself I realized I had inadvertently stumbled on the subject for the dissertation I was about to write for my systematic psychotherapy diploma (how circular questioning can help clients to create new meaning for old stories they and their families bring to therapy).

Two years after graduating, I spent three months researching and recording old and new stories told in New Zealand, and North and South America. I was curious to see what old beliefs had been transposed to new fables that still contained the 'moral meaning' for the tellers and the listeners. My discoveries made me determined to pursue this further, so on my return I became part of an organization called The Place To Be, which focused on taking therapy into schools (rather than taking children out of schools to go to therapy). The groups of primary school children (all between 9 and 11 years old) helped me to create my MISST model of working with children therapeutically through the co-creation of stories.

The aim of this storied therapy method is to enable groups of children and adults to externalize the beliefs, fears and dreams they live with on a daily basis within the safety of a co-created tale. The objective is to enable these same groups to give a voice to those previously unheard, and to hear their own voices reflected by others within the story-telling circle. The method is founded on the principle of context defining the meaning of the stories they tell. So, for example, children living within the context of first-generation, ethnically visible primary school attendees who have already been diagnosed with learning difficulties (with the almost inevitable result of threats or realities of exclusion due to behavioural problems) are given the opportunity to share their experiences of this prejudiced view. In the same way, the adults with brain damage had been given a voice, to communicate to each other and the outside world what it was like to be labelled mentally handicapped.

The following describes three groups of story-tellers who have used the MISST model. I explain the methods I use to externalize these stories and from each context give one example of a story they have told.

Context and meaning

The highest level of importance for this method is to ensure that everyone in the group has an equal opportunity to share in the process. Therefore, if there is a group of two, four, six or ten story-tellers, from the start the process must be the same. The only selective components are the opening sentences they are asked to choose from. (In other groups the choice may be an illustrated story, a magazine or a photograph in a tabloid newspaper.) The choice is determined by the context of the group. If this is a group of brain-damaged adults living in an institutional environment I will ask questions that could reflect this lack of autonomy. Often, I misjudge the story-tellers' perspective and will be contradicted (such as: 'So was he cross that the boy called him thick?' Answer: 'No, he felt sorry for the boy, the boy was the stupid one'). Opening sentences selected by a group from a cerebral palsy institute in Bombay will have to reflect the beliefs inherent in the religious contexts of the tellers and how these influence their various beliefs around disability. Equally, it could be that that particular opening has been chosen because it gives the students an opportunity to fantasize about the life they would have led if they had had more oxygen at birth. A group from a primary school in Peckham, where most of the parents are first-generation English living on income support, will not necessarily respond in the same way to a set of opening sentences created for a Catholic primary school in a predominantly white, middle-class area of south-west Clapham.

So this is the process, which any teacher in any school can follow so long as he or she remains curious and listens to what the children are saying.

Method (based on choices)

As soon as the story-tellers come into the room, invite them to form a circle and place yourself on a chair opposite. Explain that from the start everyone has to accept the majority view, that everyone has to wait their turn to add to the story and that nothing can be untold. They will be completely confused, of course, so as soon as everyone has found a place to sit (first choice) offer the second choice, the most preferred sentence, story or illustration to open their story. An example of possible openings for a group of children threatened with exclusion in the primary school in Peckham could be:

1. She had been waiting for hours, maybe something had happened.
2. He had hoped to hear from her today, perhaps the family had arrived.
3. As they walked back to their house, he thought he could hear something, but the others did not agree.

So now there is a third choice for the group, and the preferred sentence becomes the start of the story. If sentence number two had been chosen from the suggested openings, the first question you could ask, of the first person sitting at the edge of the circle might be:

'What difference might it make if the family *had* arrived?'

He or she might reply, 'Well, the family did not like the friendship.'

'Who would the family have liked him to have as a friend?'

'Someone more like them.'

Then the questioner/facilitator could move to the next teller: 'What country are we in, and what year?'

'Jamaica, 1988.'

'So was the "unsuitable" friend from Jamaica?'

'No, he had come from Britain.'

Within a few minutes the group have co-created an outline of a story that is about family beliefs; cultural beliefs; social construction of beliefs according to the period; how these levels of context may be affecting their view of themselves; and how they stand in relation to the rest of the world. The same sentences could connect to a group of teenagers living with cerebral palsy, of course, in which case the dominant theme could be disability rather than ethnicity, but most of the sentences would include some reference to the context of the group. Below, I illustrate how story-tellers in three different contexts have used this method:

1. Adult education (England, 1990s)
2. Primary education (England, 1990s)
3. Two institutions working with cerebral palsy children and adolescents (India, 1998)

Examples of stories lived and told

ADULT EDUCATION (ENGLAND, 1990s)

The story-tellers in this group were students with severe learning difficulties, living in Catholic convents in south London and attending classes close by.

Our group had been working together for quite a while when there was a major intervention in the lives of most of the story-tellers. The majority of the students were women with brain damage and Down's syndrome; a few were victims of the bombings in London during the Second World War. These women had been living in two adjacent convents in south London, some for most of their adult lives. Both convents had recently been inspected by government agencies, with a view to 'updating' the accommodation to current standards coherent with the Equal Opportunities criteria. The changes included replacing the dormitories with separate bedrooms, leaving the women shut off and isolated from their friends; separate washing facilities for each inhabitant; and small dining tables rather than communal eating. The nuns had been given a specific time to have these changes put in place before the inspectors returned to see what had been done. One convent mounted a huge appeal for money, got it and redesigned the convent from top to bottom. The other did nothing, believing that their 'girls' preferred to keep things as they were and that 'God would take care of it'. The women from this convent were in the group. Daily tragedies were enacted in front of their eyes as one by one they were being selected and sent to new homes, clutching suitcases that had sometimes arrived with them as children when they were first placed in the convent home. Every day, another woman was standing on the steps in tears saying goodbye to her long-standing friends, not understanding why her home had been declared 'an unfit place to live in'. I suggested to the group that we start a story that would reflect these troubled times.

We looked at books of fairy tales and fables. After some researching, they chose to tell their version of 'The Wild Swans'. In their story, it was the swans that were turned into people, not the other way round. They described two teenage swans, who were returning to their home with their parents after a party. All swans knew they should not fly over Winterland, where the Wicked Witch entrapped passing animals and turned them into people, to work for her, to make her even richer and even more powerful. Well, our young swans, called Finbar and Emmerline, were gossiping so much about the party that they fell behind their parents and lost their way, and ended up in Winterland after all. Finbar, being young and strong, was turned into a soldier, and his sister into a weaver. However, so powerful was their family love, and being such clever swans, they managed to find a way of communicating to each other through swan song that only they could understand. Thus they kept up their spirits and conceived a plan. Finbar set up a party in the barracks, to which everyone was invited, and the music and the laughter made such a noise that the Wicked Witch of Winterland came down from her castle to see what was going on. She was entranced by young Finbar, who was extremely handsome, and she was even more entranced when he asked her to dance. By the time the music stopped, she was so in love with the young man that she asked him to name a wish, for anything that he desired. He asked her to undo the spell that had turned all these fine beasts into people. 'Oh dear, I think I may have forgotten it,' she said, but he would have none of that and told her to go back up to the castle to find it. On her return she removed her spell and all the dancers became themselves again, slowly, one by one. Elephants, hippopotamuses, horses, bulls and, of course, swans. It made a curious ballroom scene.

The end of the story was the last metaphor for the forgiveness of these tellers. They attached no blame to the government officials who had destroyed their home. In their story, the young swans offered to come and collect the witch every year for a holiday, to sit on Finbar's back and be flown away to their own land. All the other animals were taken in a boat all round the world, being dropped off at each country that was home. The moral meaning the women gave this tale was as follows: just because we are different it does not mean that we should be changed. We are disabled, we do need special care, but just like all of you out there we need to be acknowledged and valued for who we are.

PRIMARY EDUCATION (ENGLAND, 1990s)

The following two examples are from primary schools in London.

Primary School, Peckham

There were three story-tellers in this group, two mixed race, one Scottish, all boys, in their last year of primary school. They had been referred to my group by their class teacher after behavioural problems in the classroom. All three were being threatened with exclusion, which would severely prejudice their chances of moving to the secondary school of their choice. They had very poor attendance records, and all had background stories of poor parenting, or absentee parents, or deaths in the family. It was very difficult to keep the group together, since there was also a pattern of absenteeism throughout our time together and the noise level from both children and staff made communication extremely difficult. We gradually developed a method of working with whoever was there that day, either individually, pairs or all three together. Choices for the start of the story were made from opening sentences as always, but on one occasion there was only one child present, and he chose instead to make a choice from illustrations in a wildlife magazine. This boy's history was known to the school but had not previously been externalized in the stories of the group.

His father was Nigerian, his mother Scottish. He had a younger brother, who at the time of the telling was living with their mother, along with her new boyfriend. The boy himself lived with his African grandmother, who nursed a deep anger towards the boy's mother that was reflected back to the boy on a daily basis. She regarded his mother as being responsible for her own son's incarceration in a local psychiatric hospital and could not stop identifying the boy with her own son's condition. To her, as his mother's son, the boy was no good. The boy was living with her following a violent episode with the new boyfriend. The boy had not seen his mother or brother since they, and the new boyfriend, had taken him to the psychiatric hospital and left him at the desk, saying he was now the responsibility of his father's family. It was following this episode that he began to act out in the classroom, leading to threats of exclusion.

By the time we had the solo session he had recognized the usefulness of putting his point of view to others within the safety of the group story-telling process. However, I was not sure how he would be able to develop this on his own. We looked at books for clues but he was not interested. Finally, he pointed to a giant poster of a jaguar from South America on the wall of the classroom. This is the story he told.

One day it seems a jaguar escaped from London Zoo. He had got out of the cage because his keeper had failed to close the gate properly. When asked if this had been intentional he said he was not sure (but, interestingly, the keeper had the same name as his younger brother in real life). This jaguar was not a dangerous animal as such but, like all wild cats, he needed a lot of meat. He had heard that there were a lot of good butcher shops in Brixton, so to Brixton he went. Of course people were frightened of this apparently wild beast but had no idea of how to catch him. Living just down the road, in Peckham, was Ace Ventura, the famous pet detective. Some bright lad said, 'Ring Ace', and in a trice the great detective was in his silver Maserati heading towards Brixton. He managed to catch the great beast, and then he did a very clever thing. He sent the jaguar's brain to Planet Instinct and put his body in the car so he could join all the other sweet cats Ace had sitting around his fireside at home. This way, the jaguar could follow his instincts without doing anyone any harm, because the vehicle for harm, his body, had been sent to sleep with all the other pussycats in Peckham.

At the time of this telling I was about to go to work in Bosnia, and I told him that I thought his was a great story to take to a war zone. He gave me permission and when I returned he asked me what I had done with the story. I told him I had given a copy of it to a woman who was working with a boy who had recurring nightmares about a bombing incident in his playground at school. The boy from Peckham was pleased, and hoped one day they could be pen-pals.

Primary School, Clapham

There were four story-tellers in this group: two boys, one of whom was mixed race and the other Nigerian, and two girls, both mixed European. The girls had anxiety problems and playground phobia, the boys were in the special needs group. One boy had been diagnosed with lupus on arrival in this country, so was often away sick.

The first few sessions were fruitful, but as the term progressed the boys began to tease the girls, to such an extent that neither dared make any contributions to the story for fear of being mocked. By the end of the term one girl had left the group and the other threatened to do the same. In the event, both did return the following term, but the girls laid down the condition that the boys' teasing did not continue. This was an interesting shift for the girls, both of whom had, as one of the reasons for referral, extreme timidity in the classroom. But the boys could not control their instincts, so by the end of the spring term there were only the two boys left in the group once more. The boys kept on about how it was dull without the girls, how they missed them. In my view, these two boys had not been able to contextualize their ambivalent feelings about girls. Their contributions to the stories, even when the girls were there, reflected this. Aggressive flirting, emphasis on the strong bonding (almost a sexual partnership) between boys, their inability to be comfortable with their own sexual development – which was too difficult to connect to the girls directly – all played a powerful part in the stories and, naturally, were acted out in the sessions.

This is the story they told together the week after I told them that neither of the girls was returning to the group. The telling was accompanied by one of the boys catching, killing and burying a large ichneumon fly found in the room. The 'experiment' is described as the story unfolds.

This is a story about a man called Abu Oddblob. He is ten years old at the time of the story and he lives in Africa Street. It seems that he has a wife (even one so young) whose name is Acucu. They were at school together and when they grew up a bit more they went to university together as well. They were interested in insects, they would collect them, study them, make houses for them and write about them *[one boy is making a house out of plasticine, and decorating it with spangles and shiny paper and little plastic beads]*. The story moves on to a special insect they find together, which they examine intently and then place in the special house. They make special spangled food and draw flowers for the insect to settle on, and these drawings become magic and turn into real flowers. They decide to call the insect Jim. *[During this part of the telling, the boy is tweaking and pulling at the fly, until it is immobilized.]* In the story, Abu decides that the insect's leg is too long, which is why it is not moving, so he takes it off. *[The boy is pulling at the fly's leg and wings as he imprisons it in the little jewelled house.]* Abu decides he has gone too far; he tries to revive the fly by blowing warm air on the insect but realizes it is too far gone. So he makes the fly comfortable in its little jewelled house and then goes away. *[During this part of the telling the other boy leaves the table, looking distressed.]* His wife Acucu is left alone. She wishes everyone had not left her. She wonders if she has done something to drive them away. She decides to go and look for Abu. She finds Abu, staring at the fly once more. It is nearly

dead, so Abu kills it with a brick, and then he and his wife bury it. They put a cross on the mound, such a very large mound for a very small fly, and then they go home together. *[The boy gets out of the classroom window, gathers up some earth, brings it in through the window, realizes this is no good, so climbs out again while the other boy hands him the plasticine jewelled house. It is buried in the earth, the boy comes in again, looks unhappy, goes out once more and puts two twigs in the shape of the cross, looks happier, then comes back in once more.]* Both boys told me that the moral of this story is: if you drive people away you will be alone.

TWO INSTITUTIONS WORKING WITH CEREBRAL PALSY CHILDREN AND ADOLESCENTS (INDIA, 1998)

Mumbai (formerly Bombay) and Chennai (formerly Madras) are both part of the Spastic Society of India. This is an organization started by a parent of a cerebral palsy child, and in 1998 was serving three centres (one of them a training centre) in Mumbai and one centre in Chennai. Each centre has its individual intake, and therefore the stories they tell are determined by the location of the schools and what part of the city the children live in. I describe here two of the many stories that were co-created that year. It is important to mention that during this period the staff and the parents also took part in the process, within their own groups, so the connections between all three members of the school system were represented. The story from Mumbai reflects the close community created by the children, reflecting the family patterns found in very poor slum areas of the city in contrast to the comparatively affluent neighbourhood of the sister centre. In the very poor areas, every child seems to have a function to perform in the family, even if they only have the use of a hand. The children from more privileged backgrounds are less involved with the running of the household, so have a less urgent need to stick together and feel less part of the family. In consequence, many of the stories from these groups focus on the disgrace of disability, the frustration of not being able to live a 'normal' life, whereas the other less privileged students seem more accepting of their state.

The dominant story for both is the Hindu belief that a disabled child is a manifestation of a punishment inflicted on the parents for some misdemeanour in the past. The story from Chennai reflects this stoical acceptance of their condition that so many of the story-tellers externalized. The group had more than usually disabled students and yet all the stories coming from them had the peculiar combination of 'so this is how it is' with a mystical fantasy that reflects all fairy tales worldwide and from every religious context.

It is worth noting that both these stories emerged from the sentence, 'They waited at the bus stop/train, wondering if s/he would be recognizable after all this time.'

Chennai: Vidya's Story

This is a story about a girl called Vidya, who had gone to Delhi to work in the kitchen of a grand fellow in Delhi. She was six years old when she left and now it was three years later. All her friends had gone to the railway station to meet her, wondering if they would recognize her after all this time. Well, they did, and they all went back to her house to have a party and open all the gifts she had brought home with her. The biggest parcel was for all the friends together and when they unwrapped it they found what looked like a toy aeroplane, but one so big that they could all get into it. So they did, and immediately the aeroplane flew out of the house, up into the sky, with Vidya and all her friends inside. Once they were out of sight of their homes, the aeroplane crashed, because no one knew how to fly it. But the friends did not die in the crash. Instead, they were changed into beautiful blue birds. They were quite happy to be birds for a time but then they began to be homesick and want their mothers, so they decided to fly home. Of course, their mothers did not recognize them at first and all the birds were very sad. Then Vidya had an idea. If they sang the songs their mothers sang to them when they were people, then they would be recognized. But the mothers just thought it was birdsong. Vidya decided to try one last thing. She sat on her mother's shoulder and blew into her mother's ear, just as she used to do when she was a baby. Then her mother knew her and there was great joy for the mother and child. Vidya thought she would be changed back into a girl again, and all her friends as well. But this was not possible, so all the mothers got together and they became blue birds too, so they could fly as well and so ensure that they would never be separated from their children again. The moral of this story is: there is no love stronger than a mother's love.

Mumbai: Babe and Sam

The story told is this. A group from the Spastic Society in Colaba were waiting at the bus stop, wondering if Sam would be recognizable after all this time. They had not seen him since he was three years old, only able to crawl and bunny-hop. But he had then gone to Delhi, where his father had offered

him a job. He had been away for seven years. His friends were called John, Raju, Rosie and Babe.

In fact, they did have difficulty recognizing him at first, because now he was a tall boy, walking, with only crutches for support. 'Hello Sam,' they cried, and now it was his turn to have difficulty in identifying who was who, apart from Babe, of course (alone in the group, she was the only one to be walking without any support at all). There had been a party arranged to welcome Sam back to Colaba. It was to have been at Babe's house but so many guests were invited (including all students and staff from the Colaba Centre) that they had changed the venue to the Valley Hotel in Bandra.

All Sam's family came (they all suffered from cerebral palsy, it seems) and there was lots of singing and dancing. They had fried rice, chicken, Pepsi, mangola and frooti to drink. Sam had such a good time that when he returned to Delhi he arranged to speak to his friends on the telephone every week, and he always kept his promise.

One day Sam wrote to Babe, telling her that he had met a pilot when out dancing one night. This pilot, called Rajan, had been so impressed by Sam's dancing that they had become friends, so Sam had asked him to fly to Colaba, to bring all his friends to Delhi on a visit, which he did.

It is now ten years later, and the friends are still in Delhi. All have finished school, gone to college and joined the Navy. All except Babe, who did not go to college because she was too small. Instead, she just became famous, everyone knew about Babe. She was special, she was a star.

The ending of this story embodies all the 'friends for life' themes. John becomes captain of his ship, and although a Muslim he allowed all his Hindu friends from Colaba to be part of the crew, and they set sail all around the coast of India (except Babe, of course, she was just...Babe). They enjoyed this trip so much that they decided to repeat it every year, to raise money for all students living with cerebral palsy all over India.

There was no doubt that Sam was a very popular and powerful person and the moral was that powerful people get things done, fast.

Conclusion

In retelling these stories I have tried to demonstrate how, by externalizing their innermost hope and fears, children are able to 're-author their lives and relationships'. This is a theory developed by the Australian psychotherapist Michael White, who in conjunction with his colleague David Epston, an anthropologist from New Zealand, has written a series of books and papers on the use of stories in therapy (see, for example, Epston and White 1992; White and Epston 1990).

I would like to draw a few conclusions from the stories told that connect them one with the other, regardless of the different countries and contexts that informed them. I will take the last first and work backwards.

As mentioned above, the story-tellers from India, living with difficulties unimaginable to their Western counterparts (including those with cerebral palsy), chose to tell stories that gave a positive view of their experience of poverty, with no state subsidy, no usable transport, not even pavements to run a wheelchair on should anyone possess the money to buy one. Their stories emphasized the necessity for sticking together and having loving families: 'We are all right so long as people do not separate us.' They interweave the fantasy with a reality that has no suggestion of 'I wish' in a self-pitying vein. What they are asking for is:

- recognition of their situation, validation of their right to be heard and lack of prejudice towards either their 'disability' or their ethnicity; and, most importantly,
- their right to dream of a life like other people (jobs, college, sailing round the world, flying aeroplanes, having a job, going to work, dancing till dawn).

The character Babe came into the story because one of the children was so small that she was carried everywhere. Her legs were completely atrophied but she was so pretty, everyone loved her. In the story, she could walk without any help; in reality, 'Babe' could not walk at all. But she acquired huge status; she did not need to walk.

When co-creating the Vidya story, I asked if children would be able to fly... 'Of course not, they are only children.'

'So what will happen?'
'It will crash.'
'Will the children be all right?'
'Of course not, they will die.'
'So is that the end of the story?'
'No, they become birds, blue birds.'

Then later, when Vidya finally connects with her mother:

'Will she be able to turn her back?'
'Of course not, she cannot do magic, it was just the aeroplane that was magic.'

We have to remember that none of these story-tellers would have been in an aeroplane; it must seem like magic to them. So they knew where they could fantasize and where they had to be real.

The story of the Wicked Witch from Winterland has the best connection to those from India, but that is not surprising, since both groups were living with disability, with equal lack of autonomy over their lives and the ongoing prejudice from the 'normal world'. Also, they share the transfiguration, again not surprising since Catholicism and Hinduism share this concept in many contexts. The ancient story of Noah and his Ark restores the animals to their kingdom of origin in a way that Vidya's mother was unable to do, but I think those story-tellers knew where to draw the line. Mothers joining their disabled children rather than trying to change them, on the other hand, has strong resonance to the power of the Wicked Witch, who joined her swans once a year but did not try to become a swan herself.

So, now to the boys and girls from Peckham and Clapham. The boy who said 'Leave me to my anger and distress, but take care of me so I do not do damage to others' is surely saying: 'Acknowledge that my life has been made difficult by the adult behaviour of those more powerful than me. Give me respect for what has made me but help me not to harm others.' And old Ace, who had the power to do just that, has some connection to the Wicked (turned Good) Witch.

As for Abu Oddblob and his wife Acucu, well, their story just lets us know that whatever the teachers and the parents think of the story-tellers, with their problems and phobias and fears of death, their learning difficulties and their out-of-control behaviour, they themselves have ambitions and hopes for their future and their relationships. I believe that they knew how much they were responsible for the departure of the girls they so wanted to impress, but they also let us know that they do see a future when they will be as respected and as important as the teachers who have given up on them. Yes, and be married, too.

Finally, we come to the 'girls' from the 'bad' convent, the women whose fate was put in the hands of the Lord. The way the Wicked Witch has become the people from the government – who have the power to change things, but lack judgement regarding those who choose not to acknowledge them – could be seen as the result of so many rebuffs by the outside world, and the women's anger towards those who bad-mouth them in the street is real. Somehow, I feel that these story-tellers have the closest connection with the children from India, whose religious belief is similarly the highest level of context for them and which may be in part responsible for the 'acceptance' not found among the primary school children.

I have deliberately not presented these stories as they are written, since the original versions do belong to the tellers and they may well want to publish them one day. I would just like to tell them how much I enjoyed the work we did together and how much they have taught me about the stories people tell and why.

The power of the story

- In all cultures since the beginning of time people have told stories to teach, affirm understanding, give meaning to important events and guide action.
- Story-telling is a key to relationships with others and the world.

Suggested further reading

White, M. (1995), *Re-authoring Lives: Interviews and essays*, Dulwich Centre, Adelaide, South Australia
The first recorded interview in this collection of interviews and essays examines the narrative perspective in therapy.

References

Epston, D. and White, M. (1992), *Experience, Contradiction, Narrative and Imagination: Selected papers of David Epston and Michael White*, 1989–1991, Dulwich Centre, Adelaide, South Australia
A collection of academic papers covering a range of subjects, including particular therapeutic practices and the process of questioning in the co-authorship of stories.

White, M. and Epston, D. (1990) *Narrative Means to Therapeutic Ends*, Norton, New York; London
The importance of storying in therapy is examined in this academic text.

6 Enhancing learning

– developing more effective ways of learning

Education is the drawing out of the best in the child – body, mind and spirit.
Mahatma Gandhi

Tell me and I forget. Teach me and I remember. Involve me and I learn.
Anonymous

Rhythm, repetition and reverence:
what we mean by the 3 Rs in a Steiner kindergarten

Janni Nicol

Steiner schools provide a distinctive form of education. Janni Nicol explains how Steiner Waldorf early childhood education supports the child's well-being and learning experiences with the use of rhythm and repetition. Steiner education recognizes the importance of giving children aged three to six security and stability within the familiar. Regular events punctuate the Steiner kindergarten year, week and day. Each week, for example, has its own recurring activities: baking day, painting day, crafts... Each day is structured so that there is a balance between times of rest and activity.

Rhythm

To help children to become oriented and feel safe within the structure of the kindergarten, we work with their rhythmic system, the heart and breathing. Rhythm helps to harmonize the early will forces (which drive the young child into constant activity) and to stabilize their feeling life.

Rhythm in our kindergarten is a swinging activity between contraction and expansion and we need both to become balanced:

- Contraction (a breathing in): If we have too much of this we can become quiet, retiring, inward, also antisocial, anxious and cold.

- Expansion (a breathing out): If we have too much of this we can become hyperactive, over-stimulated, also sociable, relaxed and warm.

We use rhythm within our day to aid this healthy development of the child's rhythmic system and also as a tool to make life easier for both the practitioners and parents. Preparation results in continuity and within the kindergarten morning there is little space for chaos (although we are not absolutely static or rigid in this). At this age, space and time mean little to the child. If, for example, young children ask what time it is, they do not want to know literally; they want to know if it is time for tea (they are hungry) or time for bed (they are sleepy – although they usually deny this, while yawning all the time).

The practitioner is the centre of the kindergarten and therefore must be well prepared to build up the rhythm creatively. At home, rhythm is the perfect aid to easier parenting. If the child always goes to bed at 7pm, then he or she will start yawning at that time and will usually go to bed without a fuss.

The child's rhythms are broken already by the staggered kindergarten sessions and the break at weekends. So what we offer is the rhythm of the morning, the rhythm of the week, the rhythm of the seasons, the rhythm of the festivals of the year – which provides stability in an ever-changing social and family life.

We find that the child becomes confident, strong and secure, moving freely and orienting easily within the form and structure of the kindergarten. The world becomes familiar and the child feels safe.

Repetition

Repetition is a general aid to learning and memory. When we repeat something often enough, it becomes a habit and usually becomes deeply ingrained in our memory.

Repetition strengthens and educates the will forces of the child; it takes will to repeat tasks. Like rhythm, repetition is not only daily, but also weekly and yearly. For example:

Monday is baking day; Tuesday, painting; Wednesday, crafts; Thursday, cooking; Friday, gardening and cleaning; yearly, seasonal activities and festivals are repeated. Again, this gives children security and stability within the familiar.

Daily structure

Within our kindergarten day we work with this rhythm and repetition, a constant contraction and expansion that allows a gentle flow, letting the children drift in a dreamlike, peaceful way from one activity to another without any discordant or difficult situations arising.

The children are brought in to the kindergarten (a contraction). Here, they leave the outside behind by taking off their shoes and being brought into the room and handed over to the teacher, who greets each in turn. The children often want to do a drawing, sewing, woodwork or weaving until they find where they want to go out into play.

CREATIVE PLAY (EXPANSION)

This is a breathing out within the kindergarten room. The children now have freedom (within the structure) to develop their own play constructively. We interfere as little as possible. The role of the teacher is a different one here, for we are doing adult work, such as sewing, mending or helping where required; we interrupt play only to guide the children through various social situations that might arise. During this time, they re-enact what they have observed in the outside world, learning negotiating skills, caring and sharing, establishing societies and social interaction, which are all aids to future good citizenship. Our kindergarten is a community where each member has an important contribution to make.

TIDY TIME (CONTRACTION AND EXPANSION)

Here, we come together to have a chat to the tidy gnome puppet and refuel a little by eating a few raisins or sunflower seeds (always a good opportunity for counting, social interaction, listening and sharing). After a finger game, the children go out into the room and tidy up properly, putting each item into its correct basket, container, house or shop. Tidying becomes an activity, not a chore, and caring for the environment is always an important consideration.

ACTIVITY (CONTRACTION)

All the children sit at the table and participate in a baking, painting, cleaning or craft activity. We always introduce the activity with songs and finger rhymes that are suitable for what is taking place. The craft activities, which are often seasonal, help the children to gain control and mobility of their fingers and learn new skills.

RING TIME (EXPANSION AND CONTRACTION)

Next comes ring time (or circle time), which contains both rhythm and repetition. Gesture, movement and speech must be clear, precise, beautiful and meaningful, worthy of imitation by the child. Within ring time, we repeat action songs and rhymes, learn other languages, trace the seasons or act out the stories that we have told. The children learn through the repetition and remember. It is within ring time that we develop many pre-literacy skills, such as listening, rhyme, letter sounds, counting, rhythms in music (pulse and beat) and interacting with each other in the circle games we play.

TOILET (EXPANSION)

Here the child even loses a little of himself or herself. We never have a problem getting even the youngest to go to the toilet or wash hands, it is a rhythm ingrained through constant repetition. We simply cannot eat until our hands are clean. There is no argument (in fact, the question has hardly been raised in years).

SNACK TIME (CONTRACTION)

This is a time for social interaction, to nourish our bodies, to talk and learn to listen. The new or younger children are fussy at first, but soon eat even the crustiest bread, salad from the garden, apple skins and vegetable soup (for they see the other children doing it and imitation is a powerful stimulus). We appreciate the food that we eat and nothing is wasted. Setting the table properly is always important and a good opportunity for counting, sorting and matching – the right number of chairs, bowls, cups and serviettes for each. We start with a blessing on the food, lighting a candle as a focus for our thanksgiving, and saying thank you for the meal together when we have finished. (Even the youngest children will sit at the table for over half an hour without fidgeting.) We nourish and support their physical needs through the largely organic food that they receive in the kindergarten.

OUTSIDE PLAY (EXPANSION)

Here, the children should be doing, experiencing their physical bodies and the space around them. Young children do not have a good awareness of space (noticeable by the way they often bump into things or each other, or trip over steps or other objects) so we work on this by throwing balls, playing ring games, skipping, balancing, climbing, gardening and strengthening their limbs. These all help them to become confident in their bodies and develop new skills. Sometimes we go on walks to the park, and they learn road safety awareness and listening skills, too. They work in the garden, planting, digging and harvesting their own produce.

Story time (contraction)

We gather together, sit quietly and listen. This is an opportunity for the children to completely switch off physically and enter a dream world of fantasy and imagination, where they can build pictures inwardly. We tell stories or do puppet shows, repeating them sometimes for a week or more until they become friends and companions. We choose our stories carefully (nature, folk or fairy tales) and do not shy away from adult words such as 'perceived'. The fairy stories carry deep moral truths within them. They set before the children a picture of how the human being can develop to do a task worthy of mankind. Puppet shows, the showing of books with beautiful pictures, and plays, enhance the children's understanding of stories. The children can then imitate or role-play with confidence, and working with imitation the child cannot do it 'wrong'. Children whose first language is not English are given extra help where necessary, and the repeated nature of our work supports their acquisition of English.

Goodbye (expansion)

The end of the day provides an opportunity for a few words with the parents before the children go home.

Reverence

Reverence comes into everything we do for:

- the child, as a special being with a past and a future – we acknowledge this child and the gifts he or she brings, and try to find a way to enhance these gifts;

- each other, in showing respect for each other, in our behaviour, in listening and caring and sharing, in friendships and in becoming sensitive to each other's needs and feelings;

- our environment – we take care of our kindergarten, our toys, garden and whole environment by doing things properly, mending toys and torn clothing, polishing, cleaning and tidying up;

- food, in thanking nature for providing us with good food to eat, growing it in our garden, cooking it with care, preparing and serving it properly, and sitting in a social way at the table until we have all finished.

Conclusion

Within our kindergarten day we move through the transition times with singing. When you sing, there is a rhythm to it, and it drifts from one activity to another without time for argument (the usual 'but I'm not finished playing' never seems to occur).

Our kindergartens should be a haven from the stress of the outside world, where we have time to experience others and ourselves and grow in peace and harmony, where children feel safe and not under pressure to perform or compete. They should be places where we can weave a tapestry of learning experiences for the child – that is our ideal in a Steiner kindergarten.

Key characteristics of Steiner Waldorf early childhood education

- All pupils share a broad, internationally recognized curriculum proven over 80 years, that is in accord with their developmental needs, without undue specialization.
- There is a balance of artistic, practical and intellectual content in the curriculum and an emphasis on social skills and spiritual awareness.
- Our early years approach provides time and space for development of key skills as a basis for literacy, numeracy, social and emotional competence; there is a warm and secure learning environment where the qualities of childhood are nurtured.
- Each day in the Steiner kindergarten there is some specific time dedicated to free creative play.
- Rhythm and repetition are important. Regular events punctuate the Steiner kindergarten year, week and day.

Resources

Steiner Waldorf Schools Fellowship, Kidbrooke Park, Forest Row, Sussex RH18 5JB (Tel 01342 822115)
www.steinerwaldorf.org.uk
Steiner schools are committed to the principle that a child's emotional and social skills should be at the centre of all educational practices.

Suggested further reading

Oldfield, L. (2001), *Free to Learn: Introducing Steiner Waldorf early childhood education*, Hawthorn Press, Stroud
This book explores the central principles of Steiner Waldorf early childhood education and underlines the extraordinary value to children of creative play, rhythm, movement-based learning and nourishing the senses.

Imitation

Janni Nicol

In her second contribution, Janni Nicol explains the importance of imitation in Steiner Waldorf early childhood education. This key theme provides an effective way of working with young children's natural inclination to imitate. A wide range of domestic and artistic activities is introduced in which the teacher presents herself or himself as an example rather than an instructor. This approach avoids children receiving too much early instruction and direction, which can inhibit their enthusiasm for self-initiated learning. Instead, imitation can help children to find their own situations for learning through play.

Introduction

One can think of the very young child's whole body as a sensory organ uniting external impressions with their internal world. The child's body acts as a physical substance through which his or her personality can emerge. In a way, this is similar to the function of the eyes, which let us see by acting as mediators, passing messages to the brain. This interaction of external impressions with the child's internal organic development is revealed in the wonderful power of imitation with which every healthy child is born.

Children grow through imitation of the adults and world around them, and anyone interacting with a child becomes part of the educational process of that child. If we recognize this, then two important priorities arise for parents (the child's first educators) and teachers:

- Protection of the child: This means not only physical protection (such as the right clothing) but, as far as possible, selecting the impressions that confront the child, to make them worthy of this innate developmental impulse – imitation.
- Guidance: We should guide children gently into life by letting them learn from life, by exploiting their inborn ability to imitate, rather than teaching abstractly.

These priorities require us to become good role models, encouraging the right impulses through our actions. We can become aware of our behaviour, how we apply ourselves to our work and to our daily tasks, how we communicate with others and how we develop and care for our environment.

Stages in the child's imitative behaviour

In the first six to seven years we believe that the imitative behaviour of the child passes through three distinct phases, connected with the forces of organic development that influence the whole body.

FIRST STAGE (ONE TO TWO AND A HALF YEARS)
During this time, children acquire three of the most important human abilities. They...

- stand upright and walk
- speak
- think in words (communication of needs and ideas).

SECOND STAGE (THREE TO FIVE YEARS)
In these years, children develop...

- imagination
- memory.

Children begin to use objects around them in a different way, transforming and creating things anew in play that is stimulated by external circumstances. We believe here that we should provide play objects that have the possibility of being transformed by the child's imagination –

simple toys such as a shell, which can be a ticket for a ride, a plate or simply a shell.

Rudolf Steiner said:

As the muscles of the hand grow firm and strong in performing the work for which they are fitted, so the brain and other organs are guided into the right lines of development if they receive the right impressions from the environment.

THIRD STAGE (FIVE TO SEVEN YEARS)

At this stage, children develop...

- intention.

We encourage the children to participate more in adult activities; cleaning, washing, sweeping, cooking, sewing, woodwork. Then transformation takes place and the children begin to play out of an inner picture – a pre-conceived image.

Play and imitation

Within our early years settings we create spaces, which allow children to play creatively out of themselves (child-led, not teacher-directed play) and provide the opportunity for imitation. The outside world is observed and reflected in the play of the child who then re-enacts this observation over and over until the skill is acquired. This can also work in a negative way if the child is exposed to violence or aggressive behaviour. We see this all too often played out in some form in the kindergarten. Sometimes children have to re-enact an event in order to understand it or experience it themselves, or simply to work it out of their systems (for instance, the whole kindergarten could be moved around by the children when a child has moved home).

We provide the opportunity for this in our kindergartens, and it is best achieved by the presence of adults purposefully occupied, where children can be 'securely enveloped' by the adults' work. The adults thus occupied provide a rhythmical and ordered structure – they demonstrate enjoyment of work as well as the willingness to work hard. Such efforts are never wasted when children are such good imitators.

Activities

The activities we do should also be worthy of imitation: tasks that have a purpose and an end-product that enhance the well-being of others and ourselves. Taking part in any activity helps with learning, and we make sure that we use technology that is incidental and integral to the activity (real woodwork equipment, grinders and mincers, scales, weaving looms, cookers and more). Our activities are always worth while imitating, and are divided into Domestic and Artistic.

DOMESTIC ACTIVITIES

These activities feed the physical body. When we make bread, the act of kneading the dough brings it alive. Then there are the ingredients, their feel, taste and texture. There is the sheer enjoyment of the task. (Not to forget, of course, that baking is a wonderful mathematical exercise.)

Sweeping and polishing contain rhythmic archetypal movements, and raise questions, too. Where does the dust come from? Where does it go? There is a beginning and an end, which is satisfying to the child, and a harmony in the movements.

Scrubbing and cleaning the table before eating is something we all do. Washing, mending, cooking, decorating, gardening, tidying – all are domestic tasks worthy of imitation because they have a positive outcome and are on a level the children can understand. These are good for the well-being of the physical body, the environment and each other. The child re-enacts reality until the skill is acquired, becoming a good citizen in the process.

Such activities are important in the home as well. The child has the opportunity to clean and tidy (even if it does take forever), and all children love washing up. It is the process that is important, not necessarily the outcome.

ARTISTIC ACTIVITIES

These creative activities feed the inner soul life of the child. They can be imitated freely and we all have the capacity to bring them out from within us. They include painting, drawing and modelling; crafts such as weaving, woodwork, sewing and other seasonal craft activities; and also singing and music. We tell stories, too, which allow the children to create mental pictures using their imaginative faculties, and to develop a healthy memory.

Teaching

As educators, we believe that everything we do and are, everything with which we surround ourselves and the children – our environment, gestures, language and behaviour – should be worthy of imitation. This is something we are constantly aware of and strive for.

Resources

Steiner Waldorf Schools Fellowship, Kidbrooke Park, Forest Row, Sussex RH18 5JB (Tel 01342 822115)
www.steinerwaldorf.org.uk
Steiner schools are committed to the principle that a child's emotional and social skills should be at the centre of all educational practices.

Suggested further reading

Oldfield, L. (2001), *Free to Learn: Introducing Steiner Waldorf early childhood education*, Hawthorn Press, Stroud
This book explores the central principles of Steiner Waldorf early childhood education and underlines the extraordinary value to children of creative play, rhythm, movement-based learning and nourishing the senses.

The Voices Foundation: transforming children through singing

Susan Digby

Susan Digby is principal and founder of the Voices Foundation, which puts singing at the heart of children's musical education and provides support for teachers who may feel they lack musical skills. Here, she provides an introduction to the work of the Voices Foundation. A central belief of the Foundation is that learning music through singing can be beneficial to a child's emotional, social and intellectual development. Benefits reported by headteachers whose schools have been involved in the Foundation's projects include improvements in discipline, self-confidence and academic results, and reduced playground aggression.

Introduction

I launched the Voices Foundation in 1993, after visiting Hungary as a Winston Churchill Travelling Fellow. Here, I saw how music was recognized as being fundamental and of vital importance to the development of a human being, and that there was a nationwide scheme in place to enable the vast majority of children to benefit from an excellent musical education.

The Foundation is administered from its offices in London, although regional centres are now being established. Michael Stocks, one of the UK's most respected figures in the field (formerly Music Adviser to Somerset Local Education Authority) is responsible for curriculum management and advisory teacher training. The board of management has contacts in the fields of education, teacher training and music. Our mission statement is:

To enable all children to realize their full potential through a singing-based music curriculum, and to influence national perception of the vital importance of music in education.

The Foundation's aim is to help targeted schools create a music curriculum that is accessible to all pupils, which sets properly high levels of expectation commensurate to age/stage, and which results in the school becoming a good example of teaching and learning practice.

The Voices Foundation is committed to helping schools and teachers develop the intellectual ability, emotional capacity and social skills of children through involvement in music. Musical development is known to enhance linguistic and mathematical learning. By focusing at primary level, the Voices Foundation is able to reach children at an age when they can most benefit.

The Voices Foundation in primary schools

At the heart of the Voices Foundation's work is a dynamic one-year programme. This programme is singing-based and has been designed to transform the quality of life and education of every child in school. Use of the singing voice is essential to aural development. The programmes include in-service training sessions, regular classroom visits and also a Singing Day at the end of the year that is attended by parents, staff and the local community.

Besides the one-year programme, the Voices Foundation also offers the following:

- six-day training for specialist and non-specialist teachers;
- three-day training for specialist and non-specialist teachers;

- Young Voices – after-school musicianship programmes for primary school children;
- one-day workshops for adults wishing to gain confidence in their singing.

Since Voices Foundation's inception in 1993, the innovative one-year programme has reached 233 schools nationwide and involved 2,330 teachers. Our teacher-training courses have involved 275 schools and 285 teachers, the 'Singing is good for you' workshops have been attended by 1,200 adults, and 250 children have participated in Young Voices and the Voices Foundation Children's Choir.

In addition to developing musical skills, the Foundation's projects also contribute to the development of the whole child. Schools involved in the projects have reported improvements in children's discipline, self-confidence and academic results. The one-year programme develops vital communication skills, sensitivity and tolerance at a crucial stage in the child's life. The programme has yielded particularly striking results in schools with challenging social conditions.

The work of the Voices Foundation has been supported by many charitable organizations, including the Esmée Fairbairn Foundation, the Ralph Vaughan Williams Trust, the Headley Trust, the Garfield Weston Foundation, the Po-Shing Woo Foundation, the Hedley Foundation, the John S. Cohen Foundation and the Dulverton Trust. Other awards have come from the Cecil King Memorial Fund, the Coutts Charitable Trust, the Mercers' Company, Shell UK and the Fishmongers' Company.

I set up the Foundation because I believe it is the right of every child to have a meaningful and rich music education through singing. It is our experience that every child can sing – the notion of 'tone deafness' is a myth. We are all born musicians and it is our duty as parents, carers and educators to ensure that the musician in every child is nurtured from birth. It is also our belief that the process of developing 'musical thinking' should be embarked on at the earliest possible age, preferably in utero with the mother and father singing to the unborn child. The ears are developed fully 11 weeks after conception.

The basic principles of the Voices Foundation

- To be a multidimensional human being you must have the language of music, as music can touch parts of the soul like no other form of communication.
- The singing process must start at the very earliest age – at least from birth but preferably in utero. This means that by the time children start formal education they already have a vast amount of musical knowledge in their aural banks.
- Formal music education must be highly structured and the most skilled teachers must teach the youngest children.
- Materials and repertoire have to be appropriate and of high quality. It is essential that music education begins with the voice to keep it accessible to all.

Resources

The Voices Foundation, 38 Ebury Street, Belgravia, London SW1W 0LU (020 7730 6677) www.voices.org.uk
The Voices Foundation recommends to participating primary schools the use of *Growing with Music* (Cambridge University Press) by Michael Stocks and Andrew Maddocks, who are both Voices Foundation project leaders.

Suggested further reading

Lawson, D. and Swanwick, K. (1997), *An Evaluation of the Voices Project at Oxford Gardens Primary School*, Institute of Education, London
Oxford Gardens was the first primary school to adopt the Voices Foundation's innovative music education programme. This report of a three-year research study carried out in the school assesses the effects of the programme.

Nutrition:
its effects on children's brains and behaviour

Sarah Woodhouse

Sarah Woodhouse identifies the main current concerns relating to what children are eating and how this affects their well-being. Schools can make a major contribution to the health of children by increasing their knowledge and understanding of food issues. Primary schools can help to influence eating habits formed in childhood through their participation in projects such as Grab 5! and also by establishing a parent–teacher partnership that works together to promote healthy eating.

Introduction

What children eat and drink and how the ingredients of that foodstuff have been grown and processed have a major effect – for good or ill – on their physical, mental and emotional well-being. Processed foods with chemical additives and poisonous residues from pesticides and agro-chemicals not only render children liable to degenerative diseases (such as cancer, diabetes and heart disease) later in life but can also do early damage to their developing brains. This can have detrimental effects on their personality, learning and behaviour.

One of the children in my class just brings three packets of crisps as his packed lunch. Nothing else. It really worries me. I don't know what to do about it.

Primary teacher

I only knew later that something was wrong with my child's brain by her behaviour. She can't concentrate and be absorbed in anything. She is often aggressive so other children don't want to play with her, and she throws fits of anger that seem disproportionate to some small thing that has gone wrong.

She is restless at night and can't follow even simple instructions without forgetting or being distracted. I just sense something is amiss because I know her so well – she's part of me.

Mother of a seven year old

It's so simple, so simple. Notice the child who finds it hard to sleep at night, cannot concentrate at school or at home, is hyperactive or listless, has colds, maybe an allergy, finds it hard to keep friends and tends to be overweight. Remove all refined sugar from his diet – cakes, biscuits, jam, soft drinks, ice cream, sweetened cereals – and notice energy levels increase and concentration and self-esteem improve.

Nancy Appleton PhD, author of *Lick the Sugar Habit*

The message from the Lambeth Education Authority was a strong one. At the beginning of this term we started giving the children fruit at 10.30 each morning. The staff stand out there in the playground or the hall and eat fruit with the children and they all enjoy it.

Already, six weeks later, I can see the difference in the children's health – especially those children whose packed lunch is poor in nutritional value.

Primary school head

The brain, despite being only 2 per cent of our body mass, consumes around 20 per cent of available energy. To metabolize this energy requires a range of nutrients, vitamins, minerals and essential fatty acids. These nutrients are classed as essential for the normal functioning of the brain, which means there may be consequences if we do not obtain sufficient nutrients from our diet.

Bernard Gesch, Senior Research Scientist in the Department of Physiology, Oxford University

Since the Industrial Revolution and the continuing population explosion, increasing millions have come to live in expanding cities, cut off from the knowledge of how things grow and eating foods imported from many different places, many of which have been treated chemically. The development of techniques to give foodstuffs, whether oils, dairy products, meat, fruit or vegetables, a travel survival capacity and a longer shelf-life has become a top priority for those in the food trade and the food manufacturing industry.

A long shelf-life and successful marketing strategies are of far greater concern to most food manufacturing companies than children's health. This situation will continue until there is a quiet revolution by parents and teachers who are more fully informed about children's nutritional needs and how the present damage to their brains and bodies is being brought about.

Advances in brain research and discovery in the last decade have provided a clearer picture of how different parts of the brain function. The most recent research confirms the extent to which particular parts of the brain are being physically eroded (chemically changed) by the lack of essential nutrients in the food being eaten and through the toxins that are now invading our bodies. Children's brains, because they are still growing and building new connections, suffer even more severely from this erosion than those of adults.

Current concerns about food

The main current concerns about food include those described below.

ADULTERATED FOODS

Skilful packaging and advertising of a wide range of ready-made meals, irresistible snack packs and canned sugary drinks for children have radically changed the population's diet over the last decades. Children are increasingly living off these adulterated foods that, once they become a familiar part of childhood, easily develop into 'comfort foods' to be demanded as the only acceptable things to eat. Some children hardly ever drink plain water.

Food additives can be lethal to the metabolism of children. The disturbance is caused by artificial flavouring, chemical colourants, preservatives and the antibiotic and growth hormone residues in meat. It is also caused by the extra salt, sugar or fat added to many foodstuffs and the adulterated water added to meat. Up to 30 per cent of water is injected into some meat to increase the weight and swell the profits. This is not pure water. To enable the water to remain in the raw meat and not leak straight out again, it must first be mixed with a protein powder, the animal source of which is not inspected or recorded. Only the percentage of added water is included on the label.

FATS WHICH HARM AND FATS WHICH BUILD THE BRAIN

The large proportions of animal fats that are included in many processed and manufactured foods are harmful. The vegetable oils (apart from olive oil) used in high-heat cooking or frying, as with chips, are harmful because the high heat breaks down and changes the chemical composition of the oil, producing toxins. These toxins poison children's growing brains. This can be shown by heating a tablespoon of any vegetable oil in a pan and smelling it closely just as it is on the verge of smoking. It is immediately possible to detect the unpleasant smell of toxins forming and thus recognize that this would be a dangerous ingredient in any meal.

Essential fatty acids, starting with omega 3 and omega 6, are the oils that are literally essential for normal brain function and for central nervous tissue development and repairs. We need more or less the same amount of both these omega oils, which is what our original primitive diet provided through fish, nuts, seeds and wild meat caught or gathered

Children eating organic fruit with their teacher

straight from the earth, the bushes, the trees and the water. Damage to children's brains comes through eating adulterated, processed foods rather than a variety of fresh, whole and organic food, including nuts and seeds, beans, green vegetables, fish and olive oil, all of which help to provide the essential fatty acid balance for brain building.

We are not able to make essential fatty acids in our bodies from other fats and therefore need them in our food. There is now a severe shortage of omega 3 in our diet because it is lost from the vegetable oils we buy through modern heat-processing and deodorizing treatments. These vital nutrients in vegetable oils, when stored in clear, plastic bottles, are further depleted within 48 hours by being exposed to light. No oil should be used in cooking except olive oil, and all oils should be stored in a cool place and in darkness. They should be sold in black or dark green bottles.

At Heathbrook Primary School in London the school gates have become the collection point for seasonal organic fruit and vegetables provided by an organic wholesaler. Seventy-five per cent of the fruit and vegetables are from British organic growers and 50 per cent of the price goes straight back to them. Delivery boxes are returnable. Parents place their weekly orders through a member of the Parent Teacher Association and, in return, the school receives roughly a quarter of the value of the total sales. This comes out of what the wholesaler saves by making one journey for several dozen orders, instead of delivering to individual households. This additional money has helped the PTA to fund new soft surfaces in the playground. An organic lunch is also provided without charge to staff every day.

SUGAR

The brain cannot deal with a sudden influx of excess sugar. A high intake of sugar at breakfast, added to already sweetened cereal, on bread as jam and in sweetened drinks starts a roller-coaster. Alarm bells start ringing and the pancreas takes over, pouring insulin into the bloodstream to remove this excess before it can 'burn' the brain. Then the swinging begins. Sugar levels fall rapidly and the brain tenses up again, this time for the opposite reason. A child in this situation begins to feel irritable, headachy, stomach-achy and tired. He cannot concentrate on his schoolwork, or show interest in the activities enjoyed by other children.

The child's adrenal glands may then inject cortisol into the bloodstream in an effort to bring blood sugar back up to a normal level again. This extra cortisol can give him 'false' energy, causing him to be hyperactive, obstinate and defiant. The 'memory centre' in his brain can also be disturbed and he may become confused and forgetful. The child is then likely to insist on yet more sugary food to eat, and so the cycle continues.

B vitamins and Vitamin C help to re-balance the metabolism, but if the overall range of food being eaten by the child is poor and there is a shortfall of these vitamins there will be no balancing help forthcoming. Refined flour products and white bread cannot provide these B vitamins and other important minerals. Magnesium, zinc, copper, manganese and other minerals and trace elements are also lost along the 'conveyor belt' of processing. Any 'added vitamins' message on a package is small comfort because it is never possible to put back the true value and the natural balance of what has been taken out of an original food.

Salt (sodium)
There are two minerals in our bodies, salt and potassium, which, when they are in the correct proportion to each other, pull nutrients into our cells and clear waste out of them. They achieve this through a pump-like action, which only takes place successfully if there is a very much higher amount of potassium in the body than salt. Most natural wholefoods – like carrots and lettuce – contain exactly the right ratio between potassium and salt.

In processed and packaged food, the ratio of potassium to salt is often turned completely on its head. Large quantities of salt are added and a minimal quantity of potassium remains. This imbalance is present in crisps, processed foods (tinned, frozen or bottled) and in many types of bread and cereal.

In May 2003, the Food Standards Agency, the government watchdog in the UK, accused the food industry of putting young people's health at risk through the high salt content of all processed food. Levels of salt in some crisps and snacks have almost doubled in the last 25 years. These increases have taken children, boys even more than girls, over the top limit set by the Ministry of Health. Two-thirds of salt intake is through processed foods.

Children's exposure to organophosphorus pesticides
Research (Curl et al. 2003) on pre-school children in Washington showed that children on conventional diets had a concentration of organophosphorus pesticides in their bodies six times higher than children on organic diets. This assessment was based on regular keeping of food diaries recording children's organic or non-organic intake of food and daily urine testing. The use of garden pesticides at home was also recorded. The consumption of organic fruits, vegetables and juices reduces children's exposure to organophosphorus pestides to well below the acceptable levels laid down by the US Environmental Protection Agency.

Consumption of organic products appears to provide a relatively simple way for parents and schools to reduce children's exposure to organophosphorus pesticides. Education authorities in many parts of the UK are now insisting that every child in school is given a fruit to eat during the mid-morning break.

The effects of diet on young offenders
Bernard Gesch is a Senior Research Scientist in the Department of Physiology, University of Oxford, and Director of the research charity Natural Justice, which investigates causes of antisocial behaviour. Between 1996 and 2002, through Natural Justice, he undertook an in-depth study to assess the influence of supplementary vitamins, minerals and essential fatty acids on the antisocial and violent behaviour of young offenders in prison (Gesch 2002; Gesch et al. 2002).

In such a controlled environment it was possible to set up a precise research programme, first through the random division of the 231 young offenders into two groups and then through the use of look-alike and taste-alike placebo tablets for one group and the real supplements for the other. A record was also kept of the dietary intake of each prisoner throughout the programme. Not one single person, apart from scientists away from the prison, knew who was taking the supplements and who was taking the placebos. Staff kept full records of any trouble between prisoners or between prisoners and themselves, and the disciplinary action taken.

The following findings were published in the final report:

- There were no adverse reactions to the supplements.
- There was no change in the 'trouble incident' rate in those offenders who had been on placebos.
- Those on the dose of vitamins, minerals and essential fatty acids showed a marked reduction in antisocial behaviour. Within two weeks, offences in this group were reduced by 37 per cent.

The parent–teacher partnership

In the light of so much new knowledge about children's nutritional needs and the damage being caused by anti-nutrients and missing essentials, heads, teachers, school governors and school supervisors can take a new approach to all food available to children in school, as well as ensuring the continuous availability of drinking water in class throughout the school day. Schools can also help and advise parents on what children should bring to school in their lunch boxes – individually, with parents where this can be a sensitive issue. A first move could be to gain access to the Grab 5! Project, which is described below.

THE GRAB 5! PROJECT

Sustain, an alliance of organizations supporting environmental and health issues, has set up a support scheme for schools called the Grab 5! Project. Grab 5! exists to help heads, staff and governors to develop school food policies and successful strategies for encouraging children and their families to eat more fresh, organic fruit and vegetables and wholefoods. Advice about enterprises such as the setting up of school tuck shops is also part of the project (see Resources, page 170).

The Right from the Start book *Food for Thought* (in preparation) provides a further range of ideas and information for parents, which teachers might also find helpful.

FOLLOW-UP IDEAS

A next step might be to invite parents to attend a meeting at school to talk together about food, drink and their children's behaviour at home and at school. A nutritionist could be invited to be there to speak and answer questions from both staff and parents.

It may also be useful to make available to parents articles and reports on nutrition that will help to improve children's mental and emotional well-being. This might include a short handout from the head about the reasons behind the school's food policies and the importance of working in partnership with parents.

The brain needs to be nourished in two ways: the love, nurturing and education we all need but also the nutrition to sustain our physical being. Some of these factors will act in ways that we can see, some of them will not...Clinical studies suggest that nutrition is cheap, humane and highly effective at reducing antisocial behaviour.

(Gesch 2002)

Children with poor eating habits whose diets are radically improved soon find themselves feeling noticeably less depressed, aggressive and confrontational. Good nutrition releases the positive potential in children and young people, and prevents some of the serious problems now being faced by many teachers and parents.

Working towards a healthier diet

Adopt a whole-school approach through a healthy eating policy:

- consult pupils, parents, governors and school staff;
- define roles and responsibilities of the whole-school community.

Ensure that there is a planned programme of food and nutrition education:

- start from children's ideas, ensuring that their needs inform the curriculum;
- explore attitudes and values in addition to extending knowledge.

Promote healthy eating options:

- provide food in accordance with national nutrition standards;
- provide information for parents and pupils on the content of a healthy packed lunch;
- consider setting up a breakfast club.

Promote healthy snacks at break-times:

- start a fruit tuck shop;
- encourage children to eat fruit.

Encourage all pupils to have at least three fluid breaks during the school day:

- make water available to pupils at break and lunchtime;
- explore the possibility of having water available during lessons.

Resources

Information about national nutritional standards for school lunches, healthy packed lunches, tuck shops and vending machines, and healthy breakfast clubs can be obtained from the following organizations.

British Nutrition Foundation, High Holborn House, 52–54 High Holborn, London WC1V 6RQ
(Tel 020 7404 6504); www.nutrition.org.uk

Subsidized and free school milk
www.milk.co.uk

School Nutrition Action Group (SNAG)
www.healthedtrust.com

Sustain – Alliance for Better Food and Farming, 94 White Lion Street, London N1 9PF (Tel 020 7837 1228)
www.sustainweb.org

The Grab 5! project website (www.grab5.com) provides useful information and downloadable materials.

References

Appleton, N. (1996), *Lick the Sugar Habit*, Avery Publishing Group, New York
The author shows how sugar upsets the chemistry of the body and how this can lead to various illnesses and conditions.

Curl, C. L., Fenske, R. A. and Elgethum, K. (2003), Organophosphorus pesticide exposure of urban and suburban pre-school children with organic and conventional diets, *Environmental Health Perspectives,* 111 (3), pages 377–382

Gesch, B. (2002), A recipe for peace – The role of nutrition in social behaviour. In Holden, J., Howland. L. and Jones, D. S. (eds) *Foodstuff: Living in an Age of Feast and Famine,* Demos, London

Gesch, B., Hammond, S. M., Hampson, S. E., Eves, A. and Crowder, M. J. (2002), Influence of supplementary vitamins, minerals and essential fatty acids on the antisocial behaviour of young adult prisoners, *British Journal of Psychiatry,* 181, pages 22–28

Brain Gym®: integrating mind and body through movement

Daphne Clarke

Daphne Clarke is an education consultant specializing in brain integration and has been actively practising kinesiology for the past 18 years. She teaches courses throughout Britain and lectures to various interested organizations, as well as helping people on a one-to-one basis. Daphne's contribution provides a clear and insightful introduction to several exercises that she has found to be particularly helpful to children. All of the exercises described can be done by anyone, anywhere and at any time. They can even be done as a whole-class activity and were designed to make the learning process easier and more comfortable.

Introduction

It feels really good to be able to do something well, whether it is a special performance of some kind, or simply spending a day doing more mundane things and feeling happy and satisfied at the end of it. Special performances involve special training – athletes need to train their bodies to ensure peak fitness for their chosen sport, actors and musicians need to practise techniques and rehearse plays and pieces of music with their colleagues. For a lot of children, even the simplest task becomes a 'performance', and for some just spending the day in school doing everything that a school day involves is tremendously challenging.

Back in the 1970s, in California, Dr Paul Dennison developed a programme of deceptively simple exercises to help make the learning process easier and more comfortable. Some of the exercises are designed to make electromagnetic connections in the brain more efficient, some address eye movement and hand–eye co-ordination, and some help to relieve stress and tension.

Dr Dennison called his exercises Brain Gym®, and I have found that a particular group of them provides a really good base to help children to cope on all levels with whatever crops up for them during the day. The exercises I have chosen to describe could be introduced in various ways, depending on the activity being done and the children involved.

They can be done as a whole-class activity, for instance: teachers may like to use **Brain Buttons**, **Cross Crawl** and **Thinking Caps** daily, at the beginning of morning and afternoon school, to get the children ready for learning. When there is a need for a class to calm down, **Hook Ups** are invaluable. I have taught Brain Gym® exercises to teachers in many schools, and the children in one Special Needs Unit had great fun working out different ways in which to incorporate them into their lessons. Their teacher made a video of a group of the children who had made up a dance using all the exercises, which they performed to their parents to one of the records in the hit parade.

Groups and teams can benefit: sports ability and individual and team co-ordination will be helped by doing variations of **Cross Crawl** and **Lazy Eights** (which is not solely for writing). Reading and drama groups, and choirs and orchestras, too, could use **The Reading Exercise** before a play-reading, rehearsal or performance. For all teams and groups, a few moments doing **Positive Points** and imagining a great performance is extremely beneficial.

Once children become used to using the exercises in the classroom they may find that they recognize situations, at school or at home, in which a specific exercise may be beneficial. They can just pause for a few seconds and do the exercise by themselves. Similarly, teachers may find a specific exercise particularly relevant to a child or a situation at any point during a day – in which case, it could be done there and then.

Brain Gym® exercises, then, can be done by anyone, anywhere and at any time. They need not take a lot of time out of a busy school day – nor do they need to have a special lesson assigned to them. Once children know how to do the individual exercises they can use them as and when they need to. Each exercise takes only seconds to do, and results happen quickly.

I have been using these exercises, with both children and adults, for many years, and the results have been amazing. In a very short time both sides of the brain can be activated, neural connections can be stimulated and the pupil can become motivated and focused, ready to enjoy the day. It is a good training programme to follow.

Have a drink of water

Drinking water boosts energy and mental focus

The first step along the road to efficient learning is to have a good, long drink of water, because drinking water as frequently as possible during the day helps a person to move easily and to think clearly. I know it is not always easy to allow children to leave the classroom to have a drink of water throughout the school day, but several schools in which I have taught Brain Gym® exercises are now making it a policy to have water available in the classrooms so that children can drink when they want to. Some schools allow pupils to bring individual plastic bottles to keep on their desks; some have jugs of water and a cup for each child. Generally, the plastic bottle option is the easiest and cleanest.

Now for some of the exercises.

Brain Buttons

Hold one hand over the navel, and with the other hand rub quite firmly in the hollows just under the collarbone. Change your hands over, and repeat the exercise.

Brain Buttons – 'Buzz your brain'

Brain Buttons stimulates the carotid artery which takes newly oxygenated blood to both sides of the brain simultaneously.

Cross Crawl

March on the spot for a few minutes. When you raise your right knee, touch it with your left hand, and when you raise your left knee, touch it with your right hand. It may be fun to have some music playing while doing the marching, as this helps to keep the movement going. Children often enjoy working out some other ways of moving opposite arms and legs: stretching them out to the sides is one way.

Cross Crawl – 'March to get moving'

For optimum performance in any situation, the student needs to have equal access to both the creative (right) and the organizational/language (left) brain hemispheres. **Cross Crawl** encourages both sides of the brain to work simultaneously; by moving opposite parts of the body at the same time, you are helping your brain to work in this switched-on way.

Thinking Caps

This is an exercise to get the ears ready. With your thumb and index finger, uncurl the outer part of the ear gently, starting from the top and slowly moving to the earlobe. Repeat the exercise three or four times.

Thinking Caps – 'Encourage your ears'

Thinking Caps makes listening, concentrating and remembering instructions and information easier. Just the act of physically stimulating receptors in the outer ear wakes up the whole hearing mechanism.

Lazy Eights

Here is a warm-up for the fingers, and the eyes, which helps with writing. It is called Lazy Eights because instead of being drawn upright, the number is drawn on its side, like the infinity sign. Starting at the centre, draw an eight on its side. Go upwards first, watching the movement of the fingers all the time as the eight shape is being made. Do some eights with one hand, then with the other hand, then some with both hands.

Lazy Eights is good for hand/eye co-ordination and helps the eyes to track smoothly from left to right. It does much more than that, as I found out in what for me was a very moving experience. I was invited to spend some time in a special class for children with autism, to see how their teacher was using Brain Gym®. She demonstrated how the eights exercise enabled her to gain eye contact with two of her pupils who had previously refused to have eye contact with anyone at all in the school. One little boy had a brother who was a professional clown, and who was one of the few people with whom he would communicate. The teacher borrowed a fantastic, bright red clown wig from the brother, and used it to draw eights in the air in front of the little boy. He was immediately interested, recognizing it as something to do with his brother, so his attention was gained and he watched constantly. It did not take too long for the teacher to be able to leave the wig to one side, and do the eight shapes with her hand, and still the boy watched. Eventually, she only had to lift her hand in front of the boy's face and he would look straight at her, smile and keep watching her.

The other child, a little girl, loved listening to music on a cassette recorder. The teacher followed the same procedure with her as she had with the boy, only this time she used a cassette to gain the girl's attention initially, and then used it when she drew the eights in the air for the child's eyes to follow.

It seemed that connections were made for both the children, to do with the left and right hemispheres and with eye co-ordination, too, and they continued with the progress they had made.

Lazy Eights – 'Eight's your mate for writing straight'

Hook Ups

This exercise helps banish the wriggles. It is done in two parts. Sit down and cross one ankle over the other. Cross the wrists and clasp the hands together. If it feels comfortable, fold your hands upwards so that they rest on your chest, just underneath your chin. Breathe deeply for a while, and enjoy feeling calm.

Now do part two: uncross your hands and feet, and put the tips of your fingers and thumbs together as if to make a tower. Again, breathe deeply and think about what you will be doing next.

Hook Ups – 'Cool to concentrate'

Hook Ups calms and focuses the student and aids concentration. A friend of mine used to have her turbulent Year 12 pupils do it as they came into the classroom for a French lesson. She said it never failed to calm them down, and always allowed a quiet lesson to take place.

Positive Points

I have described this exercise as if I were telling a child how to do it:

Here's a way of helping you to relax if you are feeling worried about something – reading out loud, for instance. Sit down somewhere comfortable. Hold one hand across your forehead, think about the reading you are going to do, and imagine yourself standing confidently with your book, looking relaxed, ready to read. Put in all the details you possibly can, including seeing all the people who will be there listening to you.

Next, still in your imagination, begin your reading. Hear your voice as you read beautifully, and enjoy the flow of the words as you say them. Imagine yourself smiling and feeling happy as you finish the reading and sit down, knowing that you did really well. Repeat this whole process three times, then take a deep breath and take your hands from your head. If you have a friend or parent with you, they could hold your head for you instead of you doing it for yourself. It feels good to have it done like that sometimes – it is very comforting.

This exercise is great for all sorts of things, not just reading aloud. Use it for sports – you can imagine yourself playing really well. If you are preparing music or drama for a performance, you can imagine yourself giving a superb performance. Once you have done something well in your imagination it is much easier to feel happy about doing it for real.

Positive Points – 'Relax for reading'

Positive Points is an excellent de-stresser. Holding the hands in the positions shown while either visualizing performing well, or while reviewing (and changing) something that did not go well, helps to remove stress and the fear of failure. The pupil can then feel comfortable, energized and ready to learn.

The Reading Exercise

You may also like to try this exercise, which is not from the Brain Gym® programme. This is great for warming up the eyes and the voice before reading, whether out loud or silently. With one hand on the navel and the other hand rubbing the points under the collarbone as described in **Brain Buttons**, roll the eyes in a big circle in one direction, then in a big circle back the other way. At the same time, say or

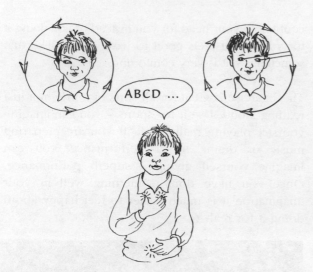

The Reading Exercise – 'Rub and roll for reading'

The Reading Exercise has a dual effect: it engages both brain hemispheres, allowing the pupil to recognize words easily and read with expression, and it also brings about efficient neural connections and tracking ability. This is one of the most stunning exercises I know, and one which seems to have instant results. The mother of a boy I did some work with did not realize it was her son reading when she came to collect him from my room, and stood outside the door listening in amazement. She told me she had never heard him read as well as that before.

sing the alphabet out loud. Change the hands over and repeat the rubbing under the collarbone, the circles and the ABC.

Conclusion

This has been a brief introduction to Brain Gym®. I am sure that if you use some of the exercises regularly with your children you will see a difference. Why not do them too, and experience the difference they can make for yourself.

Key ideas and practice pointers

- Brain Gym® integrates the mind and body through movement.
- Brain Gym® enhances learning and is based on extensive research in education, brain function, psychology and applied kinesiology.
- Brain Gym® is a programme of simple exercises. These exercises can lead to improvements in concentration, memory, reading, listening, physical co-ordination, behaviour, attitude and more.
- Brain Gym® exercises can be introduced in various ways.
- Brain Gym® exercises take only seconds to do.
- All the Brain Gym® exercises can be done as a whole-class, group or individual activity.
- Brain Gym® exercises can be done before, during or after school.
- Children can be encouraged to recognize situations where a specific exercise may be beneficial.
- Have drinking water available for children in the classroom.

Resources

Daphne Clarke has considerable experience as a Brain Gym® instructor and consultant. She can be contacted at Woodlands, Waddon Hall, Waddon, Milton Keynes, MK1 70NA (Tel 01908 501915)

Further information regarding Brain Gym® can be obtained from:
The Brain Gym® Foundation UK, 12 Golders Rise, Hendon, London NW4 2HR (Tel 020 8202 3141)
www.braingym.org.uk
Publications by Paul and Gail Dennison and other educational kinesiology books can also be purchased from the above address.

Suggested further reading

Dennison, P. E. and Dennison, G. E. (1986), *Brain Gym – Simple Activities*, Edu-Kinesthetics, Ventura, Calif. This book gives simple explanations and clear illustrations of each of the 26 Brain Gym® movements.

Dennison, P. E. and Dennison, G. E. (1994), *Brain Gym – Teacher's Edition*, Edu-Kinesthetics, Ventura, Calif. This book provides in-depth explanations of each of the Brain Gym® movements and how they can be used effectively.

Hannaford, C. (1995), *Smart Moves: Why learning is not all in your head*, Great Ocean Publishers, Arlington, Virginia
A book for teachers interested in the principles behind Brain Gym®. Neurobiologist Carla Hannaford uses her knowledge of the brain to interpret the success of the Brain Gym® exercises.

7 Vision and purpose

– right from the start

> *You are today where your thoughts have brought you; you will be tomorrow where your thoughts take you.*
>
> James Allen

Tuckswood:
the school as a community of enquiry

Sue Eagle

Tuckswood Community First School serves as an example of a school in which a range of initiatives have been implemented successfully to support children's social, emotional and cognitive development. Sue Eagle, the school's headteacher, explains the school's vision of a 'community of enquiry' through the development of Philosophy for Children as a core strategy for raising children's achievement and serving their needs as life-long learners and reflective, critical and creative thinkers. Other initiatives discussed are enquiry drama, the creative use of ICT (information, communication and technology), Class and School Council, nurture and light sensory work, learning about learning, biodiversity and the use of the school's grounds. This contribution examines the impact of the initiatives on both the children and the staff and concludes by identifying issues for future development. Sue Eagle illustrates the importance of high-quality, inspirational and practical professional development in implementing these initiatives.

Introduction

Tuckswood Community First School is physically and socially at the heart of the community, the children mostly delightful, well-behaved and engaging, and the majority of the parents extremely supportive. It was not always so, and we have been working hard at developing the school as a learning organization – a true community of enquiry – for over eight years. During this time we have had a few staff changes but have never lost sight of our focus: developing an organization where children and adults can gain knowledge, skills and understanding through questioning and enquiry in an atmosphere that is supportive, exciting and energizing, and where all concerned can foster a love and joy of learning.

Creative, critical and reflective thinking is at the heart of our work. We started as a whole staff by examining our own questioning and learning and looking closely at our individual and corporate values (see Appendix 5: Aims/Values).

There are many different aspects of the enquiry curriculum that have developed over the years. Some of these infuse the whole curriculum and are central to us. Philosophy for Children (P4C), Enquiry Drama,

and Class and School Council are powerful learning and teaching strategies that define and influence the whole curriculum. These are described below. We have developed other aspects that contribute a huge amount to our work and these, too, are described very briefly. (See Resources, page 197, for useful contact details and further information about the initiatives and organizations discussed in this contribution.)

Philosophy for Children

Philosophy for Children (P4C) is a way of encouraging children to think really well – creatively, logically and reflectively – based on questioning and enquiry. It is so straightforward that it is possible for children of all abilities to take part in and learn from and all good teachers to facilitate.

Philosophy for Children is based on the notion that everything is open to question. Children learn to question and discuss in a way that helps them build one idea from another – 'go on a journey of ideas' as one child put it. A story/picture book is usually used as a stimulus. It is read to the children and they are invited to ask a question or say what the story makes them think about. Children have such wonderful thoughts and 'wonderings' about the stories they hear.

It is easiest if the children are sitting in a circle – for one thing they can all look at each other. You need, first, to establish the conventions or rules of engagement. These are ours:

- Listen with respect to each other.
- Back up your statements with reasons.
- All ideas are open for exploration and challenge.
- Build on each other's ideas.
- Be prepared to follow an enquiry where it leads.

In the words of Jamie, aged seven years: 'It gets your brain thinking, then you can get more ideas and learn more.'

Sometimes children like to debate things they have seen on television or heard about on the news. One class of Year 2 and 3 children had an amazing debate about euthanasia following an episode of *EastEnders,* where one character (Dot) helped another (Ethel) to end her life. The children knew it was just television but, as one of them said, 'it does really happen sometimes'. During their discussion they learned something about the nature of real friendship and demonstrated a high level of mature thinking.

Whatever stimulus gets them going, we find that they quickly move into discussion of a philosophical nature – talking about the big questions of life, death and the universe. This work links closely with developing children's self-esteem and emotional intelligence.

Examples of some of our favourite books are:

Where the Wild Things Are – Maurice Sendak
Where the Forest Meets the Sea – Jeannie Baker
The Whales' Song and *The Garden* – Dyan Sheldon
Grandad's Prayers of the Earth – Douglas Wood
Anybook by Anthony Browne

Connor, aged seven years, says, 'Thinking makes your brain grow stronger' – and he's right.

On page 182 is a diagram showing the form of the session. We have been practising P4C for eight years now and it is embedded into our curriculum. All our classes have one P4C session a week, but the questioning and thinking approach is at the heart of our whole curriculum. It is exciting and challenging to teach in what is truly a community of enquiry.

Philosophy for Children is vital to our growth as educators because it is more than just a tool for teaching: it is a way of learning that influences the whole curriculum – a way of being. It has been important for all of the staff to receive training in P4C. All teachers and learning support staff at Tuckswood have been trained by Karin Murris, Joanna Haynes or Roger Sutcliffe from the Society for Advancing Philosophical Enquiry and Reflection in Education (SAPERE).

Karin runs day courses for learning support staff. Our support staff have enjoyed and benefited enormously from these days. SAPERE run accredited courses for the teaching of P4C at Levels 1, 2 and 3. Level 1 is a two-day course and Levels 2 and 3 last for four days. All our teachers are trained at Level 1, with some at Level 2 and one at Level 3. The training is thorough, exhausting but entirely energizing. Two years ago, we appointed a new deputy head who is now Level 2 trained. Our previous deputy (also Level 2 trained) is now a headteacher, running her own school that is very much a community of enquiry, with P4C at the heart. Our two new members of staff have already achieved their Level 1 status. One of these has been teaching for a very long time and felt that this training was the best she had ever attended. The other, a newly qualified teacher, felt that the P4C training typified her reasons for coming into the teaching profession.

Karin Murris and Joanna Haynes also run 'Thinking Days' in schools. Karin ran one such day at Tuckswood. We started off the new school year with it and had a wonderful day full of enquiry and community thinking. At a 9 o'clock assembly, Karin and I set a 'dramatic context' for the children and staff to work on for the rest of the day and came together at the end of the day to share and evaluate our findings. A full write-up of this can be found in the *Teaching Thinking* magazine (Eagle 2001).

We feel that it is important for us to keep refreshing ourselves and constantly talk about and evaluate what we do.

We have used Philosophy for Children for long enough to have evidence-based practice in place and to know that it is an effective and exciting way of making the curriculum inclusive and relevant. All children, whatever their particular intelligences and

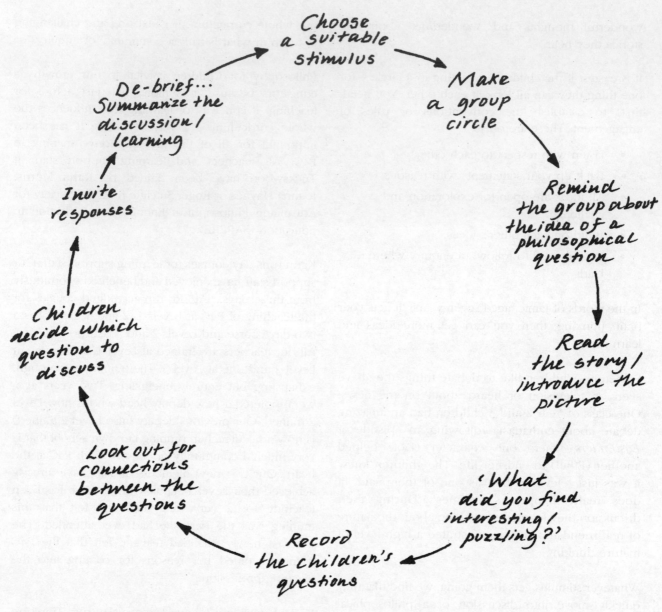

The structure of a Philosophy for Children session

special learning needs, are able to take part and all contributions are valued and used. P4C promotes independence in learning, metacognition and creative, critical and reflective thinking. We have used our experience to document what we see as a line of progression from Reception to Year 3. This is a working document and needs constant updating. The current version is as follows.

Reception year (four and five year olds) learning:

- what a question is and the difference between a question and a statement;
- what listening is and what it looks/feels like to listen and be listened to;
- what it means to agree and disagree with a person's idea;

- that it is okay to express an opinion – it is not about being right or wrong.

Year 1 learning:

- to use the format 'I agree with you because…' and 'I disagree with you because…' and be able to begin to give reasons and reflections;
- to make eye contact and to talk to each other and not through the teacher;
- what it means to agree and disagree with a person's idea;
- how to listen with care and attention.

Year 2 learning:

- to justify and explain your thinking clearly;

- to disagree with a person without falling out;
- to begin to examine and to use different types of questions;
- to think around an idea – reflect on your own thinking.

We found over the years that the level of debate is deeper and richer in Year 2 since the children have been involved in philosophical discussion from their Reception year.

Year 3 learning:

- to agree and disagree and justify your thinking with the use of the format;
- to begin to understand the difference between philosophical and scientific questions and be able to identify and use both appropriately;
- to be honest in your thinking and reflect your beliefs in your thinking;
- to display empathy in your thinking;
- to feel able to change your mind if reflection has led you to and you know your reasons for doing so;
- to reach a richness of thinking and discussion skills that will enable you to have a confident and reasoned voice in your community.

'Thinking Schools – Thinking Children'

The school was fortunate to be part of the LEA's Thinking Schools – Thinking Children project (TSTC). This was a two-year action-research-based project carried out in partnership between Norfolk schools and the Norfolk Education Advisory Service.

In September 2000, the Norfolk Association of First and Primary Headteachers held a conference attended by over 90 headteachers and led by Trevor Hawes from Optimal Learning, the co-author of *Effective Teaching and Learning in the Primary Classroom* (Shaw and Hawes 1998). Trevor led us in an exploration of new knowledge from neuroscientific research about how the brain works. The importance of this knowledge in relation to the learning and teaching was discussed. Senior advisers from the education authority also attended this conference. They were keen to share and spread the good practice already evident in this area of work within some schools.

At the end of the conference the advisers discussed with headteachers the possibility of a small-scale action-research project to be carried out in partnership between schools and advisers. Strategies for developing children's critical, creative and reflective thinking, taking into account our developing understanding of 'brain-based' learning, would be explored and evaluated. There was a huge amount of interest and enthusiasm for this – far more than we had envisaged. A joint steering group of heads, advisers and teachers was set up. Roger Eagle and Helen Banks, both senior advisers in Norfolk, led the project. The title of 'Thinking Schools – Thinking Children' was decided upon and a way of working was agreed. It was to last for two years, giving time to try out and embed some useful and innovative strategies into practice, and be supported by advisers. Each school had a key teacher as well as the headteacher leading the project and committed a small amount of money to support their work. First, primary and middle schools were mailed and we had more than 90 responses. What set out to be a small-scale project became rather large.

Termly conferences were held. These involved a variety of speakers who spoke with us about particular strategies and philosophies of developing children's thinking. We ensured that the speakers were of consistently high quality. Also, at each conference, time was made to share existing good practice in our schools and to discuss work in progress with colleagues. The conferences had a wonderful 'buzz' from teachers who were energized and genuinely enjoying what they were involved in. At the first of these conferences schools were given an overview of various strategies. Philosophy for Children, School Council work, Brain Gym®, mind mapping, use of music in learning, multiple intelligences and accelerated learning techniques were the main ones. Schools were invited to decide upon one or two of these on which to concentrate their research. Network groups were set up and advisers appointed to each group. Each school also had a named 'Thinking Schools' adviser attached to them. Action-research techniques were explored in one of the early conferences, together with ways of presenting final evidence and findings. This made the thought of researching less daunting and more possible for teachers to fit into busy schedules. Evaluations from the conferences show that people really appreciated the support from advisers and colleagues in the network groups. They were also inspired by the very high quality of the speakers. The feeling that your education authority is investing huge amounts of time and money, working and learning alongside you in exploration of innovative ideas, is very supportive. It does much to reduce the concern about fitting things into a crowded curriculum. The approach was not one of fitting in and adding more but of looking at different and exciting ways for children to learn the same curriculum content. Teaching children how to learn makes so much sense when we know that there is more knowledge to be had in the world than we could ever teach them.

Sixty-five schools submitted their final reports on the project. These were used to write the final project report published by the National Primary Trust (2003). The Norfolk Education Advisory Service's work is continuing with a School Improvement Module about developing the 'Thinking School's' approach, plus a similar module called 'Creative Schools – Creative Children'. These modules are offered to schools as a blend of training and action-research-based development.

Enquiry drama

Drama at Tuckswood Community First School involves children in an exciting exploration of many issues and is used across the curriculum in various forms. It provides opportunities for children to learn through visual, verbal and kinesthetic approaches, and uses a variety of intelligences. We find it to be a totally inclusive way of working and a vital part of our community of enquiry. Some examples of strategies used are:

- improvization
- freeze-frame and still image
- thought-tracking
- conscience alley
- enquiry/problem-solving meetings
- hot seating
- 'mantle of the expert'.

The most important element of the strategies is that children are involved in enquiry, problem solving, creative representation and thinking through issues and contexts. A vital part of the learning is that, in life, our actions/behaviours are inextricably linked to our beliefs and values. This work is of huge benefit in the pursuit of emotional intelligence.

The following is just one practical example of sessions.

RECEPTION CLASS DRAMA SESSION
This session was held in February 2001. The teacher was Mrs Jean Fraser.

Warm-up
All the children began by standing and were then asked to walk slowly about in the working space, with the teacher giving spoken signals to start and stop. After several goes the children were asked to start and stop without spoken signals but by watching each other and feeling what to do. It took about three attempts, but I was very pleased with how well the children developed the idea and took cues from each other.

Main activity
The class were then split into random groups of five. Each group was given the task of making a model (still image) with their bodies of a statue to celebrate Norwich City winning the FA Cup. Each group had adult support and after five minutes were able to produce a model. One child felt uneasy and, although she had been part of her group's model, would not join in to show the others her part in it. These models were all built on discussion between the group members. The next task was for the children to use the 'Lego' method of just placing the first 'brick' and letting the model evolve. The challenge here was to represent a group still image of the Indian earthquake (February 2001). The children set about this with due intensity. When the images were complete I questioned each group. In one group a child lay on the floor. 'I'm dead.' Another (a child with a statement of special needs) had positioned himself with his legs, arms and body distorted. 'I'm a broken house – the ground gave way.' Another group had a child hanging forward with a glum face. 'I'm a lost and broken old man.'

Conclusion of session
In unison, we all practised a simple set of movements – reaching out, catching and then throwing an imaginary ball. I then suggested that we might do it angrily, then lazily and then as if we were frightened. The children came up with their own ideas. Examples of these were: pompously, enthusiastically and, finally, as if we were on the moon.

Review
All the children really enjoyed the session, including the girl who had been reluctant at the start. They put a great deal of effort and thought into it. They all seemed to be building a greater sensitivity towards each other and the level of co-operation between the children was very encouraging. They showed a high level of understanding about emotions, responses and associated behaviours.

Information, communication and technology

Information, communication and technology (ICT) has been, and continues to be, an exciting development for us at Tuckswood Community First School. We are a mixed-ability group but lucky enough to have an excellent ICT subject leader, who has eased us through the pain barrier of our own learning and enabled us to become skilful in the creative use of the hardware we now have at school. We run an AppleMac Tech Lab, which houses eight desktop machines (iMacs) and eight laptops (iBooks). We also have an eMac, printer, a digital projector, whiteboard and mimeo board plus digital still and video cameras. Our school is wireless networked, enabling the smooth use of the hardware anywhere in the school. The iBooks can be taken into the classrooms without the need for plugs, allowing easy use of ICT as part of ongoing work. We use the equipment in a variety of ways as well as part of the ongoing curriculum. For example, as part of the children's 'early work' (basic skills work put out for children and parents to get on with when they first arrive in the morning) a spelling program is set up for identified children to work on to increase their skills.

Children are learning to use iMovie (AppleMac software) and they make short movies for various purposes. One benefit of this is that they can watch and evaluate their performances on screen. An example is a movie designed and made by Year 2 and 3 children to promote a new drink that had been created. This was part of a 'mantle of the expert' drama project. The children were able to assess, edit and redo parts of the movie as they felt appropriate. By such means, peer and self-evaluation becomes a natural part of the work. Children will be making movies of their school lives to send to link schools in other parts of the world, making decisions about content, evaluating their performance and the clarity of their messages, and editing on-screen. These skills are all very useful.

The digital camera is used by the children as part of the work they do, to record and develop projects, make posters and so on.

An exciting project during the spring and summer terms in 2003 was the ICT Club held after school on a Friday. Two sixth-form pupils from the local high school led this, acting as learning mentors to 12 of our Year 3 children. The mentors organized and ran the sessions, teaching the children a variety of ICT skills. They were wonderful mentors and all involved thoroughly enjoyed themselves. On the final session of the club, my deputy and I were invited to judge the PowerPoint presentations that our children had put together on subjects of their choice. Presentations ranged from dinosaurs to Manchester United, taking in James Bond on the way. It was an exceptionally hard job as all the presentations were well thought out, informative, humorous and an auditory and visual treat. Luckily the mentors had thought to provide prizes for all 12 children.

We will be taking our Year 3 children for a visit to Ultra Lab, Chelmsford during the autumn term to see and use the most up-to-date AppleMac equipment and learn more ICT skills from the experts. This will be a brilliant experience for us as well as the children.

Class and School Council

We have always involved the children in the life of the school; it is, after all, their community. Three years ago we all felt that they (or was it 'we'?) were ready to take on a more active and formalized role in decision making. That was the impetus for the Tuckswood Community School and Class Councils. Two members of staff received training from Schools Councils UK and fed back to the whole staff. Much discussion ensued and we decided to have a go. We have developed and tweaked our system over the years and now have a way of working which is effective and energizing. We are now part of a research project run by the University of East Anglia, exploring effective ways of including the youngest children in council work.

We felt from the start that it was important to include all the children and adults in the school. Our main aims are:

- to involve children fully in the decision-making processes of our school, thus giving them a real voice in their school community;
- to develop each child's understanding of the democratic processes of a community.

Class Councils are held in every class, once a week, any day before the School Council meeting. Each class elects a chairperson and secretary for Class Council and two representatives for the School Council.

The Class Council secretary records items discussed and any decisions made in the Class Council book. Help is provided by the teacher and support assistant as necessary, according to the age of the child. Items concerning just the class are dealt with in Class

Council. Items that come up in Class Council but concern the whole school are passed to the school secretary for inclusion in the School Council agenda. Some examples of class issues are:

- the arrangement of the furniture in the room
- children not keeping the room tidy
- development of class conventions (rules).

The sort of issues that would go forward to the School Council are:

- concern about running in the corridor
- interest in a particular charity or fund-raising initiative
- ideas for recycling.

Class Councils can put forward only two items each for the School Council agenda and so sometimes have to prioritize the importance of issues.

Election for School Council chairperson, vice-chair and secretary happens twice a year. These responsible offices are for Year 3 children. The qualities required in order to discharge these duties are discussed with the children. They are given time to decide if they would like to put themselves forward for election. Interested children are then invited to give their names to their class teacher. They prepare their promotional material – a scanned photograph of themselves plus a short paragraph describing why they feel they would make a good chairperson. Qualities the children usually emphasize are those of careful listening, confidence and good thinking skills. For one week they photocopy and place their promotional poster around the school. Each class invites the candidates in individually to ask them questions. The week following this activity we hold 'Election Assembly'. The school hall is set up with a long table at one end. This is for the 'tellers' (one adult and one existing School Council member per class list). Two secret ballot booths are set up with panels for privacy and a ballot box. We have learned that we need photographs with names of the candidates at each ballot station to remind the younger children which candidate is which.

School Council elections at Tuckswood

The children come into the hall with all the adults in the school. I remind everybody why we are gathered and what we are looking for in a chairperson for our School Council, and therefore how they need to direct their vote. We then rehearse how the voting happens. I use a large whiteboard with a ballot paper, including the children's names, drawn out on it. This is an enlargement of the real printed ballot papers we give the children. The candidates, who are sitting at the front of the hall by the stage, are then invited one by one on to the stage to give their election speeches. Each starts by saying his or her name clearly and then – 'vote for me because…' At the end of the speeches voting takes place. Each class in turn goes to the tellers to receive their ballot paper and have their name ticked off the list. They take their paper to the booth, place their cross appropriately, fold the paper and put it in the box. There is an adult at each ballot station to help the youngest children if necessary. Every adult also votes. After voting, the children leave the hall. Two adults and the existing chairperson and vice-chair carry out the vote. After a suitable interval, usually over a lunch break, we all gather in the hall again to hear the result of the vote. The chairperson is the person with the most votes, the vice-chair the next number of votes and the secretary the next. All candidates are celebrated and congratulated and the successful officers stand at the door of the hall and shake hands with everyone as they leave to return to their classes.

The School Council, then, comprises the three officers, two class representatives from each class and two staff representatives. The Council also works in committees to allow for maximum discussion of certain issues. At present we have charities, football, behaviour and environment committees. They develop according to need.

Whether working in Class, School or Committee Council, all children are encouraged to participate, verbally or in writing or drawing their ideas and thoughts. Article 12 of the United Nations Conventions on the Rights of the Child is about the right to participation. We take this very seriously and try to reflect its importance in the everyday life of the school.

We have learned a great deal about Council work along the way and have so much more to learn, but we have benefited enormously. Children feel a strong sense of ownership in the school community and their respect for each other is evident.

In the early days it became evident that the Philosophy for Children approach had enabled the children to discuss issues brought forward to Council in a very mature fashion. The children were able to see all sides of an argument and to agree and disagree with each other amicably, but they found it hard to reach any decisions. This was solved easily by giving them decision-making strategies, such as the De Bono 'PMI' format involving children in an examination of the Plus, Minus and Interesting points in any argument. They are then able to see their thinking written on paper and to reach an appropriate decision. If we had not done this, they would have been forever discussing. The Council is now a very strong part of our community of enquiry and is inclusive of all at Tuckswood. Over the last two years it has been encouraging to note that we have had several children with special learning needs feeling good enough about themselves to put themselves forward for chairperson. Watching children holding statements of special needs – and one child who is dyslexic and needed pictures to help him read his speech – feel able to get onto the stage and speak with confidence is tremendous. Candidates who are not elected to office are naturally disappointed, but none has so far suffered adversely and all have a vital part to play. An important aspect of the learning for all children is that they have moved away from voting for their friends, or for a boy or girl because of their gender. They now think carefully about the candidates' reasons for putting themselves forward. Candidates themselves think clearly about the job before writing their promotional material. The elected members find their positions exciting and challenging.

The children say:

If we have a really big problem we can sit down and discuss it.

It's made the school feel really different.

Basically, everyone brings things up to the School Council – like the apparatus in the playground that we bought.

Lots more things are properly discussed.

It makes you feel happy.

I like being on the Council because you get to read out the minutes and explain things better.

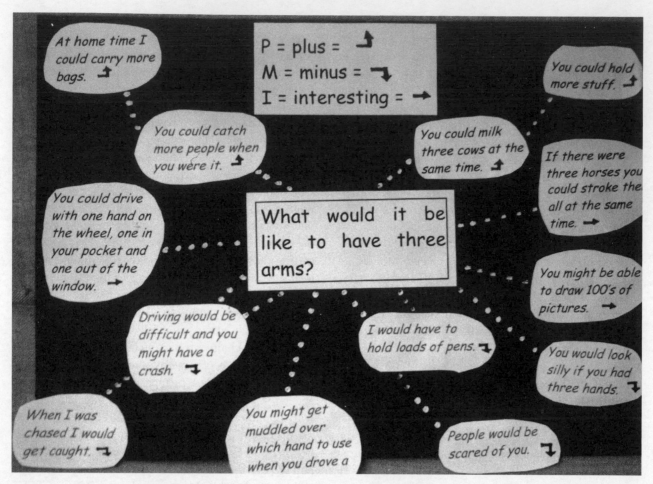

Developing children's thinking skills

Over the years the Council have solved many problems but have also served a far more proactive role. They have raised money for a variety of things, from the Indian earthquake appeal in 2001 to new outside play apparatus for the school. For the latter, they wrote to a local trust fund, raised £5,000 and then chose (within height/cost guidelines) the equipment we now have. They also have input into our school improvement priorities, provide a consultation group for school policies and are writing their own behaviour guidelines. The chairperson or vice-chair is responsible for helping me to greet and show around our many guests. They have held a meeting in the local Council Chamber at County Hall in Norwich and have observed the Norwich elected members holding their meeting. They are, indeed, treasures – what did we do without them!

Learning about learning

Much of our early training for teaching and support staff concerned our use of questioning. Of course, there are occasions when a straightforward question, to which there is a definite answer, is required. However, the use of open questions, aimed at all children, not just those who usually have the answers, is needed. To work in an inclusive way, all children need to feel that the question is for them to find an answer for, and that their response will be valued and used to find answers and solutions. Our questioning needs to help children explain, clarify, justify and be creative and lateral in their thinking and it therefore needs to be skilful in its execution. We always aim to give children thinking time and encourage every child to 'have an answer ready in your own head'. Scribble pads or small whiteboards can also be used for children to try out their answers. We do not always use 'hands up' as a signal for readiness to answer a question. If a question has been asked for everybody and the expectation is that they will all have an answer ready, then a variety of children will be chosen to share their answers. This is possible in an ethos where children's contributions are valued and used. If the children do not have an answer ready, they are given more thinking time and expected to give an answer. Questions are used in this way only if it is known that children chosen are able to answer. Children are encouraged to question, wonder and enquire all the time as a way of learning. As we have learned more about how effective learning takes place and how the brain works we have passed our learning on to the children. Books we have found most useful are Shaw and Hawes (1998), Smith (1996, 1998 and 2000) and Thompson and Maguire (2001).

As the children learn about how they learn and think they become more aware of their learning needs and can identify what to do if their 'brain switches off'. For example, they understand why they need to sip water, take time to think, be physically comfortable and take 'break states'.

BREAK STATE ACTIVITIES

The following activities are encouraged:

- free use of water bottles during learning time;
- having a 'fruit and milk or juice' break mid morning;
- talking about their work to a friend;
- taking an exercise break by doing a Brain Gym® movement;
- opening a window if too hot (or putting on a sweater if cold);
- stopping and refocusing on another task if necessary.

We do not run a formal breakfast club, but children who have not breakfasted at home are given breakfast at school as part of our Nurture Work and to make them ready for learning. Our children had always had a mid-morning break for milk or juice (no fizzy drinks). We introduced fruit or a cereal bar (no chocolate or biscuits) two years ago. Children are noticeably more alert after this break. We also notice that children who professed not to like apples or other fruit will now happily munch away at their chosen fruit.

DRINKING WATER IN SCHOOL

In line with our Statements of Aims and Values, we are concerned with maximizing children's independent learning, developing their higher order thinking and helping each child to raise his or her achievement and attainment. Our wish is to develop a community of enquiry whereby children and adults can retain the natural curiosity and joy of learning and become truly lifelong learners. Over the last few years we have looked closely at the neuroscientific research into 'brain-based learning'. This led us to continue to examine the conditions in which effective learning and teaching take place, and also the elements involved in developing brain power and children's and adults'

ability to recognize the signs of the brain being closed to learning, and to know what to do to rectify the situation.

Following a healthy eating regime and drinking plenty of water plays a large part in keeping children alert and ready for learning. Regular hydration helps to prevent headaches and fatigue. We can become mildly dehydrated quickly and our brains will not function as well as they could while we are in this state. Part of their curriculum work involves the children learning about how the brain works and how effective and sustained learning happens. This is part of their 'Brain Basics' learning.

Teachers discuss with their class the importance of drinking water regularly and keeping the brain hydrated. The children are encouraged to sip water often rather than gulp a lot at a time. The messages about the benefits of a healthy diet and drinking water regularly are backed up during assembly times.

All children at Tuckswood have water bottles on their desks and are taught how and why they should use them. The bottles are named and it is each child's responsibility to refill his or her bottle with drinking water when necessary. If the bottle is lost or spoilt within the term the family replaces it.   There are conventions about when and where to use the bottles. The water bottles are in addition to, not a replacement for, the fresh fruit or cereal bar and juice or milk that children have for mid-morning break.

Parents were informed about the introduction of water bottles in the classroom through an article in the school's newsletter. The article included straightforward information about why drinking water helps learning and the health and safety issues involved. The children were encouraged to make posters displaying similar information to put up in their classrooms and throughout the school. The introduction of water bottles has been very successful. The children are able to take a drink whenever they feel their brain 'switching off' during learning and are responsible for keeping themselves rehydrated.

BRAIN GYM® STYLE MOVEMENTS

We began our work with Brain Gym® style movements after I attended a two-day educational kinesiology course in London.

All staff then received local training and now use the movements in a variety of ways in the classroom to help children focus and concentrate on their learning. For the past three years we have run a lunchtime club during which children do Brain Gym®, style movements and juggling. The club, which is run by one of our excellent learning support assistants, includes children who are dispraxic, dyslexic and have various learning or behaviour difficulties. The children love the club, and we see great improvements in their co-ordination and learning focus. Children from the club are sometimes invited to give demonstrations at conferences and give confident performances at the Royal Norfolk Show.

MIND MAPPING

Mind mapping is another skill we have learned that we teach to our children. It appeals particularly to our visual learners and is another tool to help them organize their thinking. We use it in a variety of ways:

- to determine what children know about a subject;
- to help them organize their thoughts;
- to help them remember information;
- to assess their learning from a taught session or project.

More information can be found in *Mind Mapping for Children* (Buzan 2003) and *MapWise* (Caviglioli and Harris 2000).

CONTINUING PROFESSIONAL DEVELOPMENT

Continuing professional development (CPD) supports our work and helps us to sustain and improve what we offer to our children. As part of our CPD last year, one of our staff went to Malta to spend a week working with trainers from the Edward De Bono Institute for the Design and Development of Thinking. On her return she shared her learning with the rest of the staff and developed an excellent resource bank for us; we now use many of the strategies to help our children think effectively. We find the strategies especially useful with our youngest children. The Reception class really enjoyed doing a 'CAF' (Consider All Factors) on the question: 'What if adults came to school and children stayed at home?'

Edward De Bono has written many useful and informative books on effective thinking (see Suggested further reading, page 198).

Mind mapping – 'Everybody needs a place to think'

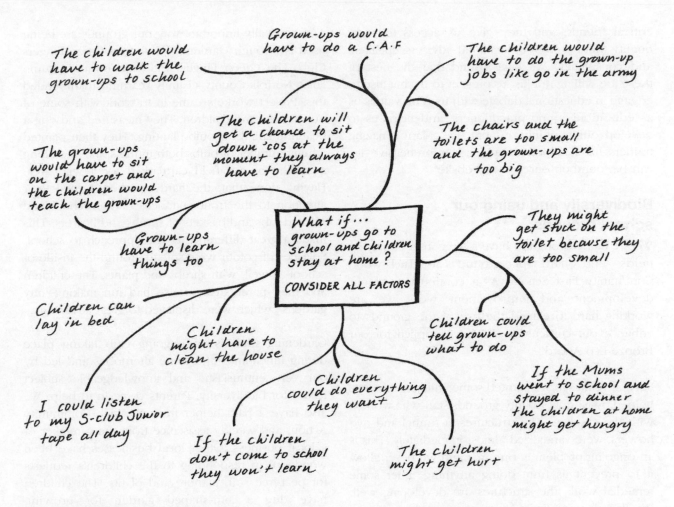

The children would have to walk the grown-ups to school

Grown-ups would have to do a C.A.F

The children would have to do the grown-up jobs like go in the army

The children will get a chance to sit down 'cos at the moment they always have to learn

The grown-ups would have to sit on the carpet and the children would teach the grown-ups

The chairs and the toilets are too small and the grown-ups are too big

Grown-ups have to learn things too

What if... grown-ups go to school and children stay at home?

CONSIDER ALL FACTORS

They might get stuck on the toilet because they are too small

Children can lay in bed

Children might have to clean the house

Children could tell grown-ups what to do

I could listen to my S-club Junior tape all day

Children could do everything they want

If the Mums went to school and stayed to dinner the children at home might get hungry

If the children don't come to school they won't learn

The children might get hurt

Reception children consider all factors

We have built up many tools and strategies to help children to think for learning. As mentioned earlier, an action research approach to CPD has been central to our work and we have utilized many opportunities to learn. The Teachers International Professional Development (TIPD) scheme has been invaluable. Information on this scheme is available from the British Council.

Over the past three years the scheme has meant that three staff have visited New Zealand, researching thinking skill development and creative use of information and communication technology, one has been to Malta to research De Bono's work, and two are about to visit Norway to research a curriculum centred around Global Biodiversity and citizenship. Our learning from these visits has been plentiful and wonderful and has benefited our children enormously. After the New Zealand visit we invited Lane Clark, a Canadian CPD provider, to England to work with many schools in Norfolk on her strategies for effective thinking and learning. We will be inviting key researchers from the De Bono Institute in Malta to Norfolk to share their work with many of our schools. In June 2003 we welcomed a New Zealand primary school principal to Tuckswood to share our work. Strong and beneficial links are made from these visits and we are very grateful to the British Council for their support.

OTHER SUPPORT

Another source of excellent support has been the Department for Education and Skills Best Practice Research Scholarship (BPRS) grants. Over the past three years we have been successful in gaining two or three grants a year. The funding has enabled us to continue to improve the learning opportunities we offer to children. The research has centred on Philosophy for Children, mantle of the expert, enquiry drama and biodiversity in our school grounds.

The Thinking Schools – Thinking Children project (Norfolk County) has been an excellent support and we are also part of the Network Learning Community in Norfolk. Opportunities like these provide funding and time to share learning with like-minded colleagues and to use each other as critical friends; and they give us access to high-quality training from educational advisers, speakers and consultants. We have found that the best of these are willing not just to present to us, but also to engage in educational debate with us. This values us as educationists and practitioners, and helps us to develop our thinking and practice. Many amazing trainers have helped us and a comprehensive list can be found on our school website.

Biodiversity and using our school grounds

We are lucky enough to have a large area of playing fields and hard playground at Tuckswood Community First School. As a continuation of our development and improvement work we are working hard to extend the use of the grounds to enhance our curriculum. We have applied for our Bronze Eco Award.

Several years ago we planted some willow structures, helped by Norfolk County grounds staff who worked with the children. The structures, a tunnel and two bowers, were vandalized almost immediately. This is an ongoing problem in our area and we never allow it to prevent us from doing anything. After some remedial work, the structures are developing well. We also planted a 'story circle' of trees two years ago. These are also growing well. We plan to inter-plant with hedge soon. Future plans include making an orchard in a section of our grounds and possibly sharing our orchard planting with neighbouring City Council land. We have two separate areas of wooden outdoor play equipment for the children's use, one funded by the Friends of Tuckswood School Association and one gained by Tuckswood School Council. We have a large shaded gazebo covering two large picnic benches. These have play tops – one being a snakes and ladders game and the other a road track. We also have a 'friendship table' where children can go if they are in need of someone to play with. Playground mentors are on the lookout to help children in need.

A recent addition is a large aluminium structure with a translucent roof. This covers the outdoor play area immediately outside the Reception and pre-school section of our school, including our paddling pool area. The paddling pool is big and deep enough for the children to practise water confidence skills, weather allowing. The structure allows children to play outside in most weathers. When we have sufficient funds we will purchase side walls for it and use it all year round.

Another really important way our grounds are being used is through Gardening Club and Green Fingers Club. The Green Fingers Club ran during autumn 2002. Norfolk County's Family Learning Team funded this. Project workers came in to work with some of our parents and children. They measured and dug a beautiful spiral for bulb planting. They then planted a huge number of bulbs both in the spiral and along a swathe of our field earmarked for a wild area. Having done that, the hardy workers turned their attention to the front entrances of our school and planted tubs and baskets of shrubs and flowers. This made a great difference to the approach to school. Splashes of colour were spread around the inside of school as well, with shrubs and plants. The children and their parents/carers also had fun making 'tray gardens', which were displayed to great advantage.

Gardening Club is an ongoing club taking place during lunchtimes and some afternoons and led by our very enthusiastic and knowledgeable subject leader for biodiversity. Parents come in to help. We also have a paid helper from Norwich Community Action, and weekly assistance from the caretaker of a local business. Other local businesses have been wonderful in responding to the children's requests for peat-free soil, manure and plants. The children have dug a sun-shaped garden for growing vegetables, a cloud-shaped garden to make a butterfly garden and are planning a further cloud-shaped garden to grow flowers for picking. The latter was in response to the children wanting to pick a glorious show of daffodils growing in the spiral and wild area, but knowing that they mustn't. Gardening Club is responsible for the composting but is helped by the whole school, who now separate their rubbish and have a good system of recycling.

All children who want to are taking part in pumpkin and sunflower growing. We plan to grow vegetables when the soil has been prepared well. When harvested, some of these will be cleaned, prepared, cooked and eaten by the children, in line with our healthy eating policy, and some will be sold for a reasonable price to parents on a market stall in our playground at the end of the school day. Money raised will be used to help fund the Gardening Club's ongoing work.

The School Council Environment Committee are very active and keep us all on our toes with recycling activities. They carried out a waste audit and put an action plan in place for the school. We now try to purchase recycled goods where possible, we recycle our ink cartridges, do back-to-back photocopying,

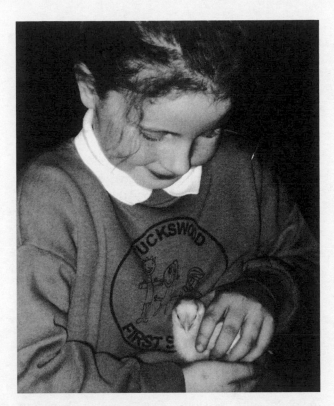

Nurturing a caring approach

re-use old envelopes and do whatever we can to save resources. The children have a growing awareness of their responsibility for their environment and community as well as their rights. If they are able to continue as they are now, they should grow up to be conscientious citizens.

Nurture and light sensory work

The staff of Tuckswood Community First School work in a way that is child-centred and follows the needs of the child. Our work is, by nature, nurturing and inclusive. However, within this context, four years ago we identified a need to offer something more and different for a significant number of children who were entering school unable to access the curriculum in the mainstream classroom as well as we felt they could. We had read about nurture work and, over a period of time, all staff took part in training concerning nurture provision in mainstream schools. This was either the four-day course (myself and the subject leader for personal, social and health education) or the short course (other teaching and support staff). Further information about nurture work can be found in Bennathan and Boxall (1998; 2000).

Having appointed a nurture group worker (initially funded by an inclusion grant, now an integral part of our budget), we set about painting and furnishing our nurture room. We did this by begging and borrowing furniture and equipment, and spending

money on certain things. We ended up with a lovely room, painted in soothing blue and lilac, providing a 'halfway house' between a nurturing home environment and a classroom. It has hot and cold running water, sink, cooking facilities, a table and chairs for the group to sit round together, a comfortable settee, a keyboard, as well as toys, books, games and more. Children work here on the same learning objectives they would in their classroom, but with a different approach and set of activities. Children will eat together as part of their work, developing social and verbal skills. Their finely tuned learning or behaviour targets are met in various ways.

We use the Boxall Profile (Bennathan and Boxall 1998) when appropriate to identify children for nurture work and assess their progress. Nurture work is part of the inclusive learning opportunities offered to our children, in the same way as we offer basic skills help to those who need it. There is no stigma attached and children simply 'go to group' in the same way that they would attend an Additional Literacy Strategy group or an art session with a support assistant. The room is not called anything special, except 'Mrs Corbett's Room' (the nurture worker). Over the years, the work changes in response to the changing needs of our children. Sometimes the work focuses on social skills and positive behaviour, sometimes on structured play opportunities, emotional literacy and sometimes on nurturing one-to-one work to ease a child into learning and help develop a positive work attitude.

An extension of this provision is our light sensory room. We have an ongoing arrangement with our local special school. Groups of their children join us weekly to share in our mainstream work – usually language and large apparatus. In return, we are able to take small groups of our children to use their light sensory room. However, several years ago we felt that we really needed that provision on our site in order to respond to immediate needs. We searched for a space and decided upon the audio-visual cupboard. The shelves were stripped out and the large cupboard painted midnight blue. We secured another inclusion grant to equip it with a fibre-optic light shower, oil-filter projector and various other sensory items and play-therapy toys (see Resources, page 197). We had a training session one evening led by a teacher from the special school and an advisory teacher from our LEA Sensory Support Team.

The room is a wonderful addition to our provision and is used in the following ways:

- One-to-one counselling sessions are held with qualified children's counsellors we buy in. This works on a contractual basis with the child, parent or carer and counsellor, and takes place one day each week.

- If a child is undergoing emotional stress or anger she or he is able to use the room with a support assistant in order to relax and regain equilibrium.

- Play-therapy sessions are held for small groups of children.

Personal, social and health education sessions are run for small groups of children.

Impact on children's learning

A vital element of any research is to explore the impact it has upon the work you are doing. It is always difficult to disentangle the impact of specific strategies when what you are aiming for is an integrated approach combining a range of underlying strategies and complementary associated techniques, tools and methods. No learning happens in a vacuum. However, within that understanding, we have noted many instances of how the work described above has impacted on our children's learning.

Children from Reception onwards display improved listening and speaking skills; our baseline assessment and record-keeping system shows this progress clearly. They develop respect for each other's ideas, plus an understanding that we can disagree with a person's ideas without 'falling out' with them. This can be seen during formal Philosophy for Children sessions, but also in other areas of school life. Children are seen and heard to use questioning and discussion in other areas of the curriculum – not just to accept things they are told. This leads us to think that some transference of learning takes place as well. Children can also be seen to be comfortable about changing their minds if they feel sufficient knowledge and reasons have been gained to do so.

We found in the Class and School Council work that philosophy had given the children an excellent grounding for reflective and reasoned debate. However, we had to teach them some simple decision-making strategies and tools in order to help them reach conclusions to their discussions. De Bono tools proved to be perfect for this and the children use these now as a matter of course in appropriate situations.

There is now an expectation on the part of most of the children that they will be consulted and involved in relevant aspects of school life. We see this as a very positive benefit of our work and a life-skill for the children. They can see that their ideas and thoughts are taken into account and that action follows – not lip service.

The majority of the children develop excellent dispositions for learning. We have heard children saying to each other 'come on – this is our learning time', 'I need some thinking time', 'I need you to help with this bit', 'I think…what do you think?' and 'I can do this better'. Very importantly, 'I'm a good thinker/learner' can be heard when it is true. There is a workshop atmosphere during the day and children are proud of their efforts and willing to talk about learning. Also, children are not keen on being held up in their learning by minor behaviour disruptions. They are understanding of the difficulties some children have with their learning but can get impatient with interruptions, particularly in philosophy sessions. Our Positive Behaviour policy focuses on minimizing behaviour disruptions to maximize learning time. During the coming year the children, through Class and School Councils, will be writing their own Positive Behaviour and Inclusion Policy for the school. I can't wait to see it.

The children demonstrate understanding of, and some independence in their use of, brain 'switch on' techniques. For example, they are happy to take thinking time to give a considered response, they use their water bottles as and when they need to, they will take a break as necessary.

Our twice-yearly School Council elections – discussed above in some detail – involve everyone in the school. The children, including Reception, seem to understand and really value the opportunity to vote. When our last chairperson was elected, the election was covered by Radio Norfolk. Interviewed on his success afterwards, Kieran said (among other things) with sparkling eyes, 'It's as exciting as…as…a day in Yarmouth!'

There has been a very definite and important improvement in the creative expression and writing of our children. There are several factors involved in this. Enquiry drama and philosophy have had a major influence on learning and teaching, in particular, 'mantle of the expert' work. In some aspects of their philosophy and drama work, children are encouraged to make notes as they explore ideas and therefore they do not 'lose' any original thoughts they have. Alternatively, they note ideas in a story they are developing through drama, ending up with a real and meaningful plan or base for their writing. Also, children who have been involved in using the 'Author Think' cycle and who have closely examined the nature of fairy stories have benefited from these opportunities. Use of 'Thinking Keys' and other strategies give children meaningful reasons for creative thinking and writing. Their use of mind mapping helps them to organize their thoughts and ideas well. The way the children are engaged in their work also more often than not provides an emotional 'hook' to enable sustained learning to take place. In 2003 we used children's creative writing for our end of Key Stage 1 SAT assessment. Previously, we had used their information writing for this. We have seen a very marked improvement in this standard assessment. What is really pleasing is the knowledge that our children are beginning to be truly confident in exploring ideas and generating something new for themselves – being truly creative.

The work has a high emotional engagement and this benefits the children in terms of their own emotional intelligence and their growth of understanding about developing their own belief systems and the relevance of those beliefs to how we live – the actions we take and attitudes we hold. This shows in their discussions: formally, in philosophy, Class and School Councils, responses to questionnaires and behaviour issues, in their drama work and their evident understanding of other curriculum issues, especially the humanities and biodiversity; and, informally, in the support most children give each other.

The children are increasingly independent in their use of technology, in particular computers, and happy to make creative use of the hardware and software. One example of this is the video that one class made concerning an area of their work – the production of a new drink. They assessed each stage of the process, using footage to evaluate their own performance, and could see clearly how important things like clarity of message and presentation were on-screen. They re-shot and edited accordingly. Technology is also used as an integral part of story production, as seen in the fairy stories some of the children produced. Presentation, font and colour were chosen individually for particular effects. The data projector is proving well worth the money in a wide variety of ways, from whole-class and group basic literacy skills work to email and internet research work. The balance of desktop machines (iMacs) and portables (iBooks) has proved to be effective. Used in the lab, the iBooks ensure that whole classes can have access to hardware (two children to one Mac or iBook). If one or two iBooks are required as part of work going on in class, then children can be seen collecting them from the lab (providing they're not in use) and taking them to their class or work base to supplement the class computers.

Impact on staff learning

Having an action research approach to school improvement is a constant learning experience. In particular, the Thinking Schools – Thinking Children project work has confirmed for us that this approach is very effective and that colleague support (peer, advisory and consultant) is extremely valuable. Dialogue with the whole staff continues, as it is part of how we work, but we must also ensure that opportunities for debate with colleagues from other schools and organizations carries on in some way. One way of this happening is through the learning networks that we belong to, and another is through the many visitors we have who come to find out about our work. Working towards a clear and coherent set of values, aims and focuses aids the process of whole-school development and improvement. As well as affirming many of the benefits of this way of working, our research work has impacted on our learning in the following ways:

- Integration of some enquiry curriculum and De Bono graphic organizers to aid thinking has very usefully added a scientific dimension to our thinking and the children's analytical skills, providing a more balanced approach.

- A Philosophy for Children background has provided our children with confidence, skills and dispositions to respond well to new learning initiatives.

- We have become increasingly aware that working a curriculum with developing critical, creative and reflective thinking at its heart makes for a very inclusive community. All intelligences are valued and all are able to take part at appropriate levels – many opportunities are provided for children to contribute to the whole and to make individual progress. None is excluded in any way.

- Our research is showing us the importance of paying close attention to approaches and strategies that infuse the whole curriculum – those that enable sustained and enduring learning to take place – and within that of providing a wide variety of tools and strategies to assist that learning. The difference is becoming much clearer for us.

- We have been affirmed in our belief in the importance of using a wide variety of CPD opportunities. These include professional readings, visits to other establishments, use of British Council international development trips and Best Practice Research Scholarships, debate led by passionate experts, attendance of all or several staff at high-quality training sessions and sharing ideas with colleagues.

- All the staff feel that working in this way is exciting and energizing. It is no easy option and working in a child-centred and needs-led way makes it a heart, mind and soul job asking a high level of commitment. It is part of our practice and part of who we are.

Future development

We need to begin the new school year by reaffirming our learning from the Thinking Schools – Thinking Children project and associated work. The following are important aspects of our future work:

- We have two new members of teaching staff. We need to ensure that, as part of their induction, both members are fully conversant with our work to date, trained in thinking skills work, and are given full opportunities to share their passions and talents with us to further our learning.

- We will continue our whole-school CPD, including the development of the integration of professional readings to facilitate debate where appropriate, and arranging more visits to other schools. We need to make more opportunities for staff to share the work they are each doing in their classrooms.

- We will broaden and extend our work with Luke Abbott in the area of enquiry drama and curriculum.

- New staff members will take part in Level 1 and 2 Philosophy for Children training. Any existing staff not yet trained at Level 2 will have the opportunity of doing so.

- Our information, communication and technology (ICT) training will continue and, as our confidence and knowledge grow, we will extend and enrich the ICT work we do with the children. We are part of an exciting project using creative digital video and plan a visit to

Enjoying the outdoor classroom

Ultra Lab in Chelmsford and a visit to an Apple Mac specialist school in London.

- We will explore different ways of effective yet straightforward planning to reflect the complexity of the work being done.

- Healthy eating is going to be part of our development work, looking at a healthy food balance and appropriate timing for snacks and meals during the day.

- We continue our work on global awareness and biodiversity. The visit by two staff to Trondheim in Norway will enhance this. During that visit the staff will also explore the utterschule, whereby Norwegian children spend one day per week with their teacher learning in the community. We have interesting lessons to learn.

- We are developing a tracking system that will show the various teaching interventions involved in children's progress – thus acknowledging the importance of seeing teaching and learning as a whole. Both the Maoris and the Welsh have only one word in their vocabularies for 'teaching and learning' – one word/one concept – an interesting discussion point.

As ever, we need to be constantly aware of curriculum richness and balance. We feel strongly that our children need a true balance of basic skills teaching, expressive arts work, and an infusion approach to the teaching of metacognition and thinking skills. Any new initiative, arising from external sources or from within the school, is evaluated against these important questions:

- What difference will this make for the children?
- What will this look like in practice in the classroom or school?
- How will it link into the Big Picture that is our vision for our school?

Resources

TIPD Team, Education and Training Group, British Council, 10 Spring Gardens, London SW1A 2BN (Tel 020 7389 4483/4826/4813); www.britishcouncil.org/learning-tipd
This site provides information about Teachers International Professional Development (TIPD) trips. The British Council fund research trips abroad for teachers. These can be local authority initiated or school determined. You will find information and contact details on the site, as well as application forms and recent reports from teachers who have returned from such trips.

www.dialogueworks.co.uk
On the Dialogueworks website you will find contact details for Karin Murris, Joanna Haynes and Roger Sutcliffe. The site is easy to navigate and full of interesting information about the training and consultancy offered in the area of citizenship, creative and critical thinking and Philosophy for Children. You will find details and online ordering for 'Storywise' on this site. Storywise is an excellent resource to help with the use of familiar stories to open up space for children's thinking. The article concerning the Thinking Day at Tuckswood is available on this site as well.

Dynamix Ltd www.seriousfun.demon.co.uk
Dynamix are a Swansea based co-operative. They work with children, young people and adults across the UK using activities promoting participation, decision making and inclusion. All the activities are fun and thoroughly engaging. Dynamix provide high-quality training for people who work with children and young people. The website gives information about all aspects of their work.

Kirton, 23 Rookwood Way, Haverhill, Suffolk CB9 8PB (Tel 0800 212709); www.kirton-healthcare.co.uk
Kirton's website is full of clear and useful information about the equipment and facilities offered. Their catalogue contains information, details and prices about light sensory and tactile equipment for use with children and adults with special needs and for equipping light sensory rooms. There is also 'Sensory-in-a-Suitcase' available for portable use. Kirton provide an advisory service and will visit your workplace if necessary.

Optimal Learning (contact Trevor Hawes or Sara Shaw, Tel 0116 271 7217)
The organization runs a highly motivating and successful one-day course called 'Optimal Learning in the Primary Classroom'. This is based on brain-compatible learning and draws on current thinking and research about how the brain works and how effective learning happens. The course can be tailored to local needs.

SAPERE www.sapere.net
This is the Society for Advancing Philosophical Enquiry and Reflection in Education. The comprehensive website provides background information, details of training, conferences, contacts and articles about Philosophy for Children.

www.tuckswoodfirst.norfolk.sch.uk
The Tuckswood First School website contains contact details and information about its enquiry curriculum, value statement and aims. The site also contains numerous examples of the children's work and parents' comments.

Ultralab www.ultralab.anglia.ac.uk/
Ultralab is an AppleMac-based learning technology resource centre at Anglia Polytechnic University run by
Stephen Heppell. The website gives full information about the very many creative and interesting projects
carried out there and the research and training available.

Suggested further reading

De Bono, E. (1993), *Teach Your Child How to Think*, Penguin, London
A guide to show parents how to teach their children to think for themselves.

De Bono, E. (2000), *Six Thinking Hats*, Penguin, London
A best-selling guide to better thinking for solving problems and making decisions.

Farrer, F. (2000), *A Quiet Revolution: Encouraging positive values in our children*, Rider, London
This book describes the introduction of a positive values programme into an Oxfordshire primary school.

Jeffrey, B. and Woods, P. (2003), *The Creative School*, Routledge Falmer, London
This book is about the success of the Coombes School in Reading, which, despite increasing pressure put
on it by changes in the curriculum, has maintained the creative values that won it widespread recognition.

Sutton, F. (2000), *The School Council: A children's guide*, Save the Children, London
A step-by-step guide to being on a School Council featuring children's own words, expressions and
artwork. It also includes information on the UN Convention on the Rights of the Child.

References

Bennathan, M. and Boxall, M. (1998), *The Boxall Profile: A guide to effective intervention in the education of
pupils with emotional and behavioural difficulties – handbook for teachers*, Association of Workers for
Children with Emotional and Behavioural Difficulties, Maidstone
The Boxall Profile provides a framework for assessing the areas of difficulty of severely disadvantaged and
deprived children so that teachers can plan focused interventions.

Bennathan, M. and Boxall, M. (2000), *Effective Intervention in Primary Schools: Nurture groups*, David
Fulton, London
A useful text for teachers across the whole age range.

Buzan, T. (2003), *Mind Mapping for Children*, HarperCollins, London
This book provides clear and straightforward guidance for introducing and using mind maps with children.
The information is presented in a lively way and includes many examples of mind maps.

Caviglioli, O. and Harris, I. (2000), *MapWise*, Network Educational Press, Stafford
This book examines the background and use of model mapping and provides a step-by-step approach to
developing the skills involved in the process.

Eagle, S. (2001), Celebrate, good times, come on, *Teaching Thinking*, 3, pages 35–37
This article describes the Thinking Day at Tuckswood, which was devoted to an enquiry based on a single story.

Greenlalgh, P., Cheshire LEA (2000), *Reaching Out to All Learners*, Network Educational Press, Stafford
This publication is presented in large booklet form and gives an easy-to-read overview of the Mind Friendly
Framework for Learning. Its focus is on the process of learning and includes current research, information
and strategies for positive learning experiences to take place.

National Primary Trust (2003), *That's What Your Brains Are For*, National Primary Trust, Birmingham
The 'Thinking Schools – Thinking Children' project report.

Shaw, S. and Hawes, T. (1998), *Effective Teaching and Learning in the Primary Classroom: A practical guide
to brain-compatible learning*, The Services, Leicester
This book, based on neuroscientific research, identifies the conditions required for effective learning and
provides practical guidance for teachers on how to facilitate optimal learning.

Shephard, C. (2002), *Participation – Spice It Up!: Practical tools for engaging children and young people in planning and consultations*, Save the Children, London
This is a wonderful resource full of background information and practical tried and tested activities to help children of all ages work together developing decision-making skills and co-operation. The whole approach put forward in this book is one of serious fun.

Smith, A. (1996), *Accelerated Learning in the Classroom*, Network Educational Press, Stafford
This book applies understandings about the role of the brain in learning to the classroom context.

Smith, A. (1998), *Accelerated Learning in Practice: Brain-based methods for accelerating motivation and achievements*, Network Educational Press, Stafford
This book offers nine principles for brain-based approaches to accelerating learning, improving motivation and achievements.

Smith, A., Lovatt, M. and Wise, D. (2003), *Accelerated Learning: a User's Guide*, Network Educational Press, Stafford
This book focuses on the 'learning' in accelerated learning. It provides over 200 ideas and activities for putting theory into practice.

Thompson, T. and Maguire, S. (2001), *Mind Your Head: And get to know your brain and how to learn*, North Eastern Education and Library Board, Antrim Centre, Antrim
This paperback book is written to use with older pupils to teach them how the brain functions and how positive learning happens. It is straightforward and colourful. There are illustrations on every page and clear text. We have found it very useful with four–eight-year-old children and also for training purposes with colleagues.

Notes on contributors

John Airs read history, English and psychology at Edinburgh University. This was followed by three years as a monk with the Dominicans and then, more happily, a post-graduate course in English and drama in Liverpool. He taught in secondary schools for 18 years and then for eight years was advisory teacher to the LEA. He is now a freelance drama teacher and lecturer of both teachers and drama students, including children of all ages. John is particularly concerned to help children cope with domestic violence. He has co-written with Chris Ball three books for schools: *Speaking, Listening and Drama for Years 1 and 2*; *Speaking, Listening and Drama for Years 3 and 4*; and *Speaking, Listening and Drama for Years 5 and 6* (all published by Hopscotch).

Priscilla Alderson is a Professor of Childhood Studies in the Social Science Research Unit at the Institute of Education, University of London. She has worked for many years on studies of children's and young people's lives, including the experiences of children with chronic illnesses, and those with special educational needs. She is known for developing ethical research procedures that safeguard the rights of children who participate in research.

Kevin Avison is married with two grown-up children, who were educated in Steiner Waldorf schools. He was trained for and worked in maintained schools before moving to a Steiner 'home school' for children with special needs. Subsequently, he became a Waldorf class teacher, working in both 'established' and founding situations. Kevin Avison served for many years on the executive of the Steiner Waldorf Schools' Fellowship as co-ordinator of the schools' advisory and accreditation service, in addition to full-time teaching. He now works full time for SWSF. He is also a member of the Executive Committee of Human Scale Education.

Liz Brooker was an early years teacher for many years, and now lectures at the Institute of Education, University of London. Her study of young children's learning, *Starting School: Young children learning cultures* (2002), was published by the Open University Press. More recently, she has been studying the lives and educational experiences of teenage parents and their babies.

Andrew Burrell is a class teacher who is also a tutor and researcher at, and an associate member of, the School of Early Childhood and Primary Education at the Institute of Education, University of London. Andrew has worked on research projects studying the teaching of language and literacy, art and design education, class size and formative assessment. He has recently been involved in a study examining Reception children's speaking and listening abilities and for the past five years has worked as an English consultant for a children's book publisher.

James Butler is passionate about empowering individuals and businesses to realize their full potential – to identify their vision and smash through the obstacles that have previously held them back. Drawing on his previous career with consultants Babtie Group and waste management company Biffa, James coaches individuals, managers and business owners to take their lives or businesses, or both, to a new level. His wife worked in secondary education for 11 years and now trains adults, helping James understand the pressures and pains faced by those in education. He firmly believes life is meant to be fun and we should seek to fully enjoy our work – we spend enough time there!

Daphne Clarke undertook her teacher training at Kesteven College in Lincolnshire, which was followed by 20 years of teaching in schools. Her interests in natural health and potential improvements in educational methods led her into the world of kinesiology. She studied kinesiology in England and the USA, where she took advanced courses in specialized kinesiology techniques, especially those with relevance to learning difficulties. She is now an educational consultant specializing in brain integration, and has been actively practising kinesiology for the past 18 years. She chaired the Kinesiology Federation and was on the Board of Directors of the International Association for Specialized Kinesiologists for a number of years. Daphne has been pioneering the use of brain integration techniques in schools in Sussex. She teaches throughout Britain and lectures to various organizations, as well as helping people on a one-to-one basis.

Emma Craigie trained as a religious education and English teacher. She has enjoyed many kinds of teaching: in comprehensives, in adult education – from Basic Skills to A levels, Open University, at a Steiner parent and toddler group. She has four children and has been very involved as a parent in establishing a new Steiner school in Bruton, Somerset. In 1999, with Susan Mantell, she set up the group 'Let the Children Play' to campaign for play-based early years education. She is currently home educating her eldest child.

Susan Digby founded the Voices Foundation following the award of a Winston Churchill Travelling Fellowship, which enabled her to visit Finland, Hungary, Canada and the USA to study methods of music teaching and choral training. Having first studied music at King's College, University of London, Susan Digby has since trained with Péter Erdei, Head of Choral Studies at the Franz Liszt Academy in Budapest and Director of the Kodály Institute in Kecskemét, Hungary. She spent many years as a primary teacher in Hong Kong before returning to England.

Phil Doyle trained at Christ's College, Liverpool, 1970–1973. This led him into teaching and two headships. St Margaret Mary's, his second headship, is a four-form junior school with 500 children. He believes passionately that children should have every chance to develop their talents and that what children remember most from school is friendships, sporting achievements, residential visits and the school play! Phil has been married for 30 years and has three grown-up children; family interests include football, cricket, reading, music and walking.

Anne D'Souza gained her BEd degree at the West Sussex Institute of Higher Education, now University College Chichester. She taught in an international English school in Cologne for two years and then at a Church of England primary school near Swindon, where she was responsible for design and technology, art and maths. She introduced and taught tai chi in the playground, which had a wonderful effect on the school's atmosphere and helped to provide a sense of belonging for all the children.

Sue Eagle has been headteacher at Tuckswood Community First School for 9 years, a position she finds exciting, challenging and hard. She has run a multicultural nursery school in Hong Kong and worked with adults while with Norfolk Advisory Service. She is passionate about the benefits of a balanced, child-focused approach to education where children can develop a lifelong love of learning, a positive self-image and a sense of their place and value in the community, and where teaching is a continuing and enjoyable learning experience for adults.

Virginia Gordon died tragically just before publication of this book. She taught sculpture and self-advocacy to adults and children with special educational needs. Her work as a qualified systematic therapist led to her research on the differences between the stories individuals create about the same event. She was fascinated by the ways in which the co-creation of stories evolve and develop a new overall meaning and belief embedded in the story told. This enables clients to develop their unique and personal moral interventions that fit their particular needs and allow them to move forward. Using this model, she worked with primary school children perceived by their teachers and parents to be potentially at risk. Virginia presented workshops in Scandinavia and the UK, and was involved in many international education initiatives, including a story-telling programme for street children in Bombay. Her ability in communicating with children who were alienated or hurt, and her skill in bringing to all children a tangible measure of self-understanding, inner growth and self-healing through creating stories together, were extraordinary.

Laura Hyde has been headmistress of St James Independent School for Senior Girls in west London since 1995. She taught at a church primary school, then St James Junior Girls, and subsequently for Leon MacLaren, founder of the School of Economic Science. Later, she took time off to bring up her family, before returning to teaching – initially in the junior school.

Sally Jenkinson is an advocate for the importance of children's play. Mother and former Steiner Waldorf kindergarten teacher, Sally lectures, writes and advises on early childhood issues. She is a founder member of the Alliance for Childhood and author of *The Genius of Play: Celebrating the spirit of childhood* (Hawthorn Press).

Joan Lister has been headteacher of Ashfield Nursery School in Newcastle since 1973. She gained a teacher training certificate with distinction in 1960, specializing in the three to nine age range. She was chairperson of the National Association of Primary Education (1984–1987) and was made an honorary fellow of the Royal College of Preceptors in 1990 for services to early years education. In 2002, she was awarded the Lifetime Achievement award for the northern region by the National Teaching Awards. She has written and contributed to training materials and children's books on drug awareness, racial awareness and child protection.

Penelope Moon has been teaching for over 28 years. In particular, her interests lie in special needs and behaviour management. She is a qualified hypno-psychotherapist and is involved in training others. She is a founder member of Cherion – A Quiet Place, which offers a range of innovative and holistic services for education and business. Its work aims to develop the full potential of individuals within the context of their environment, thus enabling them to function optimally. She co-ordinates the Early Years Behaviour Team for Liverpool Local Education Authority, from where she is seconded out to develop a Quiet Place.

Jenny Mosley has for the past 20 years worked in primary, secondary and special education, developing her unique circle time approach. She works all over Britain running highly practical courses. She is the author of many books, including the best-selling *Turn Your School Round* (LDA) and *Quality Circle Time in the Primary Classroom* (LDA). She has created a very successful INSET model. Jenny Mosley's unique approach has been featured on television, and in Open University programmes, the national press and numerous educational journals.

Janni Nicol trained as a Steiner kindergarten teacher in 1969 after attending a Steiner school in South Africa. Since then, she has taught in various kindergartens and helped to found the Rosebridge Kindergarten and Cambridge Steiner School, UK. She has worked in marketing and PR, published articles and books, and become a puppeteer and children's entertainer. She is also the early childhood representative for the Steiner Waldorf Schools Fellowship, UK. She has also lectured on many aspects of Steiner education, multiculturism and puppetry. Most importantly, she is a mother, stepmother and wife.

James Park is the founding director of Antidote, an organization he dreamed up with Susie Orbach in 1994 to campaign for emotional intelligence. In the period before setting up Antidote, he wrote *Sons, Mothers and Lovers* (1995) and *Shrinks: The analysts analyzed* (1992). He is a UKCP-registered psychotherapist with the Centre for Attachment-based Psychoanalytic Psychotherapy (CAPP).

Susan Piers-Mantell experienced childhood on a remote farm in Zambia, which gave her great security and freedom to play and explore. It was this valuable beginning that has directed her ever since to find ways to provide all children with the opportunity to play freely. After gaining a BA Honours degree in English Literature from London University and enjoying a few years teaching, she married and had four children. Watching her own four sons grow up convinced her of the vital role play has on developing happy, healthy and competent children. This led her to help pioneer and develop the Steiner Waldorf school in Bruton, which she remained involved in for ten years, ensuring a truly play-based early education for the children. In 1999, with Emma Craigie, she helped form a pressure group called 'Let the Children Play'.

Martyn Rawson was born in Glasgow in 1954 and was educated in Edinburgh and Hull. He read English and History at York University. After some years in farming he became a Steiner Waldorf teacher and was co-founder of the York Steiner School. Over the last 25 years he has taught in North Yorkshire, Stuttgart in Germany and currently in Forest Row in Sussex. Martyn has been a visiting lecturer at Greenwich University, Rolle School of Education, University of Plymouth, Tai Po University, Hong Kong and at Steiner teacher training centres in Stuttgart, St Petersburg and Dornach in Switzerland. He has published a wide range of books on Steiner Waldorf education as well as *Ready to Learn* with Michael Rose (Hawthorn Press) and *Free Your Child's True Potential* (Hodder and Stoughton).

Jeni Riley is Reader in Literacy in Primary Education and Head of the School of Early Childhood and Primary Education at the Institute of Education, University of London. Before being appointed to the Institute, Jeni's main teaching experience was in the early years and the advisory service in Oxfordshire. Since her appointment to the Institute in 1986, Jeni has focused her research energies into the teaching and learning of literacy in the early years of education. Currently, she is directing a research project that is studying the ways of effectively enhancing the spoken language skills of Reception children. She has written and edited several books including *The Teaching of Reading: The development of literacy in the early years of school* (Paul Chapman Publishing).

Ray Rumsby has had a varied career entirely in education – in schools, advisory services, human resources, and latterly with Worklife Support Ltd. He has worked in various schools in Southampton and Hertfordshire, and in LEA advisory services in Suffolk and Norfolk. As a senior adviser in Norfolk, he had numerous roles in support of schools but was also responsible for staff development in the advisory service itself. He developed and ran the Norfolk Well-being Project for two years from 1999–2001 before becoming Well-being Services Manager for Worklife Support Ltd, the commercial arm of the Teacher Support Network.

Gill Taylor began her career as a primary school teacher in inner London. She has been actively committed to developing inclusive classrooms and school communities since that time, as a teacher, educational psychologist and senior LEA officer. Gill first developed Circle of Friends as an approach in UK schools in 1994, and is a national presenter, consultant and trainer in this approach.

Elspeth Thompson is a writer with a particular interest in gardening and nature. For the past seven years she has had a weekly gardening column in the *Sunday Telegraph* and has written four books on different aspects of gardening. She studied history and history of art at Trinity College, Cambridge, and has since completed a four-year course in psychosynthesis counselling. She lives and gardens in London and on the south coast. She grows her own organic fruit, vegetables and flowers on two allotments in south London, where her five-year-old niece and various godchildren are frequent visitors.

George Varnava is a former headteacher who now works with many groups across the education and voluntary sectors, including such bodies as the National Children's Bureau, the College of Teachers and Sport England. He is a former president of the National Association of Headteachers. In addition to the publications he has written for the Checkpoints series, he is author of *How to Stop Bullying in Your School: A guide for teachers* (David Fulton Publishers).

Joan Webster sadly died of cancer just as this book went to the publishers. Her contribution to it will stand as a memorial to her 16 years as a truly magical head of Cavell First and Nursery School in Norwich. Having won a scholarship to Halesowen Grammar School and undertaken her teacher training in Birmingham, she spent the years until she married and had her family, first as a supply teacher and then as deputy head of a first and middle school, finally becoming head of Cavell First and Nursery School until her retirement. Cavell became a beacon to other local heads, a focus for educational research and was titled 'The Happiest School in East Anglia' by the local press.

Sarah Woodhouse is chief executive of Right from the Start. She studied social sciences at Exeter University. Sarah worked briefly with the Probation Services and the CAB then became a home tutor for Rugby Education Authority to teenagers in the borough who were too disturbed or violent to be in school. She has also worked in a voluntary capacity with physically and mentally disturbed and special needs children for 27 years. During the 1980s she was lead author of the first Amnesty International education pack for secondary schools. Her book *Your Life, My Life*, an introduction to human rights and responsibilities for 8 to 12 year olds, followed and became a forerunner to the Right from the Start education project which she set up in 1988. She is author of *Sound Sleep: Calming and helping your baby or child to sleep* (Hawthorn Press).

Appendices

THE YOUNG MAN AND THE STARFISH

A story inspired by Loren Eiseley

A wise man was taking a sunrise walk along the beach. In the distance he caught sight of a young man who seemed to be dancing along the waves. As he got closer, he saw that the young man was picking up starfish from the sand and tossing them gently back into the ocean.

'What are you doing?' the wise man asked.

'The sun is coming up and the tide is going out: if you don't throw them in they'll die.'

'But young man, there are miles and miles of beach with starfish all along it. You can't possibly make a difference.'

The young man bent down, picked up another starfish, and threw it lovingly back into the ocean, past the breaking waves.

'It makes a difference for that one,' he replied.

Source: United Nations Association of Great Britain and Northern Ireland correspondence to schools (February 1995) to mark the 50th anniversary of the founding of the United Nations.

Appendix 1
Summary of the UN Convention on the Rights of the Child

This summary of the UN Convention on the Rights of the Child is from UNICEF UK.

Article 1
Everyone under 18 years of age has all the rights of this Convention.

Article 2
The Convention applies to everyone whatever their race, religion, abilities, whatever they think or say, whatever type of family they come from.

Article 3
All organizations concerned with children should work towards what is best for each child.

Article 4
Governments should make these rights available to children.

Article 5
Governments should respect the rights and responsibilities of families to direct and guide their children so that, as they grow, they learn to use their rights properly.

Article 6
All children have the right to life. Governments should ensure that children survive and develop healthily.

Article 7
All children have the right to a legally registered name and nationality; also the right to know and, as far as possible, to be cared for, by their parents.

Article 8
Governments should respect children's right to a name, a nationality and family ties.

Article 9
Children should not be separated from their parents unless it is for their own good; for example, if a parent is mistreating or neglecting a child. Children whose parents have separated have the right to stay in contact with both parents, unless this hurts the child.

Article 10
Families who live in different countries should be allowed to move between those countries so that parents and children can stay in contact, or get back together as a family.

Article 11
Governments should take steps to stop children being taken out of their own country illegally.

Article 12
Children have a right to say what they think should happen, when adults are making decisions that affect them, and to have their opinions taken into account.

Article 13
Children have the right to get and share information, as long as the information is not damaging to them or to others.

Article 14
Children have the right to think and believe what they want, and to practise their religion, as long as they are not stopping other people from enjoying their rights. Parents should guide their children on these matters.

Article 15
Children have the right to meet together and to join groups and organizations, as long as this does not stop other people from enjoying their rights.

Article 16
Children have a right to privacy. The law should

protect them from attacks against their way of life, their good name, their families and their homes.

Article 17

Children have the right to reliable information from the mass media. Television, radio and newspapers should provide information that children understand, and should not promote materials that could harm children.

Article 18

Both parents share responsibility for bringing up their children, and should always consider what is best for each child. Governments should help parents by providing services to support them, especially if both parents work.

Article 19

Governments should ensure that children are properly cared for, and protect them from violence, abuse and neglect by their parents, or anyone else who looks after them.

Article 20

Children who cannot be looked after by their own family must be looked after properly, by people who respect their religion, culture and language.

Article 21

When children are adopted the first concern must be what is best for them. The same rules should apply whether the children are adopted in the country where they were born, or if they are taken to live in another country.

Article 22

Children who come into a country as refugees should have the same rights as children born in that country.

Article 23

Children who have any kind of disability should have special care and support, so that they can lead full and independent lives.

Article 24

Children have the right to good-quality health care, to clean water, nutritious food and a clean environment, so that they will stay healthy. Rich countries should help poorer countries achieve this.

Article 25

Children who are looked after by their local authority, rather than by their parents, should have their situation reviewed regularly.

Article 26

The government should provide extra money for the children of families in need.

Article 27

Children have a right to a standard of living that is good enough to meet their physical and mental needs. The government should help families who cannot afford to provide this.

Article 28

Children have a right to an education. Discipline in schools should respect children's human dignity. Primary education should be free. Wealthy countries should help poorer countries achieve this.

Article 29

Education should develop each child's personality and talents to the full. It should encourage children to respect their parents, and their own and other cultures.

Article 30

Children have a right to learn and use the language and customs of their families, whether these are shared by the majority of people in the country or not.

Article 31

All children have a right to relax and play, and to join in a wide range of activities.

Article 32

The government should protect children from work that is dangerous, or that might harm their health or their education.

Article 33

The government should provide ways of protecting children from dangerous drugs.

Article 34

The government should protect children from sexual abuse.

Article 35

The government should make sure that children are not abducted or sold.

Article 36

Children should be protected from any activities that could harm their development.

Article 37

Children who break the law should not be treated cruelly. They should not be put in prison with adults and should be able to keep in contact with their families.

Article 38

Governments should not allow children under 16 to join the army. Children in war zones should receive special protection.

Article 39
Children who have been neglected or abused should receive special help to restore their self-respect.

Article 40
Children who are accused of breaking the law should receive legal help. Prison sentences for children should only be used for the most serious offences.

Article 41
If the laws of a particular country protect children better than the articles of the Convention, then those laws should stay.

Article 42
The government should make the Convention known to all parents and children.

The Convention on the Rights of the Child has 54 Articles in all. Articles 43–54 are about how adults and governments should work together to make sure all children get all their rights.

Resources

UNICEF (see page 231) produce a number of resources for schools about children's rights. These include the above summary in leaflet form, a full-colour booklet utilizing illustrations from *For Every Child* (Castle 2002) and a full-colour A2 line illustration of a park scene depicting groups of children and adults who are engaged in activities that illustrate aspects of children's rights.

Appendix 2
Children's books

The following is a selection of children's books for exploring human values and issues concerned with spiritual and emotional well-being. The list draws on Young with Commins (2002, pages 174–178). Many of the books are recent publications although some are older, but nevertheless remain invaluable. They have been arranged under the following headings:

Sense of self, personal qualities, feelings and emotions
Social justice and equity
Appreciation of diversity
Peace and conflict resolution
Wonder, appreciation and care of the natural world

Within these headings, the books been ordered by age. The suggested age-ranges are approximate and are intended only as a guideline.

Sense of self, personal qualities, feelings and emotions

FOUNDATION STAGE, PRE-5/EARLY YEARS

Granpa (1988)
John Burningham
Picture Puffin
This story is about a little girl and the happy experiences she shares with her Granpa in the year before he dies. The book's theme is handled in a subtle and sensitive manner.

Hug (2000)
Jez Alborough
Walker Books
Little chimp feels lonely and desperately in need of someone to hug him. This tale of love and acceptance is told with very few words and poignant, colourful illustrations, making it an ideal book for the very young.

The Kissing Hand (1993)
Audrey Penn
Child and Family Press

When Chester the racoon is reluctant to go to school for the first time, his mother teaches him a way to carry her love with him.

L is for Loving – An ABC for the way you feel (1999)
Ken Wilson-Max
David Bennett Books
A colourful picture book capturing 26 moods.

Rachel's Roses (1995)
Karen Christensen
Barefoot Books
A gentle story to help children realize the importance of patience.

KS1/P1–3

Alexander and the Terrible, Horrible, No Good, Very Bad Day (1987)
Judith Viorst
Macmillan Publishing
When everything goes wrong for him, Alexander is consoled by the thought that other people also have bad days too.

Children dressed as book characters to celebrate World Book Day

Badger's Parting Gifts (1992)
Susan Varley
Picture Lion
When Badger dies, the other animals are grief-stricken. However, one by one they remember the special gifts that Badger taught them, which they would treasure for always.

Boxed In (1991)
Vyanne Samuels
Red Fox
When Leon gets shut in the toy cupboard, he thinks his family will soon find him. But then his imagination gets to work and soon he's picturing the search extending beyond the house.

Can't You Sleep, Little Bear? (1988)
Martin Waddell
Walker Books
Like many children, Little Bear is frightened of the dark. In this story, Big Bear finds a most ingenious way to reassure him and overcome Little Bear's fear.

Crusher is Coming! (1990)
Bob Graham
Collins Picture Lions

Peter, the little boy in the story, invites home his new friend Crusher but is terrified that his family will embarrass him in front of his 'tough' schoolmate.

Daddy Will You Miss Me? (2000)
Wendy McCormick
Orchard Books
Celebrates the love between a father and his son.

Guess How Much I Love You? (1994)
Sam McBratney
Walker Books
Little Nutbrown Hare and Big Nutbrown Hare discover that love is not an easy thing to measure!

The Grandad Tree (2000)
Trish Cooke
Walker Books
A gentle tale about the enduring power of love.

Hello, Sailor (2003)
Ingrid Godon and Andre Sollie
Macmillan Children's Books
Matt is a lighthouse keeper. He watches the sea every day for ships...and for his friend Sailor to return.

I Don't Like It! (1990)
Ruth Brown
Arrow Books
A story told in rhyme of a doll's jealousy when her owner is given a puppy.

I'll Always Love You (1985)
Hans Wilhelm
Hodder and Stoughton
This story sensitively portrays the close relationship between a boy and his dog, Elfie.

KS2/P4–7

Belly Flop (2001)
Morris Gleitzman
Macmillan Books
The author writes about important life issues in a way that has you laughing and crying simultaneously.

Carrie's War (1973)
Nina Bawden
Gollancz
A semi-autobiographical story about personal growth, which focuses on the experience of being evacuated during the Second World War as seen through the eyes of Carrie.

The Julian Stories (1981)
Ann Cameron
Pantheon
Six domestic stories about childhood misunderstandings.

The Owl who was Afraid of the Dark (1968)
Jill Tomlinson
Methuen
This classic book offers a gentle way into looking at children's fears.

Rosa's Singing Grandfather (1992)
Leon Rosselson
Puffin
Four stories about a single mother, her father and daughter.

Secret Friends (1997)
Elizabeth Laird
Hodder Children's Books
A moving and powerful short novel. Themes of friendship, loneliness, betrayal, bullying and death are sensitively tackled.

Stories can stimulate the imagination, the intellect and the emotions

Social justice and equity

FOUNDATION STAGE, PRE-5/EARLY YEARS

An Angel Just Like Me (1997)
Mary Hoffman
Frances Lincoln
Carl wonders why none of the Christmas angels is black or male. A good story with an explicitly anti-racist message. Not just for Christmas.

Bootsie Barker Bites (1993)
Barbara Bottner
Heinemann
The story of how one child's meanness is experienced by another.

Clown (1995)
Quentin Blake
Jonathan Cape
After many adventures, Clown finds new friends and a home for himself and his fellow toys.

Farmer Duck (1995)
Martin Waddell
Walker Books
In this tale, a farmer who exploits his animals wakes up to a surprise when they take over.

I'm Sorry (2001)
Sam McBratney
HarperCollins
A story about the highs and lows of childhood friendship.

Little Rabbit Foo Foo (1990)
Michael Rosen
Walker Books
The tale of a wild and wicked bully-boy bunny who likes nothing better than to ride through the forest bopping everyone on the head.

KS1/P1–3

Aldo (1993)
John Burningham
Red Fox
A poetic tale about a special friendship between a lonely girl and her secret friend, Aldo. With her secret friend around, the little girl is able to forget her everyday fears.

Hurrah for Ethelyn (1991)
Babette Cole
Mammoth
Ethelyn is so clever, she wants to be a brain surgeon. However, a nasty gang of jealous rats try to prevent her from succeeding.

Stories can help children to examine different viewpoints, recognize unfairness and promote a sense of injustice

Stories can help children empathize with others' experience and feelings

The Rainbow Fish (1992)

Marcus Pfister

North-South Books Inc

Rainbow Fish has to choose between his friends and a lonely little fish when a hungry and dangerous shark threatens the reef.

The Sneetches (1965)

Dr Seuss

Collins

A classic Dr Seuss story that tackles the idea of racial differences and prejudices in a way that young children can understand.

KS2/P4–7

Amazing Grace (1991)

Mary Hoffman

Frances Lincoln

The story of Grace, who, with the support of her mother and grandmother, discovers that you can do anything you want to.

A Candle in the Dark (1995)

Adele Geras

A and C Black

A moving story that deals with the transportation of two Jewish children who are forced to leave their family and travel to England in 1938.

The Friendship and other stories (1991)

Mildred Taylor

Puffin

Based on the author's experience, these stories tell of a black family's struggle for survival against oppressive racism, set in the southern states of the USA in the 1930s. Thought-provoking for top KS2.

The Legend of Freedom Hill (2000)

Linda Jacobs Altman

Lee and Low Books

A story of love, bravery and friendship. During the Californian Gold Rush, Rosabel, an African–American, and Sophie, a Jew, team up and send for gold to buy Rosabel's mother her freedom from a slave-catcher.

Nobody Rides the Unicorn (1999)

Adrian Mitchell

Picture Corgi Books

A gentle moral story of a frightened king's deceitful use of a girl to lure a unicorn and her righting of that wrong.

The Peacock Garden (1991)

Anita Desai

Mammoth

Set in India in the time of the Partition. Tells the story of a young Muslim girl isolated from her Hindu friends.

Smart Girls (1994)

Robert Leeson

Walker Books

A collection of folk tales from across the world.

The Wild Washerwoman (1979)

John Yeoman

Hamish Hamilton

A folk tale about a group of washerwomen and how they escape poor treatment from the laundry owner.

Stories can help children to reflect on moral and social issues

Appreciation of diversity

FOUNDATION STAGE, PRE-5/EARLY YEARS

ABC I Can Be (1993)
Verna Wilkins
Tamarind
This alphabet book provides positive role models and the message that you can be whatever you want to be.

Handa's Surprise (1994)
Eileen Browne
Walker Books
Handa puts a collection of fruits in her basket to take to her friend Akeyo. The animals have other ideas. A delightful story full of dramatic irony.

Skip across the Ocean (1995)
Collected by Floella Benjamin
Frances Lincoln
A selection of playful rhymes and lullabies from six continents and 23 countries. Many are shown in their original language, in addition to English.

Susan Laughs (1999)
Jeanne Willis
Andersen Press
A life the majority of children can relate to, except at the end it is revealed that Susan is disabled.

KS1/P1–3

Down by the River (1996)
compiled by Grace Hallworth
Heinemann
Rhymes, songs, chants and lullabies from the author's Caribbean childhood.

Stories can help children to develop respect for their own cultures and beliefs and those of other people

Frog and the Stranger (1995)
Max Velthuijs
Andersen Press
A tale dealing with prejudice and fear of the outsider.

Hue Boy (1992)
Rita Phillips Mitchell
Victor Gollancz
Hue Boy may be the smallest boy in the village, but he's big news – everyone has suggestions, from pumpkin soup to special baths, for making him grow.

Lily's Secret (1994)
Miko Imai
Walker Books
Lily is a little cat with funny paws. She thinks that they are ugly. But how can she keep them secret from her special friend Joey?

Oliver Button is a Sissy (1981)
Tomie de Paola
Methuen Children's Books
The story of Oliver, a young boy who would rather tap dance than play ball games, who is teased for being different.

The Paper Bag Princess (1999)
Robert Munsch
Little Hippo
A non conventional fairy story about a princess, prince and dragon.

Prince Cinders (1997)
Babette Cole
Picture Puffin
The story of Prince Cinders, who has to spend all his time cleaning up after his three brothers who bully him.

Seal Surfer (1998)
Michael Foreman
Red Fox
A gentle story about a disabled boy and his developing friendship with a seal.

The Sissy Duckling (2002)
Harvey Fierstein
Simon and Schuster
Elmer the duck is teased because he is different. However, he proves to be a hero by saving his father who is wounded by a hunter's shot.

The Sparrow's Story (1983)
Judith Crabtree
Oxford University Press
A resourceful sparrow delivers the story-teller's last story to the king.

Stories can help children to develop a positive attitude towards difference and diversity

Something Else (1994)
Kathryn Cave
Viking
Something Else tries to be like the others. But everything he does just shows how different he is. Then Something turns up and wants to be friends. But Something Else isn't sure he's at all like him.

Some Things are Scary (2000)
Florence Parry Heide
Walker Books
Some things are scary, but they can be pretty funny, too.

KS2 / P4-7

A Child's Book of Prayers: from many faiths and cultures (1997)
compiled by Tessa Strickland
Barefoot Books
A collection of prayers showing the diversity of prayer reflecting different faiths and cultures.

Fly, Bessie, Fly (1998)
Lynn Joseph
Simon and Schuster Books
A short biography of the woman who became the first African–American to earn a pilot's licence.

The Jessame Stories (1994)
Julia Jarman
Mammoth

Jessame is a young Afro-Caribbean girl who lives with her mother and grandparents in a flat in Bethnal Green. Deals with everyday realities and celebrates racial and cultural diversity.

Panda's Puzzle and his Voyage of Discovery (1977)
Michael Foreman
Hamish Hamilton
The story of Panda's voyage to find the answer to a puzzling question: is he black with white bits or white with black bits?

Six Perfectly Different Pigs (1993)
Adrienne Geoghegan
Hazar Publishing
A piglet with a straight tail feels he is no longer a proper pig, until he meets a purple frog and learns that it is okay to be yourself.

Talking Turkeys (1995)
Benjamin Zephaniah
Puffin Books
Accessible to older primary children, Zephaniah's collection is lively and politically challenging.

A World of Poetry (1991)
compiled by Michael Rosen
Kingfisher
A book of world poetry representing cultures from all over.

Peace and conflict resolution

FOUNDATION STAGE, PRE-5/EARLY YEARS

Eat your Dinner! (1994)
Virginia Millar
Walker Books
Bartholomew, a baby bear, doesn't want to eat his dinner!

Snap-happy Annie (1999)
June Crebbin
Puffin Books
The story of Snap-happy Annie who, realizing she has spoiled the fun at a birthday party, apologizes and is kind to everyone.

Two Monsters (1985)
David Mckee
Andersen
Two monsters – one blue, one red – live on opposite sides of a mountain and hold opposing views.

KS1/P1–3

Dogger (1977)
Shirley Hughes
Bodley Head
Dave had a toy dog called Dogger. He was very fond of Dogger and took him everywhere. One bedtime Dogger went missing. No matter how hard the rest of the family looked he was nowhere to be found, until Dave spotted him for sale on the toy stall at the Summer Fair!

Giant Hiccups (1995)
Jacqui Farley
Child's Play
A folk tale in which a giant's hiccups disrupt the inhabitants of a quiet town

Jamaica and Brianna (1994)
Juanita Havill
Heinemann
A story about a child who hates wearing her brother's hand-me-downs.

Lucy's Quarrel (1997)
Jennifer Northway
Scholastic
Lucy falls out with her best friend just before her birthday party...will they make up in time?

The Rabbit Who Couldn't Say No (2000)
Elena Goldoni
Siphano Picture Books
A tale about the problems encountered by Marcus, a rabbit who just couldn't say 'no'!

Stories can help children to think about the causes and impact of conflict

Stories can help children to think about how differences can be resolved through compromise and co-operation

Tusk, Tusk (1978)
David Mckee
Arrow Books
This fable centres on ideas about the causes of social conflict.

The Two Giants (1983)
Michael Foreman
Hodder and Stoughton
A tale of two giants who live in a remote part of the world where everything is perfect...until they start a quarrel.

KS2/P4-7

The Iron Man (2001)
Ted Hughes
Faber Children's Books

Modern fairy story in which the Iron Man is befriended by Hogarth and finally saves the world from destruction. Deals with human weakness in responding to those things we do not understand.

The Selfish Giant (1982)
Oscar Wilde
Puffin Books
In this much-loved fairy story a selfish giant builds a high wall around his garden to keep the children out.

Tales of Wonder and Magic (2001)
Berlie Doherty
Walker Books
Stories from different countries, which tell of our hopes and dreams.

Wonder, appreciation and care of the natural world

FOUNDATION STAGE, PRE-5/EARLY YEARS

Oi! Get off our Train (1989)
John Burningham
Cape
In this story, endangered animals climb aboard a steam train that is driven through a dream landscape by a small boy and his pyjama-case dog. The rhyming text highlights the plight of each animal.

Pi-shu the little panda (2002)
John Butler
Orchard Books
A story to introduce young children to one of the world's most endangered species - the giant panda.

Sally and the Limpet (1992)
Simon James
Walker Books
Sally is playing at the beach when a limpet latches onto her finger and no one is able to remove it. Gentle humour is used in this tale to convey the importance of respecting the natural world.

The Wild Woods (2003)
Simon James
Walker Books
Jess would like to keep a squirrel as a pet. However, while walking through the woods with her grandad she realizes that the squirrel belongs in the wild woods.

KS1/P1–3

The Big, Big Sea (1994)
Martin Waddell
Walker Books
This picture book describes a moonlit walk by the sea made by a child and her mother.

Dear Greenpeace (1991)
Simon James
Walker Books
A young girl, Emily, discovers a whale in her pond.

Dinosaurs and all that Rubbish (1972)
Michael Foreman
Hamish Hamilton
A modern fable about what happened when the dinosaurs came back to life and tidied up the rubbish that Man had left behind.

Stories can help children to gain a sense of wonder and appreciation of the natural world

The Garden (1995)
Dyan Sheldon and Gary Blythe
Red Fox
How a child finds history as well as beauty in the garden and has a wonderful dream.

Peter's Place (1995)
Sally Grindley
Andersen Press
A story of nature's struggle to overcome the damage caused by coastal pollution.

The Whales' Song (1993)
Dyan Sheldon and Gary Blythe
Red Fox
This stunningly beautiful, poetic and mysterious picture book captures a child's wonder at the richness of our natural world.

Where the Forest Meets the Sea (1989)
Jeannie Baker
Walker Books
In this story, a boy explores a prehistoric rain forest and wonders whether it will still exist if he wants to visit it in the future.

KS2/P4–7

One Tiny Turtle (2001)
Nicola Davies
Walker Books
This story illustrates the journey made by loggerhead turtles. After travelling thousands of thousands of miles they return to the same beach where they were born, to lay their eggs.

A Pocketful of Stars: poems about the night (1999)
compiled by Nikki Siegan-Smith
Barefoot Books
A collection of poems exploring the mysteries of the night. With illustrations that reflect our multiracial society.

The Silver Swan (2001)
Michael Morpurgo
Picture Corgi
A beautifully illustrated tale of a boy's developing friendship with a swan and the inner workings of nature.

The World Came to My Place Today (2002)
Jo Readman
Eden Project/Random House
This Eden Project book has two interlinked sources of information: a story element and an information text. Helps children to discover that plants from all over the world affect their daily lives.

Specialist book suppliers

Barefoot Books, 124 Walcot Street, Bath BA1 5BG (Tel 01225 322400); www.barefootbooks.com
Barefoot Books take their inspiration from many different cultures and focus on themes that encourage independence of spirit, enthusiasm for learning, and acceptance of other traditions.

Letterbox Library, 71–73 Allen Road, London N16 8RY (Tel 020 7503 4801); www.letterboxlibrary.com
Letterbox Library are suppliers of non-sexist and multicultural books for children. Books in their catalogue reflect the incredible diversity of human beings and the multicultural world we live in.

Words of Discovery, Unit 33, Vulcan House, Vulcan Road, Leicester LE5 3EF (Tel 0116 262 2244)
www.wordsofdiscovery.com
Words of Discovery stock a wide range of books that develop children's positive beliefs and values, self-esteem, creativity, communication, spiritual awareness, awareness of nature, emotional literacy, and personal and social awareness.

Appendix 3
Teachers' books and curriculum materials

Books

Brown, B. (1998), *Unlearning Discrimination in the Early Years*, Trentham, Stoke-on-Trent
This book deals with all areas of discrimination. Relevant theory and research are clearly explained and examples of good practice are provided.

Claire, H. (2001), *Not Aliens: Primary school children and the citizenship/PSHE curriculum*, Trentham, Stoke-on-Trent
Based on research with 7 to 11 year olds, the author demonstrates how the citizenship curriculum has been written with little regard for children's views and experiences and underestimates the level of debate that is possible with young children.

Farrer, F. (2000), *A Quiet Revolution: Encouraging positive values in our children*, Rider, London
This book describes the introduction of a positive values programme into an Oxfordshire primary school. See also *How to Inspire and Develop Positive Values in the Classroom* (Hawkes 2003), under Practical handbooks and classroom resources on page 222.

Gammage, P. and Meighan, J. (eds) (1993), *Early Childhood Education: Taking stock*, Education Now Publishing, Nottingham
An analysis of the conflict between the control model and developmental model of early childhood education and the gains to be made from high-quality teacher training.

Hallowell, E. (2002), *The Childhood Roots of Adult Happiness*, Vermilion, London
The author, a child and adult psychiatrist, examines recent research suggesting that teachers and parents can greatly increase the chances of children growing up to be happy, responsible adults by instilling certain inner qualities and developing childhood-based skills.

John, M. (2003), *Children's Rights and Power: Charging up for a new century*, Jessica Kingsley, London
The author considers how children learn about power and compares the situation of children to that of powerless minority groups.

Klein, R. (2001), *Citizens by Right: Citizenship education in primary schools*, Trentham, Stoke-on-Trent
The author describes how a human rights approach trialled in four inner city primary schools can be adopted by teachers to involve children in citizenship at Key Stages 1 and 2.

Klein, R. (2003), *We Want Our Say: Children as active participants in their education*, Trentham, Stoke-on-Trent
This book examines the benefits for teachers and children in creating a power-sharing ethos in our schools.

Lantieri, L. (ed.) (2001) *Schools with Spirit: Nurturing the inner lives of children and teachers*, Beacon Press, Boston
A collection of 14 essays from teachers and other educationists urging schools to recognize that the dilemmas of our times are deeply spiritual ones, and that the teaching of children must go beyond emotional intelligence into deeper dimensions of meaning, purpose and children's spiritual experiences and lives.

Lantieri, L. and Patti, J. (1996), *Waging Peace in our Schools*, Beacon Press, Boston
A powerful, practical guide presenting the Resolving Conflict Creatively Program; the largest and most successful initiative in the United States teaching children to empathize, mediate, negotiate and create peace.

Maranatha Community (1996), *What on Earth are We Doing to our Children?*, The Maranatha Community, Manchester
'An appeal to the nation' and call for action from all the churches, giving clear and chilling evidence of the remorseless and destructive influences that are at work today, shaping the lives of children and the future of civilization.

Miller, A. (1983), *The Drama of Being a Child*, Virago, London
Wise and perceptive insights into children's emotional needs; how the roots of cruelty and violence lie in unsympathetic, controlling and humiliating upbringing or harsh and erratic discipline; how these impede children's creativity, vitality and integrity.

Neall, L. (2002), *Bringing the Best out in Boys: Communication strategies for teachers*, Hawthorn Press, Stroud
A teacher's handbook of positive and practical strategies and communication skills.

Powell, R. (2001), *The Danish Free School Tradition*, Curlew Productions, Kelso
A booklet about the Danish approach to freedom and democracy in education.

Richardson, G. (1985), *Education for Freedom*, Gavemer Foundation, Sydney
This book offers vivid insights into the consciousness of a child and the hidden curriculum in every aspect of a child's life. It suggests a framework for changing our approach to education so that the touchstone is humanness for everything that goes on in a school. Garry Richardson founded the Korowall School in Australia, based on this vision.

Ross, C. and Ryan, A. (1990), *Can I Stay in Today Miss? Improving the school playground*, Trentham, Stoke-on-Trent
This book describes strategies and procedures that seek to change behaviour on the playground and is based on ideas and issues developed from work in Islington primary schools.

Siraj-Blatchford, I. (1994), *The Early Years: Laying the foundations for racial equality*, Trentham Books, Stoke-on-Trent
An overview of the issues that need to underpin the thinking and practice of teachers working with young children.

Tyrrell, J. (2002), *Peer Mediation: A process for primary schools*, Souvenir Press, London
This book is based on the Peace Education Programme developed in the 1990s for use in primary schools in Northern Ireland.

Weare, K. (2000), *Promoting Mental, Emotional and Social Health: A whole-school approach*, Routledge, London
This book examines the evidence for the importance of social and emotional education. It demonstrates how and why whole-school approaches to mental, emotional and social health not only improve morale and well-being but also raise academic achievement.

Weaver, A. (1988), *Making for Peace: Patterns in education*, Brentham Press, St Albans
Demonstrates how a feeling for community and the experience of creativity can be harnessed to the upbringing of children for a peaceful world in which human beings are motivated to take care of each other and of the planet. Offers a way forward to reduce the violence in society.

Practical handbooks and classroom resources

Alexander, T. (2001), *Citizenship Schools: A practical guide to education for citizenship and personal development*, Campaign for Learning/UNICEF, London
This guide shows democracy working within schools.

Bakyayita, J. (ed.) (1998), *Stand Up for Your Rights: A book about human rights – written, illustrated and edited by young people of the world*, Two-Can Publishing, London
A book about human rights written by and for young people.

Brown, A. (1987), *Active Games for Children with Movement Problems*, Paul Chapman, London
This handbook of resource material for teachers presents a careful and systematic approach to teaching and organizing or adapting games to include children with movement problems and ensure their integration.

Brown, M. (ed.) (1996), *Our World, Our Rights: Teaching about rights and responsibilities in the primary school*, Amnesty International, London
A handbook for learning about the Universal Declaration of Human Rights.

Burns, S and Lamont, G. (1995), *Values and Visions: A handbook for spiritual development and global awareness*, Hodder and Stoughton, London
An excellent resource of practical ideas.

Call, N. with Featherstone, S. (2003), *The Thinking Child: Brain-based learning for the foundation stage*, Network Educational Press, Stafford
This accessible book for early years practitioners describes the recent research that lies behind brain-based learning theory and gives practical techniques based on the theory, including helping children to develop good attention skills, managing behaviour positively, teaching and learning through movement, and addressing children's physical needs.

Call, N. with Featherstone, S. (2003), *The Thinking Child Resource Book*, Network Educational Press, Stafford
A highly practical book that builds on the theoretical and practical advice given in The Thinking Child, listing more than a thousand ideas on how to use brain-based learning techniques to enrich the learning experience of young children.

Castle, C. (2002), *For Every Child*, Red Fox in association with UNICEF, London
The UN Convention on the Rights of the Child in words and pictures. Eight world-class children's illustrators have contributed their work to the book. (UNICEF produce a free 16-page full-colour booklet, which utilizes illustrations from this book.)

Collins, M. (2001), *Circle Time for the Very Young 3–8*, Lucky Duck Publishing, Bristol
Activities for nursery, Reception and Key Stage 1 children. The five themes covered are friends and friendship; growing up; feelings; keeping safe; citizenship.

Corrie, C. (2003), *Becoming Emotionally Intelligent*, Network Educational Press, Stafford
This book encourages the reader to 'go deeper,' dealing with all aspects of emotional intelligence, from environment and motivation to self-esteem and identity, and includes case studies and activities to support the development of children's emotional intelligence.

Farrington, L. (1999), *Playground Peacemakers*, Loxley Press, Devon
Written for Key Stages 1 to 3, this series provides activity sessions, based on a circle time approach, to develop emotional literacy and help children to identify and express their feelings.

Fountain, S. (1994), *Learning Together – Global Education 4–7*, Stanley Thornes in association with the WWF and the Centre for Global Education, York University, Cheltenham
This book provides teaching ideas, classroom activities and games designed to foster co-operation, self-esteem and communication skills.

Hawkes, N. (2003), *How to Inspire and Develop Positive Values in the Classroom*, Learning Development Aids, Wisbech
This book offers guidance on how to introduce positive values into the classroom by developing a values-based approach to teaching and learning. See also *A Quiet Revolution: Encouraging positive values in our children* (Farrer 2000) under Books on page 220.

Hicks, D. (2001), *Citizenship for the Future: A practical classroom guide*, World Wide Fund for Nature UK, Godalming
This handbook provides practical support for teachers in preparing young people for their role as global citizens.

Human Values Foundation (1994), *Education in Human Values: Manual for schools*, Human Values Foundation, Ilminster
This manual, together with the accompanying lesson plans, has been developed as a universal, values-based programme for ethical, moral and spiritual education.

Human Values Foundation prepared by Auton, J. (1994), *Education in Human Values: Lesson plans 1–3: truth, love, peace*, Human Values Foundation, Ilminster
These lesson plans, together with the accompanying manual, have been developed as a universal, values-based programme for ethical, moral and spiritual education.

Human Values Foundation prepared by Auton, J. (1994), *Education in Human Values: Lesson plans 4–5: right conduct and non-violence*, Human Values Foundation, Ilminster
These lesson plans, together with the accompanying manual, have been developed as a universal, values-based programme for ethical, moral and spiritual education.

Lamont, G. and Burns, S. (1993), *Initial Guidelines for Values and Visions*, Manchester Development Education Project, Manchester
A practical handbook to encourage spiritual development and global awareness in primary schools. *Values and Visions: A handbook for spiritual development and global awareness* (Burns and Lamont 1995) was based on this handbook.

Levin, D. E. (2003), *Teaching Young Children in Violent Times: Building a peaceable classroom* (second edition), Educators for Social Responsibility, Cambridge, Mass.
This guide explores the cultural context for violence. It also provides practical ideas and activities for working with young children on non-violence issues. This edition has been extensively revised and updated. It includes a new chapter on helping children deal with violence in the news.

Lucas, B. and Smith, A. (2002), *Help Your Child To Succeed: The essential guide for parents*, Network Educational Press, Stafford
This practical, accessible and colourful book inspires parents to get involved in helping their children to enjoy learning, with activities, games, tips and suggestions for all the family.

Lucas, B. and Smith, A. (2003), *Help Your Child To Succeed Toolkit*, Network Educational Press, Stafford
This pack provides learning professionals with everything required to run a programme for parents on helping children to learn and succeed, and includes a handbook, CD-ROM and game cards. The Toolkit is easily accessible, with each section containing a balance of information, reflective activities and practical suggestions.

Masheder, M. (1986), *Let's Co-operate*, Peace Pledge Union, London
This booklet contains a lively collection of ideas for encouraging self-esteem, communication and co-operation.

Masheder, M. (1989), *Let's Play Together: Over 300 co-operative games for children and adults*, Green Print, London
A collection of over 300 games to encourage the development of co-operative skills. Traditional, circle, board and parachute games are among some of the games included in the book.

Masheder, M. (1993), *Windows to Nature*, World Wide Fund for Nature UK, Godalming
This book is designed to encourage young children to learn about and enjoy the wonders of the natural world and develop a caring and responsible attitude towards it.

Melichar, J. (2000), *Saying No to Violence – Children and Peace: Activities for a peaceful world*, Peace Pledge Union, London
This booklet contains suggestions and lesson plans for encouraging children to act and think non-violently.

Melicharova, M. (1998), *Working Together: A handbook for co-operation*, Peace Pledge Union, London
This handbook provides practical suggestions for developing skills in working together and is supplemented with more theoretical material to provoke thought and discussion.

Mole, S. (1997), *Colours of the Rainbow: Exploring Issues of Sexuality and Difference: A resource for teachers, governors, parents and carers*, Health Promotion Service, Camden and Islington Community Health Services NHS Trust, London
This resource provides materials for use with the four Key Stages. It contains sections on: feeling good, feeling different, the spectrum of sexuality, and homophobia and its effects.

Mosley, J. and Sonnet, H. (2001), *Here We Go Round: Quality circle time for 3–5 year olds*, Positive Press, Trowbridge
This book contains stimulating and enjoyable activities in easy-to-use format.

Mosley, J. and Sonnet, H. (2002), *101 Games for Self-esteem*, Learning Development Aids, Wisbech
A comprehensive collection of innovative games designed to help children learn to relate to each other, feel more positive about themselves and to teach skills such as empathy and co-operation. *101 Games for Social Skills* (LDA), written by the same authors, is also available.

Mosley, J. and Sonnet, H. (2002), *Making Waves: Exciting parachute games to develop self-confidence and team building skills*, Learning Development Aids, Wisbech
This handbook is based on Jenny Mosley and Helen Sonnet's extensive experience of developing parachute games. Parachutes can be purchased from LDA, Duke Street, Wisbech, Cambridgeshire PE13 2AE (Tel 01945 463441).

Olsen, S. and Parker, J. (1992), *Parachute Games*, Peace Pledge Union, London
A collection of co-operative games played with a parachute.

Peace Child International (2001), *Stand Up – Speak Out: A book about children's rights*, Two-Can Publishers, London
A peace child international project celebrating children's rights around the world. This fully illustrated book has been compiled by children from around the world. It includes stories and poems and offers a unique commentary and re-interpretation of the Convention on the Rights of the Child.

Peace Pledge Union (1993), *Co-operative Games: Activities for a peaceful world*, Peace Pledge Union, London
This booklet contains over 40 games, which are arranged in practical lesson plans.

Plummer, D. (2001), *Helping Children to Build Self-esteem*, Jessica Kingsley Publishers, London
This book offers over 100 activities aimed at helping children build and maintain self-esteem.

Sage, R. (2004), *A World of Difference: Tackling inclusion in schools*, Network Educational Press, Stafford
The author explores the elements of diversity, providing practical whole-school inclusion strategies. This book also includes a comprehensive overview of common learning difficulties and medical conditions in children and explains how to deal with them in the classroom

Save the Children (1998), *Rights and Responsibilities: Teachers' handbook*, Save the Children, London
This handbook contains a range of stories, facts and activities for finding out about the relationship between rights and responsibilities.

Save the Children (1998), *Partners in Rights: Creative activities exploring rights and citizenship for 7–11 year olds*, Save the Children, London
This resource contains a wide range of activities and also includes a set of photo cards to explore rights and citizenship across the curriculum and with mixed ability groups.

Save the Children (2002), *A Time for Rights: Activities for Citizenship and PSHE for 9–13 year olds*, Save the Children and UNICEF, London
A resource for teachers to help children think about rights and responsibilities and what this means in their own and in others' lives.

Selby, D. (1995), *Earthkind: A teacher's handbook on humane education*, Trentham, Stoke-on-Trent
Teaching the theory and practice of compassion to animals. Presents an extensive range of practical and lively activities for the classroom.

Smith, A. and Call, N. (1999), *The ALPS Approach: Accelerated Learning in Primary Schools*, Network Educational Press, Stafford
Using research and hands-on techniques, this book contains hundreds of practical examples of success, where primary teachers have used the ALPS Method™ to motivate, stimulate and inspire children. The book includes valuable sections on memory improvement, developing attention skills and improving performance in tests.

Smith, A. and Call, N. (2001), *The ALPS Approach Resource Book*, Network Educational Press, Stafford
This extremely practical title contains over 1000 useful ideas for teachers to 'accelerate' the learning of their children and photocopiable resources to use in the classroom. It extends the theoretical and practical advice given in The ALPS Approach and provides hands-on materials for classroom teachers and for those who teach children outside of the classroom.

Smith, C. A. (1998), *The Peaceful Classroom: Compassion and co-operation – activities for three to five year olds*, Floris Books, Edinburgh
This resource contains over 160 activities that promote skills such as friendship, compassion and kindness. These activities, organized by age and skill, emphasize how children's beliefs about themselves and others influence their relationships.

Stanley, S. with Bowkett, S. (2004), *But Why?: Developing philosophical thinking in the classroom*, Network Educational Press, Stafford
This resource pack provides everything you need to introduce Philosophy for Children (P4C) to the primary classroom. With a Teacher's Manual, Philosophy Bear toy and four colour-illustrated storybooks specifically designed to provoke philosophical enquiry, the pack makes philosophy accessible to even the very youngest children.

Stone, M. (1995), *Don't Just Do Something: Sit There: Developing children's spiritual awareness*, Religious Moral Education Press, Norwich
This handbook provides a range of activities for developing children's imaginative and spiritual awareness.

Young, M. with Commins, E (2002) *Global Citizenship: The handbook for primary teaching*, Chris Kington Publishing, Cambridge; Oxfam, Oxford
This handbook develops the principles of Global Citizenship into clear, practical pointers for use in school. An excellent and valuable resource for promoting social justice and equity.

Specialist book suppliers

Incentive Plus, PO Box 5220, Great Horwood, Milton Keynes MK17 0YN (Tel 01908 526120) www.incentiveplus.co.uk
Incentive Plus stock a wide range of carefully selected books and curriculum resources to promote positive behaviour, tackle disaffection, and develop emotional literacy and self-esteem. They supply the UK's only catalogue dedicated exclusively to promoting positive behaviour.

Religious and Moral Education Press (RMEP), St Mary's Works, St Mary's Plain, Norwich NR3 3BH (Tel 01603 612914); www.scm-canterburypress.co.uk/rmep.asp
RMEP has a good selection of books for primary teachers on religious, moral, personal and social education.

Words of Discovery, Unit 33, Vulcan House, Vulcan Road, Leicester LE5 3EF (Tel 0116 262 2244) www.wordsofdiscovery.com
Words of Discovery stock a wide range of books that develop children's positive beliefs and values, self-esteem, creativity, communication, spiritual awareness, awareness of nature, emotional literacy, and personal and social awareness.

Music for peaceful activities, imagination and meditation

Classical
Pianoforte, Eric Daub
Dance of the Blessed Spirits, Gluck (from Orfeo ed Euridice)
Piano Concerto No. 21 (K467), Mozart
Pachelbel's Canon and other Baroque Favourites, Toronto Chamber Orchestra
Prelude a l'Apres midi d'un Faun, Debussy
The Baroque Lute, Walter Gerwig
Oboe Concertos, Vivaldi
Air on a G String, J. S. Bach

Contemporary
Oceans, Peacock
Christofori's Dream, David Lanz

No Blue Thing, Ray Lynch
The Impressionists, Windham Hill Sampler
Piano Solos, Narada Lotus
Silk Road, Kitaro
Velvet Dreams, Kobialka
Crystal Silence, Chick Corea
Sunsinger, Paul Winter
A Piece of Heaven, Maia
Spectrum Suite, Steve Helpern
Natural States, Steve Halpern
Adagio for Strings, Samuel Barber
Tunhuang, Kitaro
Music for Airports, Brian Eno
Inside the Taj Mahal, Paul Horn

Performing arts

Thursday's Child – a different way to learn about children's rights worldwide
A full length musical available from UNICEF. All roles can be played by children aged 8 to 18 years. The story follows a group of children who make a journey to happiness.

Peace Child 2000 – script and study guide
An update of the *Peace Child* musical, which sought to bridge the gulf between East and West during the Cold War. This version allows young people to explore ways of bridging the gap between North and South. Children are encouraged to re-write the script and develop their own story-lines, characters and songs. This resource is available via Peace Child International's website (www.peacechild.org).

Kids for Peace – Singing in a brighter future
Kids for Peace developed out of the work of pupils at Darvell School in East Sussex, who were studying the conflict in Northern Ireland. The movement has worked on numerous projects worldwide. It aims to bring hope to places where people are saddened by conflict and grief. Cassette, video and CD available from Plough Publishing House, Darvell Bruderhof, Brightling Road, Robertsbridge, East Sussex TN32 5DR. Further information about Kids for Peace can be found at www.kidsforpeace.net

Appendix 4
Contacts

The following organizations provide advice and information. Please note that this is only a small selection of organizations, but it attempts to cover a wide range of issues relating to children's well-being, some of which have been highlighted in this book. The list draws on Young with Commins (2002, pages 184–186).

ActionAid
ActionAid's vision is a world without poverty, in which every person can exercise his or her right to a life of dignity.
Hamlyn House
Macdonald Road
Archway
London N19 5PG
Tel 020 7561 7561
www.actionaid.org

Amnesty International
Works worldwide to promote human rights, for the release of prisoners of conscience, fair trials for political prisoners and an end to torture, political killings, 'disappearances' and the death penalty.
The *Junior Urgent Action Guide* for schools and families from the Urgent Action Team is a valuable resource for teachers. It provides clear and sensitive instructions for 8 to 11 year olds to write on behalf of people, particularly children, who are suffering at the hands of cruel and repressive regimes. Joining the Junior Urgent Action Scheme gives children a sense of connection by turning places into people for them and enabling them to develop empathy and compassion.
99–119 Rosebery Avenue
London EC1R 4RE
Tel 020 7814 6200
www.amnesty.org.uk

British Red Cross Society
Cares for people in crisis and works with local communities to help prepare them for potential emergencies.
9 Grosvenor Crescent
London SW1X 7EJ
Tel 020 7235 5454
www.redcross.org.uk

ChildLine
A free 24-hour helpline for children and young people in the UK.
Helpline 0800 1111
www.childline.org.uk

Children Are Unbeatable!
Campaigns for children to have the same legal protection against being hit as adults and promotes positive, non-violent discipline.
Secretariat CAU!
94 White Lion Street
London N1 9PF
Tel 020 7713 0569
www.childrenareunbeatable.org.uk

Children's Rights Alliance for England
A coalition of over 180 statutory and voluntary organizations committed to the fullest possible implementation of the United Nations Convention on the Rights of the Child – involving children in the work being undertaken. CRAE keeps a watching brief on all parliamentary bills concerning child welfare, and drafts CRAE's response to the UK government's report to the inspecting UN Committee on the Rights of the Child. It has campaigned for and

will work closely with a Children's Rights Commissioner for England. Publishes *Children's Rights Bulletin*.
94 White Lion Street
London N1 9PF
Tel 020 7278 8222
www.crae.org.uk

The Children's Society

An innovative charity working with some of the country's most marginalized children and young people.
Edward Rudolf House
Margery Street
London WC1X 0JL
Tel 020 7841 4400
www.childrenssociety.org.uk

Christian Aid

Christian Aid provides resources and support for UK schools, enabling them to explore issues of Global Citizenship and to develop the skills to identify and take appropriate relevant action for a just global society.
35 Lower Marsh
London SE1 7RL
Tel 020 7620 4444
www.christian-aid.org.uk
www.globalgang.org.uk

Comic Relief

Provides free curriculum resources to support teaching around issues behind Red Nose Day, for example, Fair Trade, race.
5th Floor
89 Albert Embankment
London SE1 7TP
Tel 020 7820 5555
www.comicrelief.org.uk

Commission for Racial Equality

A non-governmental body that tackles racial discrimination and promotes racial equality.
St Dunstan's House
201–211 Borough High Street
London SE1 1GZ
Tel 020 7939 0000
www.cre.gov.uk

Commonwealth Institute

Focuses on expanding cultural horizons by working with young people on diversity, Global Citizenship and the modern Commonwealth through providing printed and online resources.
Kensington High Street
London W8 6NQ
Tel 020 7603 4535
www.commonwealth.org.uk

Council for Environmental Education

Works to ensure that the principles of sustainable development are at the heart of education policy and practice.
94 London Street
Reading RG1 4SJ
Tel 0118 950 2550
www.cee.org.uk

Family Links – The Family Links Nurturing Programme for Schools

Publishes *The Parenting Puzzle: How to get the best out of family life* by Candida Hunt in consultation with Annette Mountford.
The Family Links Nurturing Programme for Schools develops relationship skills and improves children's behaviour and achievements in the classroom. It trains teachers and supporting staff to use the Nurturing Programme. The structured ten-week course is tailored to match the national curriculum. Repeated each term, the programme teaches children to handle their anger, to treat others with respect and kindness, and to make responsible choices and decisions. The matching parents' programme is offered to every parent in the school.
Peterley House, Peterley Road
Horspath Industrial Estate
Cowley
Oxford OX4 2TZ
Tel 01865 401800
www.familylinks.org.uk

Friends of the Earth

An international network of environmental pressure groups, with local active groups.
26–28 Underwood Street
London N1 7JQ
Tel 020 7490 1555
www.foe.co.uk

Greenpeace

Undertakes campaigning work from promoting solutions, to direct actions, political lobbying and scientific research.
Canonbury Villas
London N1 2PN
Tel 020 7865 8100
www.greenpeace.org.uk

The Guide Dogs for the Blind Association
Provides information for teachers and pupils on issues of blindness and the work of guide dogs.
Hillfields
Burghfield Common
Reading RG7 3YG
Tel 0118 983 5555
www.guidedogs.org.uk

Human Scale Education
An educational charity promoting small schools and small classes.
Unit 8
Fairseat Farm
Chew Stoke
Bristol BS40 8XF
Tel 01275 332516
www.hse.org.uk

Human Values Foundation
Publishes *Education in Human Values* (see Teachers' books and curriculum materials, page 223). The foundation provides ongoing support through teacher training courses, symposia, lectures, conferences and publications.
Lower Wallbridge Farm
Dowlish Wake
Ilminster
Somerset TA19 0NZ
Tel 01460 52499
www.ehv.org.uk

Kidscape
Kidscape is a national charity that is dedicated to preventing bullying and child sexual abuse.
2 Grosvenor Gardens
London SW1W 0DH
Tel 020 7730 3300
Helpline 08451 205204
www.kidscape.org.uk

Life Education Centres
Through it's drug prevention programme, Life Education provides a yearly visit to a mobile classroom for primary school children. A resource pack is provided for teachers together with children's activity books and a parents' video.
1st Floor
53–56 Great Sutton
London EC1V 0DG
Tel 0870 770 2455
www.lifeeducation.org.uk

Minority Rights Group
An international non-governmental organization working to secure rights for ethnic, religious and linguistic minorities and indigenous peoples world-wide, and to promote co-operation between communities.
379 Brixton Road
London SW9 7DE
Tel 020 7978 9498
www.minorityrights.org

Musik Garten
A European programme specializing in music and movement in early childhood. Provides travelling workshops for teachers in the school holidays, and quality instruments and materials that complement the *Musik Garten* method of teaching. Also provides a CD pack, 'Everyone can Make Music', containing a teacher's guide to instant accompaniments to children's songs that anyone can play on a variety of percussion instruments or keyboards.
Chapel House
Bow
Crediton
Devon EX17 6HN
Tel 01363 82913
www.musikgarten.co.uk

The National Deaf Children's Society
An organization of families, parents and carers that exists to enable deaf children and young people to maximize their skills and development.
15 Dufferin Street
London EC1Y 8UR
Tel 020 7490 8656
Freephone helpline 0808 800 8880
www.ndcs.org.uk

National Society for the Prevention of Cruelty to Children (NSPCC)
Specializes in child protection and the prevention of cruelty to children.
NSPCC National Centre
42 Curtain Road
London EC2A 3NH
Tel 020 7825 2500
www.nspcc.org.uk

Pax Christi
Peace education resources and training.
Christian Peace Education Centre
St Joseph's
Watford Way
Hendon
London NW4 4TY
Tel 020 8203 4884
www.paxchristi.org.uk

The Place to Be (P2B)

An innovative and growing charity that provides effective emotional and therapeutic support to children in primary school – helping them to cope with crises such as family breakdown, violence, illness and death – and also addresses the trauma of war zone refugees.

Wapping Telephone Exchange
Royal Mint Street
London E1 8LQ
Tel 020 7780 6189
www.theplace2be.org.uk

Positive Parenting

Developing a nurturing programme and teacher training combined for parents and teachers to develop a closer relationship in terms of improving children's behaviour, school achievement, citizenship skills, and the skills of parenting and child nurture.

2A South Street
Gosport PO12 1ES
Tel 0239 252 8787
www.parenting.org.uk

Quaker Peace and Social Witness

The Peace Education Advisory Programme of Quaker Peace and Social Witness encourages peace education within schools nationally, exploring issues such as human rights, citizenship and social justice, and promoting skills of conflict resolution, mediation and problem solving. They offer visits to schools and advice on all issues relating to peace education and how to bring it alive in a classroom. Quaker Peace and Social Witness also provide resources, training, workshops and an annual newsletter.

Friends House
Euston Road
London NW1 2BJ
Tel 020 7663 1135
www.quaker.org.uk

Refugee Council

Gives help and support to refugees and asylum seekers arriving and surviving in Britain.

Refugee Help and Support Team
3 Bondway
London SW8 1SJ
Tel 020 7820 3000
www.refugeecouncil.org.uk

Re:membering education

A network of teachers from across the educational spectrum who believe that:

- There is a need to widen and deepen the current educational debate.

- All children's faculties need to be developed and nurtured.

- The moral and spiritual dimensions need to find expression in a curriculum that encourages responsibility, questioning, creativity and empathy.

66 Beaconsfield Villas
Brighton
East Sussex BN1 6HE
Tel 01273 239311
www.remember.mcmail.com

Royal National Institute of the Blind (RNIB)

Provides information and support for anyone with a serious sight problem and those working with them.

105 Judd Street
London WC1H 9NE
Tel 020 7388 1266
www.rnib.org.uk

Royal Society for the Prevention of Cruelty to Animals (RSPCA)

Campaigns on a variety of welfare issues affecting animals in the UK and throughout the world.

Wilberforce Way
Southwater, Horsham
West Sussex RH13 9RS
Tel 0870 333 5999
www.rspca.org.uk

Royal Society for the Protection of Birds (RSPB)

Provides a range of classroom resources suitable for primary and secondary teachers.

Education Department
The Lodge
Sandy
Bedfordshire SG19 2DL
Tel 01767 680551
www.rspb.co.uk

Runnymede Trust

UK-based think tank on ethnicity and cultural diversity. Challenges racial discrimination and aims to influence anti-racist legislation.

Suite 106
The London Fruit and Wool Exchange
London E1 6EP
Tel: 020 7377 9222
www.runnymedetrust.org.uk

SAPERE (Society for Advancing Philosophical Enquiry and Reflection in Education)

The SAPERE website provides background information, details of training, conferences, contacts and articles about Philosophy for Children.

Westminster Institute of Education
Oxford Brookes University
Harcourt Hill Campus
Oxford OX2 9AT
tel 01865 488340
www.sapere.net

Save the Children UK
Works with schools and youth groups in the UK to promote children's rights in the context of Global Citizenship through the production of resources, websites and outreach programmes.
1 St John's Lane
London EC1M 4AR
Tel 020 7012 6400
www.savethechildren.org.uk

School Councils UK
A training and support agency in the area of school and class councils, working with teachers and pupils to set up effective structures for pupil involvement.
2nd Floor
Lawford House
Albert Place
London N3 1QB
Tel 0845 456 9428
www.schoolcouncils.org

SCOPE
A national disability organization whose focus is people with cerebral palsy; works to achieve equality and civil rights for disabled people.
PO Box 833
Milton Keynes
MK12 5NY
Tel 0808 800 3333
www.scope.org.uk

Strategy Against Violence in Education (SAVE)
SAVE is an independent group that brings together representatives from education, teacher training, psychology, counselling, and research into social policy and the protection of children and young people. It works to create the process of intervention from school, to the home, to the community.
Roehampton University of Surrey
School of Psychology and Therapeutic Studies
Whitelands College, West Hill
London SW15 3SN
Tel 020 8392 3278
www.savecircle.co.uk

Totnes Community Family Trust
Introduces relationship training at all levels.
The Mansion
36 Fore Street
Totnes TQ9 5RP
Tel 01803 868519
www.tcft.freeserve.co.uk

United Nations Association
Campaigning and educating to turn the ideals of the UN into reality.
3 Whitehall Court
London SW1A 2EL
Tel 020 7766 3444
www.una-uk.org

United Nations Children's Fund (UNICEF)
Has regionally based Education Officers covering England, Wales, Scotland and Northern Ireland who run free INSET sessions on how to integrate the Convention on the Rights of the Child into the citizenship curriculum. (Young people can participate in discussions with children all around the world on UNICEF's international online service Voices of Youth at www.unicef.org/voy/.)
Africa House
64–78 Kingsway
London WC2B 6NB
Tel 020 7405 5592
www.unicef.org.uk

Worldwide Alternatives to ViolencE (WAVE)
WAVE was founded in 1996 to research the causes of violence in society and promote effective means to reduce it. *Right from the Start* is working in partnership with WAVE towards this end.
Email: wavetrust@aol.com
http://wwwave.co.uk

World Wide Fund for Nature (WWF)
Campaigns for the protection of endangered spaces and species, and addresses global threats.
Panda House
Weyside Park
Godalming
Surrey GU7 1XR
Tel 01483 426444
www.wwf-uk.org
www.wwflearning.co.uk

Appendix 5
Tuckswood Community
First School – Aims/Values

Our aims

We aim to create a secure, caring, happy and stimulating learning environment in which all will develop their aptitude and abilities to the full.

We wish to:
- develop lively and enquiring minds;
- enable children to acquire knowledge and the relevant skills in order to lead full and useful lives;
- work hard to ensure each child makes a good rate of progress to achieve the highest possible standards in all national curriculum subjects plus religious education;
- help children to respect the views of others;
- encourage good manners, moral awareness and a degree of self-reliance;
- help children to understand the world in which they find themselves, prepare for the future and enjoy the present at a pace appropriate to themselves.

We work to achieve these aims through:
- providing a curriculum appropriate to each child's ability and needs;
- providing opportunities for children to develop skills of investigation, enquiry, communication and co-operation;
- promoting the dignity, worth and status of all people and providing equality of opportunity regardless of gender, race and ability;
- creating an awareness of, and respect for, religions and moral attitudes and values;
- fostering and maintaining strong home–school and community links;
- using the school budget to provide effective education for our children and value for money for their parents.

It is our aim to educate the 'whole' child and enable him/her to go forward equipped to deal with the ever-changing world.

Our values

Our school is committed to promoting a sense of community as well as an individual sense of self-worth. Our school is to be a community of caring and fairness, of lifelong learners, for whom access to knowledge is both a right and a critical achievement.

The following coherent set of values have grown from our learning about the most effective way to achieve our school aims.

The values that the whole staff at Tuckswood Community First School base our practice on include the following:

- learning for its own sake
- developing each person's individual potential
- working in a collaborative way
- consistent coherence to an agreed set of policies
- being learners alongside the children
- self-analysis and openness with each other
- trust in each other's professional judgements
- improvement in the quality of our children's experience and attainment.

The values we wish to influence and promote in children's learning include the following:

- enthusiasm for learning
- persistence in learning
- enquiry and curiosity in learning.

The personal values we wish to promote include the following:

- openness and optimism in approach
- sharing and learning together
- self-respect, integrity, honesty and trust
- acceptance, courtesy and compassion.

We are committed to the promotion and development of human dignity and human potential.

REFLECTIONS

A time to think
A time to reflect
A time to be still

This sculpture was presented by Ros Asher
to Tuckswood Community First School.

Further books in the Right from the Start series

The following *Right from the Start* resource books for teachers and parents will be published to complement and extend *The Right from the Start Handbook: Promoting Children's Well-Being in the Primary Years*.

The Power of Music for You and Your Children
Why music and sound are vital to you and your children, and how music and singing can help children to become happier, healthier and well-rounded human beings. Why listening matters and what it can do. How music can heal and calm, and how it can help children to learn.

Touch, Massage and Movement: *Deepening the connection with children*
Answering the universal hunger for touch, from baby massage and baby yoga to the happiness and respect that develop through peer massage in primary school. Understanding how movement, rhythm and music give the best possible impetus to healthy and balanced brain development and therefore a child's capacity to build warm relationships and to learn.

Food for Thought: *What children eat and its effect on their intelligence, personality and behaviour*
The importance of good nutrition – the essential knowledge and skills. The nutrients that may be missing and the pollutants that may be absorbed. The damage that can be done to children's sensitive, still-growing brains.

Natural Wonder: *The enchantment that feeds the human spirit*
Ways to encourage children's understanding, enjoyment and care of the natural world, especially city children. Increasing children's sense of connection and belonging.

Rainbow Colours: *A source of children's energy and contentment*
The physical and psychological effects of different colours and of daylight and darkness. Using this knowledge to help children's concentration, composure and happiness and to reduce their feelings of threat and helplessness.

Helping Children with Yoga: *Suppleness, balance, and self-respect*
Introducing yoga for children. Energy for life, through inner calm, self-confidence and self-control.

Stillness, Imagination and Meditation for Children
Helping children to develop their inner life and to realize their power to love, to give comfort and to create beauty. Healing through meditation and art.

Understanding Disablement
Helping children over the fear-and-uncertainty barrier. Encouraging empathy, inventiveness and adventure. Disabled children tell their own stories.

Your Life, My Life (for use with 8–12 year olds)
A children's introduction to human rights and responsibilities. Ideas to explore and questions for discussion and role play. Stories told, in their own words, by street children and refugee children from different parts of the world.

The following books will be published especially for parents:

A Right and Gentle Beginning
Understanding the sensitivity, intelligence and memory in unborn and newborn babies and how parents can respond in the way they welcome, calm and care for their babies in the first months.

Playing for Life: *Protecting children from hurtful influences and violence*
A child's need to play, in different ways, from birth onwards. A child's right to be able to play outside. The encouragement that parents can give to help a child learn to concentrate, cope well with difficulties and grow up rich in imagination, optimism and understanding.

Calmer, Easier, Happier Parenting
Children behave well when they feel right. Helping them to feel right, to be open and honest and to make amends. Forgiving ourselves and each other. Setting boundaries and helping children's confidence and self-discipline.

Network Educational Press – much more than publishing…

NEP Conferences – Invigorate your teaching

Each term NEP runs a wide range of conferences on cutting edge issues in teaching and learning at venues around the UK. The emphasis is always highly practical. Regular presenters include some of our top-selling authors such as Sue Palmer, Barry Teare and Steve Bowkett. Dates and venues for our current programme of conferences can be found on our website www.networkpress.co.uk.

NEP online Learning Style Analysis – Find out how your students prefer to learn

Discovering what makes your pupils tick is the key to personalizing learning. NEP's Learning Style Analysis is a 50-question online evaluation that can give an immediate and thorough learning profile for every student in your class. It reveals how, when and where they learn best, whether they are right brain or left brain dominant, analytic or holistic, whether they are strongly auditory, visual, kinaesthetic or tactile … and a great deal more. And for teachers who'd like to take the next step, LSA enables you to create a whole-class profile for precision lesson planning.

Developed by The Creative Learning Company in New Zealand and based on the work of Learning Styles expert Barbara Prashnig, this powerful tool allows you to analyse your own and your students' learning preferences in a more detailed way than any other product we have ever seen. To find out more about Learning Style Analysis or to order profiles visit www.networkpress.co.uk/lsa.

NEP's Critical Skills Programme – Teach your students skills for lifelong learning

The Critical Skills Programme puts pupils at the heart of learning, by providing the skills required to be successful in school and life. Classrooms are developed into effective learning environments, where pupils work collaboratively and feel safe enough to take 'learning risks'. Pupils have more ownership of their learning across the whole curriculum and are encouraged to develop not only subject knowledge but the fundamental skills of:

- problem solving
- creative thinking
- decision making
- communication
- management
- organization
- leadership
- self-direction
- quality working
- collaboration
- enterprise
- community involvement

"The Critical Skills Programme… energizes students to think in an enterprising way. CSP gets students to think for themselves, solve problems in teams, think outside the box, to work in a structured manner. CSP is the ideal way to forge an enterprising student culture."
Rick Lee, Deputy Director, Barrow Community Learning Partnership.

To find out more about CSP training visit the Critical Skills Programme website at www.criticalskills.co.

Other titles from Network Educational Press

ACCELERATED LEARNING SERIES

Accelerated Learning: A User's Guide
    by Alistair Smith, Mark Lovatt & Derek Wise
Accelerated Learning in the Classroom by Alistair Smith
Accelerated Learning in Practice by Alistair Smith
The ALPS Approach: Accelerated Learning in Primary Schools
    by Alistair Smith & Nicola Call
The ALPS Approach Resource Book by Alistair Smith & Nicola Call
ALPS StoryMaker by Stephen Bowkett
MapWise by Oliver Caviglioli & Ian Harris
Creating an Accelerated Learning School by Mark Lovatt & Derek Wise
Thinking for Learning by Mel Rockett & Simon Percival
Reaching out to all learners by Cheshire LEA
Move It: Physical movement and learning by Alistair Smith
Coaching Solutions by Will Thomas & Alistair Smith

ABLE AND TALENTED CHILDREN COLLECTION

Effective Provision for Able and Talented Children by Barry Teare
Effective Resources for Able and Talented Children by Barry Teare
More Effective Resources for Able and Talented Children by Barry Teare
Challenging Resources for Able and Talented Children by Barry Teare
Enrichment Activities for Able and Talented Children by Barry Teare
Parents' and Carers' Guide for Able and Talented Children by Barry Teare

LEARNING TO LEARN

Let's Learn How to Learn: Workshops for Key Stage 2 by UFA National Team
Brain Friendly Revision by UFA National Team
Creating a Learning to Learn School by Toby Greany & Jill Rodd
Teaching Pupils How to Learn by Bill Lucas, Toby Greany, Jill Rodd & Ray Wicks

PRIMARY RESOURCES

Promoting Children's Well-Being in the Primary Years:
    The Right from the Start Handbook edited by Andrew Burrell and Jeni Riley
But Why? Developing philosophical thinking in the classroom
    by Sara Stanley with Steve Bowkett
Foundations of Literacy by Sue Palmer & Ros Bayley
Help Your Child To Succeed by Bill Lucas & Alistair Smith
Help Your Child To Succeed – Toolkit by Bill Lucas & Alistair Smith
That's English! by Tim Harding
That's Maths! by Tim Harding
That's Science! by Tim Harding
The Thinking Child by Nicola Call with Sally Featherstone

The Thinking Child Resource Book by Nicola Call with Sally Featherstone
Numeracy Activities Key Stage 2 by Afzal Ahmed & Honor Williams
Numeracy Activities Key Stage 3 by Afzal Ahmed, Honor Williams
       & George Wickham

EXCITING ICT

New Tools for Learning: Accelerated Learning meets ICT by John Davitt
Exciting ICT in Maths by Alison Clark-Jeavons
Exciting ICT in English by Tony Archdeacon
Exciting ICT in History by Ben Walsh

CREATIVE THINKING

Think it–Map it! by Ian Harris & Oliver Caviglioli
Thinking Skills & Eye Q by Oliver Caviglioli, Ian Harris & Bill Tindall
Reaching out to all thinkers by Ian Harris & Oliver Caviglioli
With Drama in Mind by Patrice Baldwin
Imagine That... by Stephen Bowkett
Self-Intelligence by Stephen Bowkett
StoryMaker Catch Pack by Stephen Bowkett

EFFECTIVE LEARNING & LEADERSHIP

Effective Heads of Department by Phil Jones & Nick Sparks
Leading the Learning School by Colin Weatherley
Closing the Learning Gap by Mike Hughes
Strategies for Closing the Learning Gap by Mike Hughes with Andy Vass
Transforming Teaching & Learning
       by Colin Weatherley with Bruce Bonney, John Kerr & Jo Morrison
Effective Learning Activities by Chris Dickinson
Tweak to Transform by Mike Hughes
Making Pupil Data Powerful by Maggie Pringle & Tony Cobb
Raising Boys' Achievement by Jon Pickering
Effective Teachers by Tony Swainston
Effective Teachers in Primary Schools by Tony Swainston

EFFECTIVE PERSONNEL MANAGEMENT

The Well Teacher – management strategies for beating stress, promoting staff health &
    reducing absence by Maureen Cooper
Managing Challenging People – dealing with staff conduct
    by Maureen Cooper & Bev Curtis
Managing Poor Performance – handling staff capability issues
    by Maureen Cooper & Bev Curtis
Managing Recruitment and Selection – appointing the best staff
    by Maureen Cooper & Bev Curtis
Managing Allegations Against Staff – personnel and child protection issues in schools
    by Maureen Cooper & Bev Curtis

*Managing Redundancies – dealing with reduction and reorganisation
    of staff* by Maureen Cooper & Bev Curtis
Paying Staff in Schools – performance management and pay in schools
    by Bev Curtis

VISIONS OF EDUCATION SERIES
Discover Your Hidden Talents: The essential guide to lifelong learning
        by Bill Lucas
The Power of Diversity by Barbara Prashnig
The Brain's Behind It by Alistair Smith
Wise Up by Guy Claxton
The Unfinished Revolution by John Abbott & Terry Ryan
The Learning Revolution by Gordon Dryden & Jeannette Vos

EMOTIONAL INTELLIGENCE
Becoming Emotionally Intelligent by Catherine Corrie
Lend Us Your Ears by Rosemary Sage
Class Talk by Rosemary Sage
A World of Difference by Rosemary Sage
Best behaviour and Best behaviour FIRST AID
        by Peter Relf, Rod Hirst, Jan Richardson & Georgina Youdell
        Best behaviour FIRST AID also available separately

DISPLAY MATERIAL
Move It posters: Physical movement and learning by Alistair Smith
Bright Sparks by Alistair Smith
More Bright Sparks by Alistair Smith
Leading Learning by Alistair Smith

NEWLY QUALIFIED TEACHERS
Lessons are for Learning by Mike Hughes
Classroom Management by Philip Waterhouse & Chris Dickinson
Getting Started by Henry Liebling

SCHOOL GOVERNORS
Questions School Governors Ask by Joan Sallis
Basics for School Governors by Joan Sallis
The Effective School Governor by David Marriott (including audio tape)

For more information and ordering details, please consult our website
www.networkpress.co.uk